The **ITN** *Guide*
ELECTION 1992

The ITN *Guide* to the ELECTION 1992

Introduction by
Jon Snow

Edited by
David Cowling

Written by
*Malcolm Boughen, David Cowling,
Glyn Mathias, Nadine Mellor, Carole Saunders,
Anthony Prangley and Robert Waller*

ITN

B⊞XTREE

This book is dedicated to

Sir David Nicholas and Sir Alastair Burnet

First published in the UK 1992 by
Boxtree Limited
36 Tavistock Street
London WC2E 7PB
1 3 5 7 9 10 8 6 4 2

Design, typesetting and diagrams by ML Design
Jacket design by Millions Design
Printed and bound in Great Britain by Richard Clay Ltd, Bungay, Suffolk

A CIP catalogue record for this book is available from the British Library

ISBN 1 85283 127 8

CONTENTS

INTRODUCTION

Not since 1974 has the outcome of a General election looked so uncertain. The only certainty is that we have a very real electoral battle on our hands. The challenges for each of the main parties are clear.

The Parties

The **Conservatives** have to do something that no Party has achieved since the Napoleonic era, they have to win a fourth term. The Tories have to break the spell cast by dipping at one stage to below twenty points behind the opposition in the polls. Traditionally no party has ever returned from such depths to clinch victory. Yet there's been a change of leader from Margaret Thatcher to John Major. Has he done enough in eighteen months to convince the voters that effectively there has already been a change of government since the gloomy days of Mrs Thatcher's final autumn? The Conservatives' core problem is that the recession has hit skilled workers in Tory strongholds.

Labour too has to do something that no other party has done in recent voting history. It has to produce a swing in its favour of around eight per cent to produce a majority Labour government. On the other hand many of the issues which troubled Labour in the last three elections – defence in particular – have been revised, abandoned, or have been rendered irrelevant by a fast-changing world. Has Neil Kinnock been in opposition too long to win? He is the longest serving leader of the Opposition this century. And does a seasoned team with less controversial policies offer enough of a choice from the one that's already doing the job? Labour's core problem is that the opinion polls suggest that the party's greatest strength is the capacity to stack up still more votes in the areas where they are already strong – the party appears less able to do so in the areas that might once have given them outright victory.

Then there are the **Liberal Democrats**. They are safely through their messy divorce from the Owenite rump of the SDP and happily remarried to the Jenkinsite mainstream of their partner in the Alliance that performed so strongly in the '83 and '87 elections. David Steel has stepped down, Paddy Ashdown has had long enough to establish himself as an identifiable national leader. The Liberal Democrats' difficulty is that so far they have failed to return to the dizzy polling heights of the old Alliance, even though they could hold on to their existing seats or increase them on a smaller share of the vote than last time. Their core problem is that the 'first past the post' electoral system makes it immensely difficult for them to beat the two bigger parties at their own game.

The Leaders

The spotlight is bound to focus on the party leaders during the campaign. **John Major** has proved himself a nice man, a competent operator on the world stage and a less aggressive figure than his predecessor. But he has never played a leading role in a General Election. He is a sensitive man and resents personal attacks. He is best in question-and-answer sessions at news conferences and this a role he will be used extensively to play at the regular morning conferences throughout the campaign. He is no great orator and not the most natural of campaigners on the stump. Watch to see if he succumbs to invitations to debate Labour and Liberal Democrat leaders head to head on television. His people don't want him to, his inclination is to do it if the going gets really tough.

Neil Kinnock is the only one of the three who has been here before. By common consent he fought an attractive campaign in 1987, even if it only resulted in limiting the Conservative majority to 101. He is less effective than John Major at the campaign news conferences, but is a more accomplished orator on the set-piece occasions. Llandudno and Birmingham town halls saw almost Bevan-like performances during the last campaign. The other parties will be on the lookout for slips and any loss of cool. His people are keen for him to debate against John Major in a television encounter and have been looking for an opportunity since the New Year.

Paddy Ashdown is perceived to have had a good Gulf War and a good Soviet coup. It was during these two episodes that he proved himself an adept purveyor of the television 'sound-bite'. His problem is to steer the argument beyond " what will you do if there's a hung Parliament?" He too is keen to debate, but both the other leaders would like to cut him out and turn the whole campaign into a straight battle between Labour and Conservative. The difficulty the party faces is that it will be expected and will want to compete nationally with both Labour and the Conservatives, yet its best prospect for increased representation will be concentrating resources and energy into a small number of targeted seats.

The Marginals

The number of marginal seats has been declining since the War. In one way it should make election night easier to follow. But to say that is to understate the potential for change this time. The electorate is more volatile these days and we may well see different parts of the country defying 'national swings'. There could yet be some dramatic changes in seats with more than ten per cent majorities.

The 'Fifty' and a Hung Parliament

Not since before the Second World War have there been so many MPs from parties other than Conservative and Labour – fifty in all. Besides the Liberal Democrats, there are the Scots and Welsh Nationalists, the rump of the SDP, assorted Ulster Unionists, a Sinn Feiner, and the SDLP. No one can really be sure how the Northern Irish parties will react should a hung parliament result. The Liberals are unlikely to want to be seen keeping a Tory Government in power if it has had a majority of 87 (following by-election losses since the last election) wiped out at the ballot box. The nationalists have no affinity for keeping the Conservatives in either. History suggests that the non-Labour, non-Conservative MPs are more likely to tolerate a minority government made up of the former opposition than sustain a minority one composed of the former government that has lost its overall majority. So that even a failure by one or two seats to win an overall majority could eventually prove disastrous for the Conservatives.

The Characters to Watch Out For

An unusually large number of MPs are retiring at this General Election. Because they will have no seats to nurse we can expect to see plenty of them on our screens throughout the campaign. For the red corner, the 'Old Bruiser' **Denis Healey**. For the Blue corner, 'the dead sheep' **Sir Geoffrey Howe**, the man whose oratorical knife was so telegenically and dramatically plunged between Mrs Thatcher's political shoulder blades. **Sir Cyril Smith** is not contesting Rochdale again so he will be footloose for the gold camp of the Liberal Democrats . **Dr David Owen** has no party to lead and is not running with any other, but that does not mean he will vanish from the campaign scene. **Mrs Thatcher** herself, and her retiring acolyte, **Cecil Parkinson**, will be forces for both Labour and Conservatives to reckon with. **Michael Foot**, Labour leader in the '83 campaign will be shoring up other peoples' hustings and the Euro-sceptic faction will be well represented by the former Trade Secretary, **Nicholas Ridley**.

The Country

The back-drop is one of recession and promised but non-evident recovery. Mortgage repossessions peaked at over eighty thousand in 1991. Company closures were running at 200 every working day by the beginning of '92.

Unemployment was tracking on back up past the two-and-a-half-million mark. Yet the opinion polls in late 1991 and early 1992 rarely put much daylight between the two biggest parties. The pound was bumping along the bottom of the European Exchange Rate Mechanism's wide band. The Green Party's blooming in the European Elections of 1989 seems to have died away. Support for the Liberal Democrats rarely crept into the mid-teens in the opinion polls but their results in local and Westminster by- elections continued to defy national polling trends. In Scottish by-elections the SNP worked its way back into second place behind Labour but well above the Liberal Democrats and even further above the Tories who are battling to save even a few of the nine seats they still hold there.

Election Night
Finally to the night. Ten o'clock will find ITN's Harris exit poll predicting the result. But if it is as close as the polls suggest it might be, then there's a fascinating night ahead. Those moments of 1987, the camera inside Mrs Thatcher's car observing her triumphal return from Finchley to a third term in Downing Street – Neil Kinnock at home in Wales watching the results on television and learning the true scale of his party's third defeat in a row, are vivid memories of that campaign. There will be equally memorable images in 1992. Technology, satellites, graphics and electronics will do their bit but nothing can blunt or exaggerate the full drama of it all. I and the rest of the ITN team – Alastair Stewart, Trevor McDonald, Julia Somerville and John Suchet – are determined to bring you a fast and clear account of what is happening and the earliest picture of the Prime Minister and Government-elect. I look forward very much to being with you and sharing the excitement of what is bound to be another watershed in our political history.

JON SNOW

THE STATE OF THE PARTIES

Overall, not a great deal changed in the 1987 general election. The table below sets out the total number of seats won by the parties in both the 1983 and 1987 general elections:

	1983	1987
Conservative	397	376
Labour	209	229
Liberal Alliance	17	17
SDP Alliance	6	5
SNP	2	3
Plaid Cymru	2	3
Ulster Unionist	11	9
DUP	3	3
PUP	1	1
SDLP	1	3
Sinn Fein	1	1

The Conservatives lost 29 seats and gained 12 (including three by-election losses since 1983). Labour made 27 gains but also suffered six losses (three of them in London – including Fulham, their one by-election gain in the previous Parliament). The Alliance partners gained three seats but lost eight, whilst among the nationalists the SNP gained three but lost two and Plaid Cymru took Ynys Mon. In Northern Ireland, the SDLP took Enoch Powell's seat from the Unionists and held their 1985 by-election gain of Newry & Armagh.

Voting across the U.K. in the 1987 general election was as follows:

Conservative	13,760,583	42.3%
Labour	10,029,807	30.8%
Lib/SDP	7,341,633	22.5%
SNP	416,473	1.3%
Plaid	123,599	0.4%
Green	89,753	0.3%
Others	767,730	2.4%

When the dust settled the electoral landscape looked remarkably similar to that which had existed before polling day. The Conservatives had been battered in

Scotland and bruised in Wales, but in England (which comprised 80 per cent of Westminster seats) their opponents had hardly laid a glove on them.

Since June 1987 there have been 23 parliamentary by-elections in Britain and these are listed below:

VOTING IN PARLIAMENTARY BY- ELECTIONS
(Compared with the 1987 general election)

Seat	Con	Lab	LD	
1987/92 Parliament	%	%	%	
Kensington 14.7.88	-5.9	+5.0	-6.4	Con Hold
Glasgow, Govan 10.11.88	-4.6	27.8	8.2	**SNP Gain**
Epping Forest 15.12.88	-21.4	+0.3	+6.6	Con Hold
Pontypridd 23.2.89	-6.0	-2.9	-15.0	Lab Hold
Richmond (Yorks.) 23.2.89	-24.0	-6.9	-4.9	Con Hold
Vale of Glamorgan 4.5.89	-10.5	+14.2	-12.5	**Lab Gain**
Glasgow, Central 15.6.89	-5.4	-9.9	-9.0	Lab Hold
Vauxhall 15.6.89	-10.2	+2.6	-0.7	Lab Hold
Mid Staffordshire 23.3.90	-18.3	+24.4	-12.0	**Lab Gain**
Bootle 24.5.90	-11.0	+8.5	-4.0	Lab Hold
Knowsley South 27.9.90	-6.3	+4.3	-5.4	Lab Hold
Eastbourne 18.10.90	-19.0	-3.8	+21.1	**L-D Gain**
Bradford North 8.11.90	-22.7	+8.9	+7.6	Lab Hold
Bootle 8.11.90	-10.9	+11.5	-5.1	Lab Hold
Paisley North 29.11.90	-1.0	-11.5	7.5	Lab Hold
Paisley South 29.11.90	-1.	-10.1	5.3	Lab Hold
Ribble Valley 7.3.91	-22.4	-8.3	+27.1	**L-D Gain**
Neath 4.4.91	-7.5	-11.6	-8.3	Lab Hold
Monmouth 16.5.91	-13.5	+11.6	+0.8	**Lab Gain**
Liverpool, Walton 4.7.91	-11.5	-11.3	+14.8	Lab Hold
Hemsworth 7.11.91	-6.7	-0.7	+4.3	Lab Hold
Kincardine & Deeside 7.11.91	-10.1	-8.2	+12.7	**L-D Gain**
Langbaurgh 7.11.91	-2.6	+4.5	-3.8	**Lab Gain**

Kensington was assured its place in history before a single vote was cast. It ended the longest period this century without a parliamentary by-election. Caused by the death of Sir Brandon Rhys Williams, it saw the Conservative majority fall from 4,447 to 815. Labour, in second place, performed quite well and saw off the challenge of the old Alliance partners who fought each other for the first time since their split in March. However, only four months later, Labour crashed in flames when they lost the safe seat of **Glasgow**, **Govan** to the SNP. The Labour MP, Bruce Millan, had been designated one of Britain's two European Commissioners and Labour decided to cut and run before the SNP could build up a head of steam in the constituency. All to no avail. The achievement of the victorious Jim Sillars was truly remarkable: on a swing of 33 per cent he overturned a Labour majority of 19,509 and produced his own of 3,554. The **Epping Forest** by-election one month later (caused by the death of Sir John Biggs-Davison) did not offer Labour much of a prospect for restoring its fortunes. However, it was the type of seat where the old Alliance partners would have been favourites to take a scalp in the previous two parliaments. As it was, the Democrats and the SDP fought each other again, with their combined votes coming just 428 short of winning the seat. The Conservative share fell 21.4 per cent and Labour was not squeezed as expected, increasing its share by 0.3 per cent. In February, 1989, both Labour and the Democrats faced major challenges.

In **Pontypridd**, caused by the death of Brynmor John, Labour was defending a safe seat but, following Govan, it could not afford another collapse in its vote. In **Richmond (Yorks.)**, caused by Sir Leon Brittan's appointment as an EEC Commissioner, the Democrats needed a gain in order to recreate the spectacular Alliance bandwagon of previous years. Labour's vote in Pontypridd fell, but only by 2.9 per cent, as Plaid Cymru mopped up most of the disaffected voters (its share rose by 20 per cent). In Richmond, while the Conservative share fell 24 per cent, their candidate survived because of the divided centre vote. The SDP came second and the Democrats third but their combined share amounted to 54.3 per cent (compared with 37.2 per cent for the surviving Conservative). Labour desperately needed a success to wipe away their Govan disaster and this occurred in the **Vale of Glamorgan**, caused by the death of Sir Raymond Gower. Although a South Wales seat, it had always eluded Labour since they lost it in 1951. The result proved to be their best by-election gain from the Conservatives since Liverpool, West Toxteth in 1935. Labour faced another 'shoot-out' with the SNP in **Glasgow Central** caused by the death of Robert McTaggart but this time they did not suffer the humiliation of Govan. Labour's share of the vote certainly fell (by 9.9 per cent) but, compared with their loss of 27.8 per cent at Govan, they had genuine grounds for relief. In **Vauxhall** caused by Stuart Holland's university appointment in Italy, Labour faced a messy candidate selection with some local activists asserting that the vacancy should be filled by a black candidate. In the event, Labour slightly increased their share of the vote. Also, this was the first parliamentary by-election where the Green Party saved their deposit. The first by-election following Labour's revival in the European elections came in 1990, when the Conservatives defended **Mid Staffordshire** caused by the death of John Heddle. In 1987, it was their 230th safest seat, registering a majority of 14,654 (or 25.9 per cent).It proved an astonishing contest with Labour winning by a majority of 9,449 on a swing of 21.4 per cent. It was portrayed as a referendum on the Poll Tax and in some measure this was true. However, it was also a serious rebellion by the middle and skilled working classes of middle England against a raft of Government policies. The death of the Ulster Unionist, Harold McCusker, caused a by-election in **Upper Bann**. The main interest here was in the fate of the Official Conservative candidate, given the doldrums in which Unionist politics seemed becalmed over the Anglo-Irish Agreement. The seat was easily held by the Ulster Unionists and the Conservatives came sixth with only 3 per cent of the vote. Labour faced the prospect of a political banana skin in the **Bootle** by-election caused by the death of Allan Roberts. It was one of their safest seats and complacency could easily have resulted in a drop in their share of the vote. In the event they fought it like a marginal and secured a 9.8 per cent swing from the Conservatives. The latter were well pleased to have held on to second place, narrowly ahead of the Lib-Dems. But it was the fortunes of the SDP which grabbed the headlines when their candidate polled only 155 votes compared with 418 for the Monster Raving Loony Party. The death of Labour's Sean Hughes caused a by-election in **Knowsley South** with the lowest turnout (33.4 per cent) in any by-election since Mrs Thatcher was first elected in 1979. Labour held the seat with a 4.3 per cent increase in its vote as both the Conservatives and the Lib-Dems fell back. For the latter this was a marked contrast to the by-election in Knowsley North in 1986 when the Alliance vote increased by 19.8 per cent. The murder of Ian Gow by the IRA caused a by-election in **Eastbourne**. Labour (with only 8.8 per cent of the vote at the last election) was not in contention and the Lib-Dems (with a swing of 20.1 per cent) swept away a majority of almost 17,000 to take the seat with a 4,550 majority of their own. The NOP/BBC exit poll showed that 27 per cent of 1987 Conservative voters defected to the Lib-Dems in the by-election. The Conservatives suffered another blow in the **Bradford North** by-election, caused by the death of Pat Wall. It was a seat which Labour had won from the Conservatives in 1987 and they saw their majority increase from 1,633 to 9,514 on a swing of 15.8 per cent. The Conservatives were forced into third place with only 16.8 per cent of the vote as the Lib-Dems benefited from their post-Eastbourne revival. This humiliating result for the Conservatives added fuel to the growing speculation about a challenge to Mrs Thatcher's leadership.

Another by-election occurred in **Bootle** following the death of the victor of the earlier by-election in May. With so much voter 'fatigue' (there had also been local elections in May) it could have been a problem for Labour. In fact they secured the largest majority for any by-election since 1950. To the surprise of many, the Conservatives held second place as the Lib-Dem vote fell back slightly on their share in the earlier by-election. By-elections were held on the same day for the two **Paisley** seats, caused by the deaths of Allen Adams (*North*) and Norman Buchan (*South*). Held in the immediate aftermath of Mrs Thatcher's resignation and John Major's election as Prime Minister, the Conservative vote fell only slightly in both seats as Labour and the Liberal-Democratss suffered at the hands of the SNP. These two results seemed to support the proposition that Labour did badly in Scotland when their prospects for winning nationally declined.

The first by-election in 1991 occurred in **Ribble Valley**, caused by the elevation to the Lords of David Waddington, former Home Secretary. It was an astonishing victory by the Liberal-Democratss, on a swing of 24.8 per cent, with a turnout above 70 per cent, in the fourteenth safest Conservative seat in the country. The over-riding issue of the campaign was the Poll Tax and 85 per cent of voters were dissatisfied with it. The **Neath** by-election, caused by the death of Donald Coleman, saw Peter Hain defending the seat for Labour. Mr Hain's past student protests against South African rugby tours were widely featured in the campaign but the beneficiary of any resentment caused was Plaid Cymru whose share of the vote rose by 17 per cent, as those for all three main parties fell back. The **Monmouth** by-election, caused by the death of Sir John Stradling-Thomas, left the prospect for any June 1991 general election dead in the water. It was a seat which Labour had only held once (1966-70) since it was created in 1918. Yet, to the chagrin of both the Conservatives and the Liberal-Democrats, Labout won the second safest Conservative seat in Wales – and the most English of all Welsh seats – on a swing of 12.6 per cent.

The **Liverpool, Walton** by-election, caused by the death of Eric Heffer, posed a real threat to Labour. For the first time the Militant Tendency supported a candidate (under the label 'Real Labour') against an official Labour candidate. Labour's share of the total vote fell by 11.3 per cent and the Conservative vote was squeezed to 2.9 per cent. But the principal beneficiary were the Liberal-Democrats whose share of the total vote increased by 14.8 per cent, whereas the 'Real Labour' candidate secured 6.5 per cent. In the **Hemsworth** by-election, caused by the death of George Buckley, Labour faced the potential embarassment of the national party selecting Derek Enright as their candidate, over the local party's preference for an NUM official supported by Arthur Scargill. In the event Labour's share of the vote fell less than 1per cent on a turnout of 43 per cent. The Liberal-Democrats candidate forced the Conservatives into third place but did not make the expected inroads into Labour support. In the **Kincardine & Deeside** by-election, caused by the death of Alick Buchanan-Smith, the Conservatives were routed by the Liberal-Democrats who transformed a Conservative majority of just over 2,000 votes into one for them of nearly 8,000. Labour came fourth, displaced by the Scottish Nationalists. The result, bad enough in itself for the Conservatives, also meant that the Liberal-Democratss overtook them as the party with the second largest parliamentary representation in Scotland. The **Langbaurgh** by-election, caused by the death of Richard Holt, resulted in a Labour gain and the election of a second Asian MP in Dr Ashok Kumar. Two opinion polls had forecast leads of between 11-13 per cent. ITN's own exit poll on election day indicated an 11 per cent Labour lead. The actual result was a 4 per cent Labour lead, representing a swing of 3.6 per cent.

VOTING IN PARLIAMENTARY BY-ELECTIONS
(Compared with the previous general election)

Seat	Con	Lab	SLD	
1979/83 Parliament	%	%	%	
Manchester Central 27.9.79	-10.1	-0.1	+8.9	Lab Hold
Hertfordshire S.W. 13.12.79	-8.8	0.0	+7.4	Con Hold
Southend East 13.3.80	-19.3	+6.5	+12.0	Con Hold
Glasgow Central 26.6.80	-7.6	-11.7	-	Lab Hold
Warrington 16.7.81	-21.7	-13.2	+33.3	Lab Hold
Croydon N.W. 22.10.81	-18.9	-14.1	+29.5	*Lib Gain*
Crosby 26.11.81	-17.2	-15.9	+33.9	*SDP Gain*
Glasgow, Hillhead 25.3.82	-14.5	-8.5	+19.0	*SDP Gain*
Beaconsfield 27.5.82	+0.1	-9.7	+9.7	Con Hold
Mitcham & Morden 3.6.82	-0.5	-20.8	+20.5	*Con Gain*
Coatbridge & Airdrie 24.6.82	-1.3	-5.8	-	Lab Hold
Gower 16.9.82	-8.4	-9.7	+16.0	Lab Hold
Peckham 28.10.82	-15.7	-9.5	+25.2	Lab Hold
B'ham, Northfield 28.10.82	-9.8	-8.8	+18.0	*Lab Gain*
Glasgow, Queens Park 2.12.82	-12.1	-8.4	-	Lab Hold
Bermondsey 24.2.83	-19.4	-37.5	+50.9	*Lib Gain*
Darlington 24.3.83	-8.5	-6.0	+14.3	Lab Hold

Seat	Con	Lab	SLD	
1983/87 Parliament	%	%	%	
Penrith & The Border 28.7.83	-12.8	-5.9	+16.7	Con Hold
Chesterfield 1.3.84	-17.2	-1.6	+15.2	Lab Hold
Cynon Valley 3.5.84	-6.8	+2.8	-0.7	Lab Hold
Stafford 3.5.84	-10.8	+3.7	+ 7.1	Con Hold
Surrey South West 3.5.85	-10.4	-1.5	+11.3	Con Hold
Portsmouth South 14.6.84	-15.7	+3.9	+12.2	**SDP Gain**
Enfield, Southgate 13.12.84	-8.5	-5.9	+12.2	Con Hold
Brecon & Radnor 4.7.85	-20.5	+9.4	+11.4	**Lib Gain**
Tyne Bridge 5.12.85	-14.1	+1.3	+11.4	Lab Hold
Fulham 10.4.86	-11.3	+10.4	+0.5	**Lab Gain**
Derbyshire West 8.5.86	-16.4	+2.7	+12.4	Con Hold
Ryedale 8.5.86	-17.9	-1.9	+19.8	**Lib Gain**
Newcastle-u-Lyme 17.7.86	-17.4	-1.2	+17.2	Lab Hold
Knowsley North 13.11.86	-13.8	-8.2	+19.8	Lab Hold
Greenwich 26.2.87	-23.6	-4.5	+27.9	**SDP Gain**
Truro 12.3.87	-6.6	+2.5	+3.1	Lib Hold

Opinion Polls

TRENDS IN VOTING INTENTION

Between the last general election and December 1991 some 325 individual opinion polls were published giving answers to the standard question: 'How would you vote if there was a general election tomorrow?' The table below shows the number of polls published each month since June 1987 and gives the average figures for the main parties in response to this question.

	(Polls)	Con	Lab	Alliance	
1987		%	%	%	
July	3	47	33	18	
August	2	47	36	16	
September	4	47	35	16	
October	4	49	35	14	
November	2	48	36	14	
December	3	47	36	15	
1988					
January	3	46	38	15	
February	3	45	39	14	
				SLD	SDP
March	6	45	38	10	4

	(Polls)	Con	Lab	SLD	SDP	Greens
April	4	43	41	9	5	
May	5	44	39	9	4	
June	6	46	40	8	4	
July	5	45	40	8	4	
August	3	47	37	9	5	
September	6	45	38	10	5	
October	5	46	39	9	5	
November	4	43	39	9	5	
December	3	45	36	9	6	
1989						*Greens*
January	5	45	38	10	4	
February	6	40	39	10	6	
March	4	42	40	8	6	
April	5	41	40	9	6	
May	3	43	42	7	3	
June	4	36	45	6	3	6
July	4	36	45	5	4	7
August	5	37	45	6	7	7
September	12	37	44	6	3	8
October	10	38	48	5	2	5
November	4	37	49	6	3	4
December	5	38	47	6	3	4
1990						
January	8	36	47	6	3	5
February	6	34	50	6	3	4
March	7	30	53	6	3	5
April	9	31	53	6	3	5
May	6	34	49	8	2	4
June	8	36	50	7		4
July	6	36	49	8		4
August	6	37	49	8		4
September	7	36	47	11		3
October	6	34	47	14		3
November [1]	11	36	47	12		3
November [2]	6	47	40	10		2
December	5	44	42	9		2

[1] Before and [2] after Mrs Thatcher's announcement that she would not stand in the second ballot for the Conservative leadership.

1991	(Polls)	Con	Lab	SLD	SDP	Greens
January	7	45	42	9		2
February	8	45	41	10		2
March	10	43	39	15		2
April	8	41	41	14		2
May	9	37	42	17		2
June	9	37	43	16		2
July	6	38	43	15		2
August	7	39	41	15		2
September	11	40	40	15		
October	8	40	44	13		
November	9	40	42	15		
December	4	40	42	14		

The *Glasgow Herald* regularly publishes the findings of the Scotland-wide polls produced by the System Three company. The figures since the last election are set out below:

VOTING INTENTION IN SCOTLAND (System Three/*Glasgow Herald*)

Month	Con	Lab	SNP	Lib-SDP Alliance	
1987	%	%	%	%	
July	19	53	14	14	
August	24	48	12	15	
September	23	50	14	12	
October	22	50	12	15	
November	23	45	16	16	
1988					
Early Jan	23	49	15	12	
Late Jan	22	48	16	13	
February	18	51	18	13	
				LD	SDP
March	23	48	18	8	2
April	22	49	21	6	2
May	22	46	22	6	3
June	25	40	23	8	3
July	25	44	22	6	1
August	23	49	21	2	3
September	23	47	19	6	4
October	23	45	20	8	3
November	21	39	30	7	2

1989	Con	Lab	SNP	LD	SDP
Early Jan	20	36	32	7	3
Late Jan	20	41	28	8	2
February	20	41	27	8	3
March	20	41	27	7	3
April	19	42	27	8	3
May	21	47	25	5	1
June	19	46	24	5	1
July	21	45	22	6	2
August	16	48	22	5	2
September	19	48	18	7	2
October	18	55	17	5	1
November	21	49	20	5	2
1990					
Early Jan	16	50	21	6	1
Late Jan	21	48	19	6	2
February	21	52	17	5	1
March	15	54	20	7	-
April	19	49	20	8	1
May	17	49	23	5	2

	Con	Lab	SNP	LD	Green
June	19	48	23	6	4
July	19	52	20	4	4
August	22	49	20	5	3
September	19	42	24	10	3
October	16	48	24	9	3
November	24	43	23	7	3
1991					
Early Jan	21	45	23	9	2
Late Jan	30	44	18	7	2
February	23	46	22	6	3
March	23	42	22	10	2
April	27	42	18	11	2
May	23	44	20	11	2
June	25	46	16	9	3
July	24	46	20	8	2
August	25	45	18	8	2
September	24	43	23	9	1
October	23	41	24	10	2

Press Association Regional Polls

In Autumn 1986, the Press Association published the first of their polls specifically designed to represent voting intention in the Standard Regions of Britain. In effect, a separate opinion poll was devised for each of the Regions. The table below sets out the voting intention figures for each of the four PA polls conducted between 1986-91, as well as the actual vote share for the main parties in these regions for the last two general elections. It is important to set the context of each poll. The *first*, in October 1986, showed a marked Labour recovery from the electoral earthquake which nearly flattened the party in the 1983 general election. But Labour's recovery then was at the expense of the Alliance parties rather than the Conservatives. This poll was conducted in the aftermath of the Alliance's damaging dispute over Defence in their September Party Conferences. The *second*, in April 1987, shows a collapse in the Labour vote which had gone back to the Alliance. The fieldwork for this poll followed Labour's disastrous loss of the Greenwich by-election to the Alliance in February 1987. The *third*, in September 1989, reflected the substantial change in the British political landscape following the June European Parliament elections that year. In those elections Labour had soundly beaten the Conservatives, whilst the Social & Liberal Democrats had slumped to fourth place behind the Green Party. The *fourth*, with fieldwork in the last three days of September and the first three in October 1991, occurred when the national opinion polls indicated that the Conservatives and Labour were neck-and-neck. The overall message of the fourth PA poll was a swing to Labour of 6.5 per cent since the 1987 election. This translated into a 'hung' parliament with Conservatives and Labour in close contention for the largest number of seats.

STANDARD REGION RESULTS OF PRESS ASSOCIATION POLLS
(in 1986 and 1987 (by Marplan) and 1989 and 1991 (by ICM) compared with actual votes cast in the 1983 and 1987 general elections.)

	Elec 1983	PA Oct.86	PA Apr.87	Elec 1987	PA Sep.89	PA Oct.91
Britain	%	%	%	%	%	%
Con	43.5	41	40	43.3	37	40
Lab	28.3	38	30	31.5	45	42
All/Dems	26.0	19	27	23.1	4	13
Greens					8	2
Scotland						
Con	28.4	22	24	24.0	21	23
Lab	35.1	50	37	42.4	51	47

	Elec 1983	PA Oct.86	PA Apr.87	Elec 1987	PA Sep.89	PA Oct.91
Scotland	%	%	%	%	%	%
All/Dems	24.5	13	26	19.3	2	8
SNP	11.8	15	13	14.0	21	21
Greens	0.1			0.2	4	1
Wales						
Con	31.1	32	37	29.5	24	31
Lab	37.5	47	34	45.1	58	55
All/Dems	23.2	15	24	17.9	2	8
Plaid	7.8	4	4	7.3	9	5
Greens	0.2			0.1	6	2
North						
Con	34.6	28	31	32.3	28	31
Lab	40.2	54	44	46.4	61	55
All/Dems	25.0	17	24	21.0	2	12
Greens					5	2
North West						
Con	40.0	35	34	38.0	33	36
Lab	36.0	45	39	41.2	56	52
All/Dems	23.4	19	26	20.6	2	11
Greens					6	1
Yorkshire & Humberside						
Con	38.7	31	36	37.4	29	34
Lab	35.3	49	39	40.6	57	55
All/Dems	25.5	18	25	21.7	3	9
Greens					7	2
West Midlands						
Con	45.0	44	47	45.5	38	42
Lab	31.2	37	26	33.3	48	44
All/Dems	23.4	18	26	20.8	3	12
Greens					8	1
East Midlands						
Con	47.2	46	48	48.6	43	42
Lab	28.0	36	27	30.0	40	45
All/Dems	24.1	17	25	21.0	6	11
Greens					9	1
East Anglia						
Con	51.0	48	53	52.1	48	51
Lab	20.5	30	20	21.7	32	33

	Elec 1983	PA Oct.86	PA Apr.87	Elec 1987	PA Sep.89	PA Oct.91
East Anglia	%	%	%	%	%	%
All/Dems	28.2	21	27	25.7	5	13
Greens					12	3
London						
Con	43.9	43	45	46.5	37	46
Lab	29.8	37	30	31.5	46	40
All/Dems	24.7	19	25	21.3	3	11
Greens					10	2
South East (excluding London)						
Con	54.5	49	50	55.6	56	51
Lab	15.8	23	16	16.8	27	29
All/Dems	29.0	27	34	27.2	5	18
Greens					9	2
South West						
Con	51.4	49	47	50.6	47	47
Lab	14.7	27	17	15.9	31	27
All/Dems	33.2	24	35	33.0	6	23
Greens					10	2

Sample Size		
	1986	9,000
	1987	9,170
	1989	10,101
	1991	10,159

Remembering that the national swing in the 1991 PA poll was 6.5 per cent, the table below shows the range of regional swings compared with the 1987 general election:

REGIONAL SWINGS TO LABOUR SINCE JUNE 1987
(based on the 1991 ICM/Press Association regional poll)

	%		%
East Midlands	11.0	East Anglia	6.0
South East	8.5	North	5.0
Yorks. & Humberside	8.5	Wales	4.5
South West	7.5	London	4.5
West Midlands	7.5	Scotland	3.0
North West	6.5		

The North West registered the same swing as the national average and there were five regions with greater swings and five with lesser. Four of the five with greater swings were regions where Labour was far behind the Conservatives in 1987 (South East, South West, East Midlands and West Midlands). Three of the five with lesser swings were Labour heartland regions: Scotland, Wales and the North. This seemed to reverse Labour's 1987 experience when they piled up votes in their safe seats but seriously under-performed in the key marginals across England. London represented the most worrying feature of the poll for Labour – they need a better swing than 4.5 per cent there if they are to win the next election. Because the regional samples were weighted to provide a national profile, we are able to draw a broad picture of how party voting divides regionally:

		Population	Con	Lab	Lib-Dem
		%	%	%	%
Scotland		9	5	10	6
Wales		5	4	7	3
England:	North[1]	27	23	34	21
	Midlands[2]	20	21	19	17
	South[3]	39	47	30	53

[1] *North, North West, Yorkshire & Humberside*
[2] *East and West Midlands, East Anglia*
[3] *South East, London, South West*

We can see that just under one-half of Conservative supporters in this poll and just over half of Liberal-Democrats supporters were in the South of England. By contrast, one-third of Labour supporters were found in the North of England.

Local and European elections

LOCAL ELECTIONS: 5 MAY 1988

This was the first major test of support for the parties following the general election. Every Councillor in the 53 Scottish Districts faced re-election. In England, one-third of the seats in all the 36 Metropolitan Districts and in 117 Non-Metropolitan Districts were contested. In Wales, one-third of the seats in 5 Districts were fought. The last time these, near 4,000, Councillors were elected was in May 1984. In Scotland, Labour was defending a very strong position (with 75 per cent of the electorate living in Districts they controlled). In the event, their share of the vote fell by 3 per cent compared with 1984 but they emerged with their biggest total of Councillors since 1974. The Conservatives finished with their lowest number of Councillors since 1974. The Democrats saw their share of the vote fall significantly (although they marginally increased their number of seats). The biggest change came in the SNP vote which increased by 9.6 per cent over 1984. However, this was in part due to the fact that they contested many more seats this time. In the English Metropolitan Districts, Labour won 70 per cent of the seats with 51 per cent of the total votes. Its vote share was a slight increase over 1984 but the Conservative share also held, whilst that of the Democrats fell. In the English & Welsh Non-Metropolitan Districts, the Conservatives held a 4 per cent lead over Labour in the popular vote and made a handful of net gains compared with 1984. The Democrats suffered a small number of net losses.

LOCAL ELECTIONS: 4 MAY 1989
In these elections it was the turn of 'Middle England' to vote, as every seat in the 39 Shire Counties outside London and the Metropolitan Districts faced re-election (as well as in all eight Welsh Counties). Overall, some 9.6 million people voted in these 47 Counties. The previous Shire elections were held in 1985, when both the Conservatives and Labour had suffered at the hands of the Alliance partners. In 1989 the Conservatives were the principal beneficiaries of the decline in support for the centre parties.

Voting in the English Shire County elections

	1985	1989	+/- per cent
	%	%	
Conservative	38.4	42.1	+3.7
Labour	30.0	31.1	+1.1
Alliance/SLD	28.0	20.1	-7.9
Others	3.6	6.7	+3.1

The 1985 elections had not been a good result for Labour and yet they increased their share of the vote by only 1.1 per cent. The Democrats lost more than one-quarter of the 1985 Alliance vote, and the Conservatives gained the biggest single slice of it. The most distinctive feature of the 1985 elections was the large number of Counties where no single party held overall control. However, in 1989 these were considerably reduced.

In terms of seats, 421 out of 3,005 changed hands in England (boundary changes in six of the eight Welsh Counties made direct comparisons impossible). The Conservatives and Labour made net gains of 91 and 51 respectively, whilst the Democrats suffered a net loss of 112 seats (the SDP lost 18 seats with no gains). But, because there is no immediate, central collection of local government votes (unlike most other Western European countries) the major focus of public attention was on the voting in the Vale of Glamorgan parliamentary by-election held on the same day. Labour won this seat and the subsequent national opinion polls reflected their triumph in one out of 650 constituencies, rather than the impressive mid-term Conservative performance in dozens of Counties across England.

EUROPEAN PARLIAMENT ELECTION, 15 JUNE 1989

Six weeks after the Shire County elections the political landscape of Britain altered significantly. Following their victory in the Vale of Glamorgan, Labour secured more than 40 per cent in the four published polls of May, leading the Conservatives by 2 per cent in one and at level pegging in another two. The few polls which asked specifically about voting intention for the impending European Parliament election showed an even stronger Labour performance. But the Gallup poll published in the *Daily Telegraph* on 12 June promised a dramatic result. Looking only at those respondents who said they were 'certain to vote' it showed a 15 per cent Labour lead over the Conservatives, and the Green Party in third place. The NOP/BBC exit poll, broadcast on the night of 15 June, confirmed the two most important facts of the election – Labour would win decisively and the Greens would push the Democrats into fourth place.

Result of the European Parliament election

Britain	*Votes*	*%*	*Candidates*	*Elected*
Labour	6,153,661	40.1	78	45
Conservative	5,331,098	34.7	78	32
Green	2,292,718	14.9	78	-
Democrat	944,861	6.1	78	-
SNP	406,686	2.6	8	1
Plaid Cymru	115,062	0.8	4	-
SDP	75,886	0.5	16	-
Others	41,295	0.3	26	-

Northern Ireland (*First preference votes*)				
DUP	160,110	29.9		1
SDLP	136,335	25.5		1
Ulster Unionist	118,785	22.2		1
Sinn Fein	48,914	9.1		-
Alliance	27,905	5.2		-

Northern Ireland	*Votes*	*%*	*Candidates*	*Elected*
Conservative	25,789	4.8		-
Ecology (Green)	6,569	1.2		-
Others	10,404	1.9		-

In terms of seats, the situation was the exact reverse of 1984: Labour won 45 and the Conservatives 32, with the SNP retaining their one seat. The Conservative share of the national vote was their lowest since 1859 and their loss of 13 seats was the largest suffered by any national party in the 12 member states. For Labour it was the first time they had secured the largest share of the popular vote in a national contest since the October 1974 general election. Ten of their 13 gains (along with a swing of 9.4 per cent compared with June 1987) were in England where, for most of the previous decade, they had failed to make any electoral headway. For the Democrats is was a devastating experience: pushed into a poor fourth place by the Green Party which had registered only 2 per cent in the opinion polls just one month earlier; and losing 34 deposits in the process. The European election proved a watershed. The age of the two-party system had broadly returned and the almost effortless Conservative political supremacy since June 1987 was left in tatters.

LOCAL ELECTIONS: 3 MAY 1990
Elections occurred across the whole of Scotland for the nine Regional Councils and the Islands. In addition, there were all-out elections in the 32 London Boroughs; and elections for one-third of Councillors in the 36 English Metropolitan Districts and 121 Non-Metropolitan Districts in England and Wales. outside Scotland it was the first 'Poll Tax' election. These particular Councillors had last been elected in May 1986. Even before Labour's remarkable success in winning the Mid Staffordshire by-election in March the prospects for the Conservatives seemed rather miserable. Following that defeat it looked as if the local elections would be a bloodbath for their Councillors. And so it turned out, except in London. Overall, the Conservatives made a net loss of 175 seats. In Scotland their aggressive campaign brought no real dividends: they contested more Regional Councils seats than ever before but ended the day with their smallest ever representation (winning only 52 out of a total of 445). Similarly, in the Metropolitan Districts, whilst Labour won their largest ever number of seats in one-third elections since 1973, the Conservatives won their smallest ever number (114 out of a total of 855). For the Non-Metropolitan Districts, in the words of the '1990 Local Elections Handbook' (Colin Rallings & Michael Thrasher, Polytechnic South West): 'They provided the government with its biggest shock...Labour topped the poll and won more than half the wards in the

tier of local government usually assumed to be a Conservative stronghold' (Labour won 969 seats compared with 464 for the Conservatives). The full scale of this disaster was concealed by some remarkable results for the Conservatives in London (where 40 per cent of all the Council seats were being fought on 3 May). Of the 96 seats Labour lost to the Conservatives, 90 fell in London. In the Boroughs of Brent, Ealing, Wandsworth and Westminster Labour were massacred by swings of 6 per cent or more to the Conservatives. The tide was not uniform across London (Labour made significant gains in the Boroughs of Lewisham, Havering, Islington and Merton) but the Conservatives seized the opportunity to promote these gains and play down their bad performance virtually everywhere else.

LOCAL ELECTIONS: 2 MAY 1991

These particular elections were important for two reasons: firstly, they involved more than 30 million electors and over 470 parliamentary constituencies. This is because every four years all the district authorities in England and Wales (outside London) with one-third elections coincide with all those operating all-out elections. Secondly, they were the same set of local elections which triggered the last two general elections. In 1983, the local elections were held on 5 May. On 9 May Mrs Thatcher announced she had asked the Queen to dissolve parliament. In 1987, the local elections were held on 7 May and Mrs Thatcher asked for a dissolution on 11 May.

The tables below compare the local elections results with those of May 1987:

ENGLISH NON-METROPOLITAN DISTRICTS

	May 1987	May 1991	
	%	%	(seats won)
Conservative	40.1	35.2	3,887
Labour	23.7	27.9	2,621
Lib-Dem	27.2	22.7	1,972
Others	14.2	9.0	1,616

ENGLISH METROPOLITAN DISTRICTS

	May 1987	May 1991	
	%	%	(seats won)
Conservative	31.7	31.8	184
Labour	42.6	45.1	526
Lib-Dem	23.8	18.6	109
Others	1.9	4.6	19

The elections in Wales are more difficult to interpret because in about 40 per cent of the seats Councillors were returned unopposed. With that important caveat in mind, the table below sets out the May 1991 data:

WELSH DISTRICTS

	May 1991	
	%	(seats won)
Conservative	12.5	104
Labour	35.0	570
Lib-Dem	8.7	75
Plaid Cymru	10.7	112
Others	33.1	506

Source for all three tables above: Dr Colin Rallings and Dr Michael Thrasher, Polytechnic South West, Plymouth, in their 'Local Elections Handbook 1991'

The real surprise of the election was the performance of the Liberal-Democrats. They made a net gain of 531 seats, compared with Labour's net gain of 487. What was surprising was that May 1987 represented a very good result for the old Alliance parties and the Liberal-Democrats were expected to lose seats rather reap such a harvest. Compared with May 1987, support for the centre in the national opinion polls was significantly lower; indeed, the tables above show that their share of the vote fell in May 1991 compared with May 1987. However, they succeeded in targeting the seats where their prospects were best this time.

LOCAL GOVERNMENT BY-ELECTIONS
Between the last general election and December 1991 there were some 1,770 local government by-elections throughout Britain. The table below summarises the seats gained, held and lost during that period:

	Conservative	*Labour*	*Lib-Dem*	*Others*
Seats Held	439	482	192	82
Seats Lost	204	105	110	156
Seats Gained	154	175	165	81
Net gains/ losses	-50	+70	+55	-75

The contrast with the last Parliament is quite striking. During those four years (1983-7) there were some 1,470 by-elections and the Conservatives suffered a net loss of 222 seats (46 per cent of all the seats they were defending). Over the same period, the Alliance parties made net gains of 280 seats, whilst Labour made a net gain of only *two* seats. Since June 1987 the pattern has been very different – the net Conservative losses are less than a quarter of those they suffered during the previous Parliament; and Labour out-performed the Lib-Dems.

These by-elections involved some three million voters. A number of these contests were not fought by all three main parties together but, looking at those which were, the following voting pattern emerges:

Quarterly voting in three-cornered local by-elections

	Con	Lab	Lib/SDP		Others
1987	%	%	%		%
Q3	43.1	29.2	25.6		2.1
Q4	40.6	35.5	19.0		4.9
1988			*LD*	*SDP*	
Q1	40.0	30.2	26.8	0.5	2.5
Q2	39.1	34.1	20.9	3.0	2.9
Q3	37.6	35.1	23.3	1.0	3.0
Q4	37.6	28.1	27.9	1.7	4.7
1989					
Q1	36.3	28.3	30.3	1.3	3.8
Q2	34.6	36.3	21.8	2.0	5.4
Q3	40.0	30.6	24.2	1.5	3.7
Q4	31.7	39.6	20.8	0.3	7.6
1990					
Q1	31.2	36.8	25.1	1.2	5.7
Q2	26.7	42.8	22.9	2.6	5.0
				Green	
Q3	31.2	36.4	27.6	2.1	2.7
Q4	31.0	35.9	28.5	1.3	3.4
1991					
Q1	35.4	33.6	25.0	1.6	4.4
Q2	33.5	31.8	30.4	1.4	2.9
Q3	33.9	32.2	27.2	1.6	5.1
Q4	36.5	33.8	25.0	0.9	3.8

KEY EVENTS 1979-1991

1979
May

3   • General Election.

4   • The Conservatives win with an overall majority of 43 and the nation elects its first woman Prime Minister, Margaret Thatcher, 53 years old.

8   • Sir Derek Rayner, the joint MD of Marks & Spencer, appointed to head a government efficiency drive in Whitehall.

• Jeremy Thorpe, former Liberal leader, stands trial at the Central Criminal Court for conspiring to murder Norman Scott, with whom he is said to have had a homosexual relationship.

10 • In America, a judge rules that IRA suspects accused of bombing Ripon Barracks in North Yorkshire cannot be extradited to Great Britain.

11 • Inflation reaches double figures in April after 15 months of single figures.

15 • In the Queen's Speech, Mrs Thatcher outlines her Government's plans for 'sweeping changes', including lower taxes and public spending, curbs on union powers and a law on picketing.

24 • The situation in Iraq provokes panic buying of petrol and further price increases put petrol up by as much as 6p to about £1.22 a gallon.

28 • The Government decides to admit to Britain nearly 1,000 Vietnamese boat people rescued from the South China Sea.

June

1   • Rhodesia becomes a nation, and is renamed Zimbabwe-Rhodesia.

7   • US President, Jimmy Carter, refuses to lift economic sanctions against Zimbabwe-Rhodesia because the elections were 'neither fair nor free'.

8   • Fewer than one third of Britain's electors vote in the European Parliament Elections. The result is a landslide for the Conservatives who win 60 of the 78 British seats. Labour win 17 seats and the Scottish Nationalists 1 seat. However, the Socialists remain the largest political group in the European Parliament.

12 • Geoffrey Howe's first Budget cuts the standard tax rate by 3p, lowers the top rate from 83 per cent to 60 per cent and raises VAT to 15 per cent.

18 • President Jimmy Carter and Leonid Brezhnev sign SALT-2 Treaty, limiting number of strategic nuclear missiles held by each side to 2,250 by 1981.

• Neil Kinnock becomes Shadow Education Spokesman.

22 • Jeremy Thorpe and three others men cleared of all charges relating to plot to murder Norman Scott.

July

9 • Len Murray, TUC General Secretary, calls the proposed changes in labour legislation 'a major challenge' to the rights of workers and their unions.
 • Sir Robert Armstrong becomes Cabinet Secretary.

11 • MP's vote themselves a £2,553 pay increase.

18 • The pound reaches its highest level for four years and the Treasury announces a further relaxation in exchange controls.

19 • The House of Commons votes against restoring Capital Punishment.

20 • Announcement that a minority shareholding in the state-owned British Airways is to be sold to the public.

26 • The Government announces it will sell off North Sea oil interests.

August

1 • Commonwealth leaders begin talks amid deep divisions regarding Zimbabwe-Rhodesia.

2 • An IRA landmine kills two soldiers bringing the total to 301 of Army deaths since 1969.

5 • Government's initiative to resolve the Zimbabwe-Rhodesia issue is unanimously endorsed by the Commonwealth. The next steps are for Britain to draw up a constitution for 'genuine' black majority rule and a plan for supervising the elections.

10 • Independent Television is blacked out after a series of pay disputes.

14 • Fastnet disaster. Seventeen people die as gales hit the race.

17 • The Government introduce the Tax and Price Index which shows that the rise in total household costs fell in July.

22 • TUC leaders declare total opposition to the Government's proposals for changes in trade union law.

27 • Earl Louis Mountbatten and three others die when their boat is blown up by the IRA. Thomas McMahon was later sentenced to life imprisonment for murder, and Francis McGirl acquitted of the same charge.
 • Fifteen soldiers die in an IRA ambush at Warrenpoint.

September

2 • The 'Yorkshire Ripper' murders his 12th victim.

7 • The Rt Rev Robert Runcie, Biship of St Albans, is named Archbishop of Canterbury from January.

10 • The Zimbabwe-Rhodesia consitutional conference opens in London.
 • British Leyland announces it will axe 25,000 jobs and 13 plants.

12 • The Government announces plans to split the postal service from the telephone network.

13 • Mineworkers decide to press for a 65 per cent pay rise.
21 • Bishop Muzorewa accepts the general principles of the British
consitutional proposals on Zimbabwe-Rhodesia.
23 • Soviet troops enter Afghanistan.
27 • In the first by-election since the General Election, Labour holds
Manchester Central and the Conservative candidate loses his deposit.
30 • The Pope visits Drogheda and appeals to the people to end the violence
in Ireland.

October

1 • At the Labour Party Conference Mr Callaghan is accused by left-wingers
of losing the election over pay policy.
2 • Labour delegates vote for mandatory re-selection of Labour MPs.
6 • Mr Brezhnev offers to reduce troops and tanks in Europe in return for
NATO abandoning plans to modernise nuclear weapons.
16 • The Government announces plans to sell off 5 per cent of its holdings in
British Petroleum.
24 • British exchange controls are abolished.
• Independent Television goes back on air as Thames relay an
emergency service.
29 • New curbs on immigration are announced. Husbands and fiances will
not be allowed to settle in Britain unless the women concerned are
born here.
31 • Miners Leaders reject the Coal Board's offer of an 11-13 per cent pay rise.
• The Bank of England announces Government plans to sell off shares in
BP at 363p per share.

November

2 • Government White Paper announces cuts in education grants for
overseas students.
4 • Iranian students storm the American Embassy in Tehran and take
hostages, demanding the Shah's return from exile in New York.
5 • Iranian students and revolutionary guards take over the British Embassy
in Tehran for six hours.
13 • The Miners reject a 20 per cent pay increase and decide to take industrial
action to secure their 65 per cent pay claim.
15 • Sir Anthony Blunt stripped of his Knighthood when it is revealed he was
the 'fourth man'.
• The Minimum Lending Rate is raised from 14 per cent to 17 per cent.
22 • A record mortgage rate of 15 per cent announced.

25 • Ford workers offered a record 21.5 per cent wage increase – the biggest ever given by the company.

29 • Mrs Thatcher calls for a £1,000 million cut in Britain's contribution to the EEC, saying that she is not afraid to precipitate a crisis if her demand is not met.

December

4 • The Local Government Planning and Land Bill is published, which proposes fundamental changes in the relationship between central and local government.
  • Miners ballot rejects NUM call for an all-out strike.

5 • Mr Jack Lynch, the Irish Republic's Prime Minister resigns. He is succeeded by Mr Charles Haughey six days later.

6 • The Government announces plans to reduce Civil Service staffing by 40,000 over the next three years.

7 • A national steel strike is called for January 2 over the 2 per cent wage increase offer.

10 • Britain appeals to other European members of NATO to back US plans
to site nuclear weapons in their countries. NATO later allowed 572 new American missiles to be stationed in Europe.

11 • British Steel sets a deadline of 8 months to complete cuts of 52,000 jobs, mainly in Wales.

12 • Twenty-four IRA suspects detained after a raid in London and four other English cities in an attempt to foil a pre-Christmas offensive. Despite this effort, five soldiers killed when remote-controlled bombs explode in Northern Ireland four days later.

17 • Stansted chosen as the site of London's third airport.

21 • After 14 years of illegal independence, a ceasefire agreement is signed in London and Rhodesia (or Zimbabwe, as it will be known) becomes a British colony again.

25 • The Afghanistan capital, Kabul, is taken by Soviet troops and the government overthrown two days later.

1980

January

2 • National steel strike begins, the first since 1962.

6 • Three Ulster Defence Regiment soldiers are murdered, bringing their death toll to more than 2,000 over the last decade.

24 • The Government outlines a package of anti-Soviet measures as a protest at the invasion of Afghanistan.

February

13 • Announcement that the sixpence piece will cease to be legal tender after the end of June.

14 • Mrs Thatcher says that State Benefit to strikers will be halved.

22 • Amid reports of hundreds dead, martial law is imposed on Kabul.

27 • State Elections begin in Zimbabwe.

March

4 • Robert Mugabe becomes Prime Minister of Zimbabwe, and Joshua Nkomo, Home Affairs Minister.

6 • Shell announces world record profits of £3,051 million.

12 • Clashes between police and steel strikers in South Yorkshire result in 59 arrests.

13 • Conservatives hold their seat in the Southend-East by-election, but Labour slashes their majority from 10,774 to 430.

17 • The House of Commons vote (315 to 147) for a British boycott of the Olympic games in Moscow.

18 • Mrs Thatcher threatens to withold VAT payments to the EEC if Britain's contribution is not cut.

19 • The Government approves the Channel Tunnel project, but says that it should not be funded with public money.

21 • The Underhill Report reveals a Trotskyist plan to infiltrate and control the Labour Party, under the guise of 'Militant Tendency'.

26 • Budget Day brings a rise in tax allowances, higher duties on alcohol, tobacco and petrol and an increase in prescription charges to £1 per item from December.

27 • Disaster strikes in the North Sea with the collapse of the Alexander Kielland oil rig with the loss of 123 lives.

April

2 • Fighting breaks out in the St Pauls district of Bristol between black youths and the police.

7 • The US breaks off diplomatic relations with Iran over the hostages still being held.

22 • Britain urges its citizens to leave Iran.
   • Unemployment in Britain tops 1.5 million for the first time since 1978.

25 • The US launch a disastrous attempt to rescue their citizens held hostage in Iran.

30 • Iranian gunmen hold 20 hostages after seizing the Iranian Embassy in London demanding freedom for Arabs held in Iran. Five days later, after

two of the hostages are killed, the SAS storm the Embassy freeing the hostages and killing three of the captors.

May

1 • Labour makes large gains in the local elections at the expense of the Conservatives.

2 • British Steel bring in Mr Ian MacGregor from an American bank to succeed Sir Charles Villiers as Chairman from 1 July.

14 • The TUC's call for a day of action meets with a patchy response.

16 • The inflation rate for April the highest for four years at 21.8%.

18 • Britain imposes sanctions on new trade contracts with Iraq.

27 • A verdict of misadventure is passed the death of Mr Blair Peach, a teacher who was killed at an anti-National Front rally in Southall in 1979. It was earlier alleged that he had been killed by a blow from a police truncheon.

June

2 • The Government accepts the EEC's proposal to repay £2,000 million over three years.

3 • The Court of Appeal rules that police vetting of juries is legal.

5 • The European Commission of Human Rights rules against British Rail's closed shop policy.

9 • Roy Jenkins hints at a new centre-left party.

17 • The Government announces plans to site cruise missiles at Greenham Common and Molesworth.

24 • At 1.6 million, unemployment in Great Britain is the highest since the war.

26 • In the Glasgow Central by-election, the Conservatives lose their deposit when Labour returns with a reduced majority.

July

2 • The Government's plans for devolution in Northern Ireland include an elected assembly of 80, and voting by proportional representation.

14 • Transport Secretary, Norman Fowler, announces plans to sell off Sealink and British Rail hotels.

15 • The Government announces plans to replace Polaris with Trident-1 missiles, the total cost of which will be £5,000 million over fifteen years.

19 • The Olympics open in Moscow, although British athletes do not boycott the games.

22 • Redundancies during the first half the year total 180,000, more than

double that during the whole of 1979, with unemployment standing at 1,896,634 – the highest since 1936.
- The House of Commons vote to legalise homosexuality in Scotland.
23 • The Government announces that by April 1982, the 90 area health authorities in the NHS will be abolished.
31 • Shirley Williams, Bill Rodgers and Dr David Owen urge Labour members to join them in a fight against the far left.

August
10 • Four people are killed on the tenth anniversary of Internment in Northern Ireland.
15 • The Retail Price Index falls from 21 to 16.9 per cent, while the Tax and Prices Index rises from 17.4 to 18.5 per cent.
27 • Unemployment reaches 2,000,000 for the first time since 1935.
28 • The Foreign Office denies a coverup over the death of Helen Smith, a British nurse in Jeddah.

September
1 • The Employment Act 1980 comes into force including reforms on picketing, closed shops and strike ballots.
9 • The British Embassy in Teheran is closed.
22 • 'Solidarity' is formed in Poland, led by Lech Walesa after Polish workers win the right to organise free trades unions.
24 • Iraqi troops and tanks cross the border with Iran into Abadan, and full scale hostilities begin.

October
2 • The Labour Party Annual Conference decides to convene a special conference in January 1981 to determine the method of electing future party leaders.
3 • The Housing Act, allowing people to buy their council homes, comes into force.
15 • Mr Callaghan, at 68, resigns as leader of the Labour Party, and a leadership contest begins with Denis Healey and Michael Foot as the leading candidates to succeed.
- Prison Officers start industrial action.
17 • The Soviet-USA conference on nuclear arms limitations in Europe opens in Geneva.
23 • The Soviet Prime Minister, Mr Alexei Kosygin, resigns and is succeeded by Mr Nikolai Tikhonov.

26 • Between 50,000 and 60,000 people attend a CND rally in London, the largest for almost twenty years.

27 • In the Maze prison in Belfast, seven Republican prisoners begin a hunger strike.

November

4 • Ronald Reagan wins a sweeping victory in the US Presidential Elections, beating Jimmy Carter. It is the first time since Hoover's defeat in 1932 that an elected sitting President has been defeated.
  • The pound reaches its highest level against the dollar for seven years at $2.4540.

8 • The Alternative Service Book 1980 comes into use.
  • Voyager 1 sends back pictures of the rings and moons of Saturn.

11 • Michael Foot becomes Labour leader after he defeats Denis Healey by 139 to 129 votes.

13 • Dennis Healey becomes Labour's Deputy leader.

18 • The Yorkshire Ripper claims his 13th victim.

24 • Geoffrey Howe announces cut in the Minimum Lending Rate from 16 to 14 per cent, public spending cuts and extension to 'Granny Bonds'.

December

1 • Prescription charges rise to one pound per item.

8 • Charles Haughey, the Irish Prime Minister, and Mrs Thatcher meet in what is described as 'an historic breakthrough' in Anglo-Irish relations.

18 • Northern Ireland's prison hunger strikers end their fast.

24 • Unemployment rises to a post-war record of 2,133,000.

28 • Southern Television and Westward Television lose their IBA franchies. TV-AM wins the breakfast franchise.

1981

January

1 • Greece becomes the tenth member of the EEC.

5 • Peter Sutcliffe, a long-distance lorry driver, is charged with the Ripper murders.

14 • The Nationality Bill is published, creating three categories of citizenship.

16 • British Steel workers accept a plan which includes closures, redundancies and a pay freeze.
  • Inflation falls to 15.1 per cent.
  • Bernadette McAliskey (nee Devlin) is shot seven times by masked gunmen in Northern Ireland.

20 • Ronald Reagan is inaugurated as President of the United States.
   • Iran releases 52 American hostages taken in 1979.
24 • The special Labour party Conference to decide on how to elect the party leader votes to give 40 per cent of the electoral college votes to the trade unions, and 30 per cent each to the PLP and the constituencies.
26 • Roy Jenkins, Shirley Williams, William Rodgers and David Owen criticise the Labour Party for drifing towards extremism. They form a Council for Social Democracy and are dubbed the 'Gang of Four'.
27 • William Rodgers resigns from the Shadow Cabinet.

February

4 • The Gang of Four publish a list of 100 MP sympathisers.
  • The Government announces plans to sell off 50 per cent of British Aerospace as the first step to 'privatise' nationalised industries.
9 • Shirley Williams resigns from Labour's national executive committee.
  • In Poland, General Jarulzelski replaces Mr Pinkawski as Prime Minister as labour disturbances increase.
10 • The Coal Board announces 30,000 redundancies by closing 50 pits.
17 • South Wales miners begin unofficial strike action over the Coal Boards plans to close pits. The Government withdraws plans to close 23 of the 50 envisaged in a bid to avoid a national miners strike.
24 • The Prince of Wales at 32 announces his intention to marry the 19-year-old Lady Diana Spencer.
26 • Mrs Thatcher meets President Reagan for the first time.

March

1 • In Belfast's Maze Prison, Bobby Sands begins his hunger strike.
2 • Dr. David Owen and 11 other MPs resign from the Labour Party.
9 • Civil servants begin strike action over pay.
10 • In the Budget, alcohol, tobacco, petrol, and road tax all receive substantial increases. The minimum lending rate is reduced from 14 per cent to 12 per cent. Income tax allowances are unaltered.
26 • Roy Jenkins, David Owen, William Rogers and Shirley Williams launch the Social Democratic Party.
30 • Assassination attempt on President Reagan in Washington.

April

4 • Rioting breaks out in Brixton between black youths and the police after a crack-down on street violence.
10 • Bobby Sands, the Maze prison hunger striker, is elected MP for

Fermanagh and S.Tyrone in a by-election.

13 • After a further weekend of rioting in Brixton, William Whitelaw announces that there will be an inquiry, headed by Lord Scarman.

23 • Unemployment reaches 2.5 million.

28 • The Pope announces he will visit Britain 28 May – 2 June 1982.

May

1 • The 'Peoples March For Jobs' sets out from Liverpool.

5 • Bobby Sands dies in the Maze prison. His death sparks off rioting in both Northern and Southern Ireland.

7 • Labour make gains in the County elections, and Ken Livingstone is elected Leader of the GLC.

10 • Francois Mitterand is elected President of France.

13 • An assassination attempt is made on the Pope.

22 • Ian Paisley and his Ulster Unionist party make large gains in Northern Ireland's local elections.

• Peter Sutcliffe, the 'Yorkshire Ripper", is jailed for life.

30 • The 'Peoples March for Jobs' arrives in London, but is banned from marching down Whitehall. They hold a mass meeting the following day in Hyde Park.

June

4 • Sterling falls to $1.9410.

11 • Eight IRA prisoners shoot their way out of Crumlin Road jail.

30 • Charles Haughey is replaced by Garret Fitzgerald as Irish Prime Minister.

July

2 • The Government announces it will set up an advisory committee for Northern Ireland.

6 • Police use CS gas to quell rioting in Toxteth.

7 • Rioting spreads to parts of London, and districts of Manchester.

16 • Labour holds its seat in the Warrington by-election, but with a greatly reduced majority, losing many votes to Roy Jenkins who stood for the SDP.

• Poland holds the first free elections in a Communist country.

28 • The Commons votes for the compulsory wearing of seatbelts.

29 • The Prince of Wales marries Lady Diana Spencer at St Pauls Cathedral.

August

2 • Eighth IRA hunger striker Kieran Docherty dies.

9 • President Reagan announces that the USA will proceed with building the neutron bomb.

20 • Minimum Lending Rate suspended by the Bank of England.

21 • Owen Carron elected MP for Fermanagh and S Tyrone in a by-election.

24 • The 'sus law' is abolished.

September

1 • Service stations in Britain start selling petrol by the litre.

10 • The TUC at its annual conference approves a policy of unilateral nuclear disarmament.

16 • The Liberal Party assembly votes for an alliance with Social Democrats.

27 • Tony Benn narrowly defeated by Denis Healey for deputy leadership of the Labour Party.

30 • The Labour Party conference votes for unilateral nuclear disarmament, and continuing membership of Nato.

October

1 • British Telecom takes over the telephone service from the Post Office.
  • Interest rates rise from 14 per cent to 16 per cent.

3 • After seven months and ten deaths, the hunger strike in Northern Ireland ends.

4 • The first Social Democratic Party Conference opens in Perth.
  • Windscale shuts down, after milk on local farms had become contaminated from a radiation leak.

6 • The Egyptian President, Anwar Sadat, assassinated in Cairo.

10 • Two people killed and 38 wounded, when an army coach outside Chelsea Barracks is blasted by an IRA nail bomb.

15 • Norman Tebbit addressing addressing the Conservative Party Conference, says: 'My father did not riot. He got on his bike and looked for work.'

19 • The Government announces plans to sell off 51 per cent of North Sea Oil.

22 • In their first by-election victory, William Pitt for the Alliance captures Croydon NW from the Conservatives.
  • A ruling by the European Court claims the Government has broken the Convention of Human Rights, by treating homosexuality in Northern Ireland as a crime.

November

5 • The European Court of Human Rights claims the Government has broken the Convention by denying mental patients the right of appeal.

6   • Margaret Thatcher and the Irish Premier Garret Fitzgerald agree to establish an Anglo-Irish council.

10   • Vice President, Hosni Mubarak, selected to replace the assassinated Egyptian president Sadat.

12   • The Church of England`s General Synod votes overwhelmingly to admit women as deacons.

14   • The Unionist MP for South Belfast, Rev Robert Bradford, shot dead in his home.

19   • Tony Benn loses his seat on the Shadow Cabinet.

26   • With a majority of 5,289, the SDP's Shirley Williams wins the Crosby by-election from the Conservatives.

December

2   • The price of a colour TV licence goes up £12 to £46.

8   • Arthur Scargill is elected President of the National Union of Mineworkers.

31   • Reports from New York, San Fransisco and Los Angeles suggest a new type of infection that destroys the body's immune system.

1982

January

1   • Three new ITV stations go on the air for the first time, Central, TVS and TSW.

14   • Mark Thatcher, who went missing on the Paris-Dakar rally in the Sahara two days earlier, is rescued.

26   • For the first time since the 1930s, unemployment passes the three million mark.

February

5   • Sir Freddie Laker's cut-price airline collapses.

19   • John De Lorean's car company goes into receivership in Belfast.

22   • Mercury receives a licence to operate in competition with British Telecom.

24   • Greenland votes in a referendum to withdraw from the EEC.

March

4   • Satellite television receives the go-ahead from the Government.

9   • Petrol, road tax and tobacco increase in the Budget; tax allowances and special benefits increase.

    • Mr Charles Haughey succeeds Dr Garret Fitzgerald to become the

Irish Republic's new Premier.

11 • The Government announces that it will replace Polaris with the US Trident 2 at a cost of £7,500 million.

19 • Between fifty and sixty Argentinians land on South Georgia in the Falklands.

25 • Roy Jenkins, on behalf of the SDP-Liberal alliance wins the Hillhead by-election in Glasgow from the Conservatives.

30 • Many prisons are degrading and brutalising, says a prison inspectorate report.

April

2 • After a three-hour battle, Royal Marines guarding the Falkland Islands' capital, Port Stanley, surrender to Argentinian forces.
• Britain breaks off diplomatic relations with Argentina.

5 • Mr Francis Pym replaces Lord Carrington as Foreign Secretary.
• A task force sets sail for the Falklands.

7 • Britain imposes a 200-mile 'exclusion zone' around the Falklands.

8 • US Secretary of State Mr Haig holds talks with Mrs Thatcher in London.

18 • The Queen signs a new Constitution for Canada in Ottawa, which includes a Charter of Rights and Freedoms.

25 • British troops recapture South Georgia.

30 • America pledges support for Britain in the Falklands war and imposes sanctions against Argentina.

May

1 • The RAF bomb Port Stanley.

2 • The Argentine cruiser, *General Belgrano*, is sunk. Hundreds feared dead.

4 • *HMS Sheffield* is hit and sunk by Exocet missiles with the loss of 21 lives.

7 • Britain warns that all Argentine forces more than 12 miles from Argentina were possible targets for attack.

12 • The QE2, equipped as a troop ship, sets sail for the Falklands.

14 • Self-certification for sickness comes into force.

18 • The EEC votes for a record increase of 11 per cent in farm prices.

20 • UN peace negotiations in Falklands conflict break down.

21 • British troops establish a beachhead in San Carlos Bay. *HMS Ardent* is sunk.

24 • *HMS Antelope* is sunk.

25 • Both the *HMS Coventry* and the *Atlantic Conveyor* are hit.
• The EEC agrees a rebate of at least £476 million to Britain.

27 • Conservatives hold the Beaconsfield constituency in a by-election, but with a much reduced majority.

28 • The Pope arrives in Britain for a five-day visit.
• British forces recapture Goose Green, taking 1,400 prisoners.

30 • Spain becomes the sixteenth member of NATO.

June

3 • Conservatives win Mitcham & Morden by-election from a Labour defector to the SDP.

6 • World leaders support Britain in the Falklands War in a summit at Versaille.

7 • President Reagan visits Britain. He addresses a joint session of Parliament the following day.

8 • The *Sir Galahad* and *Sir Tristram* are hit in fighting around Bluff Cove.

9 • The 20p coin comes into circulation.

12 • *HMS Glamorgan* is hit.

14 • The Argentine forces surrender when the British break their defences around Port Stanley at Tumbledown Mountain, Mount London and Wireless Ridge. The known death toll for the whole campaign is 255 Britons and 652 Argentinians. Mrs Thatcher is cheered on the steps of 10 Downing Street.

17 • General Galtieri is ousted as President of Argentina and stripped of his post as commander-in chief of the army.

18 • The Court of Appeal upholds a worker's right to choose his union.

20 • The EEC lift their trade embargo on Argentina.

21 • The Prince and Princess of Wales have an heir – he is christened William Arthur Philip Louis, 'Wills' for short.

24 • Labour hold their seat in the Coatbridge & Airdrie by-election, but with a reduced majority.

25 • US Secretary of State, Alexander Haig, resigns and is replaced by George Schulz.

July

2 • Roy Jenkins is elected leader of the SDP.

6 • Lord Franks is appointed head of the Falklands Inquiry.

9 • Michael Fagan gains access to the Queen's apartments and Her Majesty awakes to find him sitting at the end of her bed.

12 • Britain announces the end of hostilities in the South Atlantic saying that Argentine POWs will be repatriated.
• The United States lifts trade sanctions against Argentina.

13 • Gerard Tuite makes history as the first Irish citizen to be tried in Ireland for terrorist activities in Britain. He receives a ten-year jail sentence.

20 • IRA bombs in Hyde Park and Regents Park kill 11 soldiers, several horses and injure spectators.
22 • Britain lifts the 200-mile exclusion zone around the Falklands.
27 • The Government abolishes hire purchase restrictions.

August
9 • Fleet Street workers strike in sympathy with health workers, preventing the publication of six national newspapers.
16 • The inquest into the death of Helen Smith in Jeddah opens in London.

September
8 • The whooping cough epidemic reaches its highest level since 1957, the year the vaccine was invented.
16 • Labour hold their seat in the Gower by-election.
23 • Shirley Williams is elected president of the SDP.
• Nigel Lawson says 'No industry should stay in state ownership unless there is an overwhelming case."
29 • Lord Denning retires as Master of the Rolls. He is succeeded by Sir John Donaldson.

October
8 • At the Conservative Party Conference, Mrs Thatcher denies that she intends to break up the NHS, saying 'The National Health Service is safe with us'.
11 • Over 800 people are cited for awards in the full Falklands Honours list.
18 • The Church of England publishes a report called 'The Church and the Bomb' opposing nuclear weapons as a deterrent.
21 • Gerry Adams and Martin McGuinness are elected at the Northern Ireland Assembly elections.
28 • Labour narrowly wins Birmingham Northfield from the Conservatives, and holds onto Southwark, Peckham in by-elections.
31 • The Thames Flood Barrier is successfully tested.

November
2 • Miners reject a call for strike action in a ballot. 61 per cent vote against.
• Channel Four goes on the air.
4 • Charles Haughey's government collapes after a vote of no confidence in

the Irish Parliament.

11 • The SDLP and Sinn Fein boycott the opening of the Northern Ireland Assembly.

19 • Only 30 per cent of Britoil shares offered to the public are sold.

10 • Geoffrey Prime is committed to 38 years in jail for supplying Government secrets to the Russians.

12 • Reports from Russia state that President Breznev died on the 10th. He is succeeded by Yuri Andropov.

22 • The pound falls against the dollar after the government says it will not support it.

23 • Labour publishes its plans for economic recovery, commentators claim it implies a 30 per cent devaluation.

December

12 • Over 20,000 women protest outside the nuclear base at Greenham Common.

• Britain sends a reconaissance unit to join a multinational peace-keeping force in Beirut.

17 • Inflation drops to 6.3 per cent – the lowest for 10 years.

1983

January

6 • Michael Heseltine replaces Sir John Nott as Secretary of State for Defence.

8 • Margaret Thatcher visits the Falkland Islands.

17 • Early morning TV begins with the BBC's 'Breakfast Time'.

18 • The Franks report on the Falklands War says that Mrs Thatcher and her government could not have prevented Argentina's invasion. However, it criticises the machinery of government and British intelligence.

20 • The Serpell report on British Rail recommends higher commuter fares and drastic cuts in the system.

25 • The pound drops to $1.517 – a record low.

31 • The wearing of seatbelts in cars becomes compulsory.

February

1 • ITV's breakfast channel, TV-AM, goes on air.

3 • Unemployment is at a record figure of 3,224,715.

4 • The Shops Bill on Sunday trading is defeated in the House of Commons.

11 • Inflation falls to 4.9 per cent.

23 • The Labour Party expels five Militants.

24 • Peter Tatchell loses the Bermondsey by-election for Labour to Simon Hughes, Liberal/SDP Alliance.
28 • Yorkshire and South Wales miners strike at planned pit closures.

March

3 • The BMA reports that the chances of surviving a nuclear hollocaust are 'a myth'.
   • The NUM call a national strike ballot, against the wishes of the miners' leader, Arthur Scargill.
5 • Mr Bob Hawke and the Labour Party defeat Malcolm Fraser's coalition in the Australian general election.
6 • Chancellor Kohl and his Christian Democrat party are returned to power in Germany.
9 • Miners vote against strike action, and the following day abandon their year-long boycott of the NCB.
14 • OPEC cuts the price of oil by 15 per cent.
15 • The Budget sees increases in drink, petrol and tobacco. The bank lending rate is cut to 10.5 per cent.
18 • Peter Jay resigns as chairman of TV-AM.
23 • President Reagan announces his 'Star Wars' defence plans, which entail developing futuristic weapons to defend the US against Soviet nuclear attack.
25 • The European Court of Human Rights votes that Britain is violating human rights by censoring prisoners' mail.
26 • Anthony Blunt dies of a heart attack.

April

1 • The Government expels three Russians named by a defector as KGB spies.
   • Thousands of CND supporters join hands to form a 14-mile chain linking Greenham Common, Aldermaston and Burghfield.
8 • Russia expels two British journalists.
18 • The Government commits itself to lead free petrol by 1990.
21 • The pound coin comes into circulation.

May

4 • President Reagan admits that covert weapons supplied to the Contras in Nicaragua is to help overthrow the Sandinista government.
6 • Extracts from 'The Hitler Diaries' are published in *Stern* magazine. Experts are divided over their authenticity. They turn out to be a clever

hoax and *The Times* cancels plans to publish them. Konrad Kujau later surrenders to the police in West Germany, claiming to be the author.

- New police powers on drinking and driving come into force.

9
- Mrs Thatcher sets the general election date – June 9.

11
- Labour publishes its manifesto, which includes withdrawal from the EEC and unilateral disarmament.

12
- The Government backs the Security Commission's plans for lie detectors to be used on security staff.

13
- House of Commons Speaker, Mr George Thomas, retires and is replaced by Mr Bernard Weatherill.

18
- The Conservative Party manifesto is published, which includes plans to abolish the GLC and the six metropolitan counties.

24
- The Criminal Justice Act comes into force.

25
- Jim Callaghan attacks Labour's plans to abandon Polaris.

June

1
- The first prosecution for a 'video nasty' is made under the Obscene Publications Act.

9
- Conservatives win a landslide victory at the General Election with 397 seats. Labour win 209, the Liberal-Social Democrat Alliance win 23, and others 21. Tony Benn, Shirley Williams and Gerry Fitt all lose their seats.
- Debendox, the morning sickness pill, is withdrawn from circulation by its manufacturers.

12
- Michael Foot resigns as leader of the Labour Party.

13
- Roy Jenkins resigns as leader of the SDP, and recommends David Owen as his successor.

14
- Interest rates are cut from 10 per cent to 9.5 per cent.

16
- The Pope begins an historic eight-day visit to his homeland, Poland.

18
- Inflation falls to 3.7 per cent – the lowest for 15 years.

30
- A report criticises the West Yorkshire police's handling of the Yorkshire Ripper murder hunt.

July

4
- The Selby coalfield begins production.

5
- The Government 'fines' high-spending local authorities.

12
- The European Court of Justice rules that Britain's taxation of wine is illegal.
- The government promises to introduce legislation making it law for Trade Unions to hold secret ballots of their members before calling strike action, and hold elections for their top union jobs.

13 • Neil Kinnock narrowly escapes injury when his car overturns on the M4.

14 • The General Synod approves a plan for divorcees to marry in church.

26 • Victoria Gillick loses her battle to prevent doctors prescribing the Pill to girls under the age of 16 without parental consent.

28 • In the Penrith and The Border by-election, the Conservative majority is drastically cut to 552 by the Alliance candidate.

August

12 • The Argentinian Government agrees to release Britain's assets frozen during the Falklands War.

14 • The French police seize arms en route to the IRA.

16 • The USA admit they helped Nazi war criminal, Klaus Barbie, escape after the War. They apologise formally to France.

27 • Russian President Andropov offers to destroy SS20s in return for the US not deploying new missiles in Europe.

September

1 • Ian MacGregor takes over as chairman of the National Coal Board.

• The United States accuse Russia of shooting down a Korean Airlines 747 with the loss of 269 lives.

2 • Unemployment falls for the first time since 1979.

6 • Moderates gain a large majority in the TUC Council.

7 • Arthur Scargill attacks Poland's Solidarity for anti-socialist behaviour against a socialist state.

8 • The NHS is required by government to allow private contractors to tender for cleaning, catering and laundering services.

14 • John Gummer succeeds Cecil Parkinson as chairman of the Conservative Party.

15 • Neil Kinnock announces that under a future Labour government Britain would remain in the EEC.

19 • More BP shares sold, reducing the Government's holding to 31 per cent

21 • The Liberal Party vote for a United Ireland.

25 • A prison officer is killed during a mass break-out of IRA prisoners at the Maze.

26 • Patrick Gilmour, father of a 'supergrass', is released after being held captive for 11 months by the IRA.

October

2 • Neil Kinnock, at the age of 41, is elected leader of the Labour Party, with Roy Hattersley as his deputy.

5 • Cecil Parkinson admits that he had a relationship with his secretary, Sara Keays, and that he is the father of the child she is expecting.
 • Lech Walesa is awarded the Nobel Peace Prize.
7 • The Government publishes a White Paper anouncing the abolition of the GLC and metropolitan counties in 1986.
10 • Yitzhak Shamir replaces Menachim Begin as Israel's Prime Minister.
15 • Cecil Parkinson is replaced by Norman Tebbit as Trade and Industry Secretary.
20 • Reports say that acid rain is killing trees in Germany.
21 • Miners vote for an overtime ban.
22 • London comes to a halt as between 250,000 and 400,000 people protest at plans to base US Cruise missiles in Britain. Neil Kinnock addresses this, the biggest anti-nuclear weapons demostration for twenty years, and calls it 'a movement for life'. Similar demonstrations are repeated in France and Germany.
24 • American forces land in Grenada following the disappearance of Prime Minister, Maurice Bishop.
25 • The Griffiths Report recommends the appointment of 'general managers' in the NHS.
26 • The Trades Union Bill is published, making secret ballots of members over strike action compulsory.

November
1 • Michael Heseltine says that demonstrators who get near nuclear missiles are liable to be shot.
2 • Following a television programme reporting the extraordinarily high rate of leukaemia victims among children around Windscale, the Government demands an inquiry, headed by Sir Douglas Black. British Nuclear Fuels say they 'have nothing to hide'.
8 • The Government publishes the Social Security (Age of Retirement) Bill proposing equal state pensions for both sexes.
14 • The first Cruise missiles arrive at Greenham Common. 141 women are arrested.
15 • Three hundred anti-nuclear demonstrators are arrested outside the House of Commons.
 • Rauf Denktas declares the Turkish sector of Cyprus to be independent.
20 • The Official Unionist Party withdraws from the Northern Ireland Assembly following the murder of three men in a Protestant church.
23 • The Royal College of Physicians say that 100,000 people die yearly from smoking.

- The Russian delegation walks out of nuclear disarmament talks in Geneva.
26 • Thieves escape with £25 million worth of gold bars from Heathrow Airport in the Brinks-Mat robbery.

December
3 • Women peace campaigners break into the airforce base at Greenham Common.
4 • The SAS shoot dead two IRA men in Northern Ireland.
5 • The House Buyers Bill is published, allowing people other than solicitors to carry out conveyancing.
   • The Health and Social Security Bill is published which, among other things, abolishes the opticians' monopoly on supply of spectacles.
8 • Peers vote to allow television cameras into the House of Lords.
10 • Argentina inaugurates a new civilian President – Raoul Alfonsin. Mrs Thatcher unfreezes diplomatic and trade negotions.
11 • Protests continue at Greenham Common, this time with the arrest of 60 women from the 30,000 demonstrators.
12 • The US withdraws its troops from Grenada.
13 • Turgut Ozal becomes the first civilian Prime Minister of Turkey since the military coup in 1980.
15 • The European Parliament blocks the £457 million EEC rebate to Britain.
16 • The Court of Appeal demands that the *Guardian* hand over a leaked Defence document in order to identify the mole who supplied it.
17 • An IRA car bomb explodes outside Harrods in London, killing six, including three police officers.
19 • Britoil cancel an order worth £86 million from British Shipbuilders' Scott Lithgow Yard because they are 500 days behind the agreed delivery date.
20 • The Rates Bill is published, giving the Government the power to cap expenditure by individual local authorities.

1984
January
3 • Despite compensation being awarded to six cancer victims, Sellafield nuclear power plant denies any liability.
   • 7,000 men are sent home as the NUM overtime ban reaches its tenth week.
6 • Sir Keith Joseph announces plans to reform school exams.
   • Foreign Office clerk Sarah Tisdall is charged under the Official Secrets Act.

13 • On his visit to Saudi Arabia, Sir Geoffrey Howe upsets Israelis over his remarks urging them to recognise the rights of the Palestinians for self-determination.

19 • 'Unions must adapt to changing circumstances' states the TUC document 'Strategy for the Future'.
   • Inflation is at its lowest for 16 years.

21 • The first British test-tube triplets are born.

23 • Twelve Conservative MPs, including Francis Pym, abstain in vote on 1984-5 rate support grant proposals.

24 • 11,000 schools in London close for the day as teachers strike.

25 • Staff at GCHQ are deprived of their union membership.

27 • Treasury and Cabinet Office civil servants walk out in protest over the GCHQ decision.

February

2 • Britain agrees that Royal Navy should help convoy oil through the Strait of Hormuz.

8 • Britain brings home peace-keeping forces from the Lebanon.

10 • After only 15 months in office, the Russian leader Yuri Andropov dies. He is replaced by Konstantin Chernenko.

21 • Mrs Thatcher claims most staff at GCHQ have agreed to a payment in return for their right to belong to a union.
   • The Government is defeated in the Lords on phone-tapping.

29 • The Canadian Prime Minister, Pierre Trudeau resigns, and is replaced by Lestor Pearson.

March

1 • Tony Benn wins the Chesterfield by-election for Labour with a 6,264 majority.
   • Concern mounts amongst scientists that the constant use of fossil fuels will cause a 'Greenhouse Effect'.

9 • Miners' strike involving 83,000 men begins.

13 • The Budget brings radical changes in taxation, with substantial cuts in income tax.

14 • Gerry Adams is shot three times in Belfast by Loyalist gunmen.
   • Bank interest rates are cut to their lowest level for nearly six years.

20 • The EEC Summit breaks down over disagreement about Britain's contributions.
   • Miners' pickets close down 80 per cent of pits.

21 • Brenda Dean becomes the first woman to head a major trades union

when she is elected general secretary of SOGAT '82.

23 • Sarah Tisdall, a secretary in Geoffrey Howe's private office, is jailed for six months for releasing a top secret document about Cruise Missiles arriving at Greenham Common.

April

1 • The Metropolitan Police announce plans to allow some officers to carry automatic weapons.

4 • Police-backed bailiffs clear women from the Peace Camp at Greenham Common.

• Nottinghamshire miners reject the NUM's recommendation not to cross picket lines.

9 • 100 arrests are made at Nottinghamshire and Derbyshire pits.

11 • Mr Heath accuses the Government of 'Gerrymandering' over GLC.

12 • Arthur Scargill rejects proposals to hold a national ballot of miners over continuing strike action.

16 • Michael Bettany, an MI5 double agent, is jailed for 23 years.

17 • WPC Yvonne Fletcher is murdered when shots are fired from the Libyan People's Bureau in St James's Square, London.

18 • British Rail and British Leyland both announce they are back in profit.

22 • Students and diplomats of the Libyan People's Embassy are told to leave within seven days as Britain cuts off diplomatic links with Libya.

23 • The discovery of the AIDS virus is announced in Washington.

26 • British diplomats and families return from Tripoli.

May

2 • TUC General Secretary Len Murray announces he will retire in the autumn.

3 • The Conservatives lose Birmingham City Council in local elections.

8 • The Thames flood barrier is officially opened.

14 • 20,000 take part in a miners protest march in Mansfield, 55 were later arrested.

21 • Len Murray says sympathy strikes for the miners will be disowned.

23 • Arthur Scargill and Ian MacGregor meet for their first talks. The talks break down after only an hour.

25 • Nottinghamshire miners win the 'right to work' from the High Court.

29 • 84 pickets are arrested, 41 policemen and 28 picketing miners are injured during violence at Orgreave Pit, South Yorkshire.

30 • Arthur Scargill is arrested at Orgreave and charged with obstruction.

June

2 • President Botha visits Britain amid protests, the first visit by a South African leader for 23 years.

7 • 120 are arrested at a mass lobby of striking miners outside Parliament.

8 • World leaders hold an Economic Summit in London to discuss the international debt crisis.

14 • In the nationwide elections for the European Parliament, Labour doubles its representation by gaining 16 seats from the Conservatives.

• Michael Hancock wins Portsmouth South for the Alliance, with a majority of 1,341, in a surprise defeat for the Conservatives.

20 • The Government announces that 'O' levels and 'CSE's will be abolished and replaced with 'GCSEs.

July

2 • Steel unions reject a plea by the NUM to strike in sympathy.

• The National Coal Board implement plans which will make 20,000 miners redundant.

4 • The Government announces the abolition of licences for dogs.

6 • David Jenkins is consecrated as Bishop of Durham.

7 • Chief of Defence Staffs and service heads appeal directly to the Prime Minister over service cuts.

9 • Start of the national docks strikes.

• 700-year-old York Minster is devastated by a bolt of lightning.

10 • The General Synod approves second marriages in churches.

11 • The NUM defies the High Court by implementing disciplinary measures against non-strikers.

12 • Britain receives a rebate from the EEC of £475 million.

17 • The NUM leadership is challenged with the formation and launch of the National Working Miners Committee.

28 • Seven out of the ten largest ports join the dock strike.

• Electricians union leader, Frank Chapple, accuses Arthur Scargill of 'setting worker against worker'.

August

1 • Proceedings begin to seize the assets of the South Wales miners for refusing to pay a fine.

• Geoffrey Howe announces plans to hand back Hong Kong to the Chinese in 1997.

2 • The Government pledges to introduce laws on phone-tapping after the European Court of Human Rights condemns it.

- Ken Livingstone resigns as Leader of the GLC.
6 • The Government wins its fight to overturn a High Court ruling that the ban on unions at GCHQ is illegal.
15 • A former MI5 officer alleges that he is 99 per cent certain that Sir Roger Hollis, former Director General of Security Services, was a spy. Mrs Thatcher had formally exonerated him in the Commons.
18 • Clive Ponting, a senior civil servant at the MoD, is charged with an offence under the Official Secrets Act. The charge is connected to Labour MP Tam Daylell's campaign to hold an inquiry into the sinking of the Argentine cruiser, the *General Belgrano*.
23 • Building Societies are given the go-ahead to compete with high street banks and provide customers with cheque books, overdrafts and personal loans.
24 • Talks are held in London and at 12 coalfields to discuss the miners' return to work.
  • Patrick Jenkins announces in the Commons that 18 councils will be rate-capped next year.
30 • Mrs Thatcher attacks Neil Kinnock and the Labour Party as 'the allies of wreckers of the coal industry'.

September
3 • The NUM receives an overwhelming vote of support at the TUC for extending strike action into other industries.
4 • Norman Willis is elected to succeed Len Murray as General Secretary of the TUC.
13 • Michael Heseltine, Secretary of State for Defence, agrees to appear before the Commons Select Committee on Foreign Affairs to talk about the sinking of the *General Belgrano*.
14 • Talks between the Coal Board and the NUM break down for the last time when the NUM refuse to accept a settlement which allows the Coal Board to close down uneconomical pits.
16 • Prince Harry is born to the Prince and Princess of Wales.
18 • The three-week dock strike ends.
19 • Mrs Thatcher says she is prepared for the miners strike to continue for another year if the NUM won't allow the Coal Board to close uneconomical pits.
  • A report states that the MoD knew of the *Belgrano*'s change of course before it was sunk, but that this information was withheld from ministers.
20 • The Liberal Party Assembly votes, against the wishes of David Steel, to remove cruise missiles from British soil.

21 • The Bishop of Durham attacks the Government's handling of the miners strike, and urges the removal of Ian MacGregor, calling him 'an imported, elderly American'. The Archbishop of Canterbury later writes to Ian MacGregor apologising for the Bishop's remarks.
   • The TUC Finance and General Purposes Committee agree to underwrite the NUM's fight by raising £150,000 a week.
26 • Documents on the future of Hong Kong are exchanged in Beijing.
30 • Two miners win their battle when the High Court declares picketing around collieries in Yorkshire is 'unlawful'.

October

1 • The Labour Party Conference rejects Neil Kinnock's proposals for 'one member, one vote' for the reselection of MPs.
7 • The Archbishop of Canterbury criticises the Government's handling of the miners' strike.
10 • The High Court fines the NUM £200,000 and Arthur Scargill £1,000 for contempt of court. Despite this, the 31-week strike is still said by the NUM to be official.
11 • An IRA bomb explodes at the Grand Hotel in Brighton during the Conservative Party Conference. Three are killed and 32 are injured.
25 • The High Court orders sequestration of the NUM's assets as payment of the £200,000 fine.
28 • The TUC criticise the NUM for allowing one of its leaders to 'consort' with Colonel Gaddafi.
30 • The Soviet Union embargoes fuel exports to Britain in sympathy with the striking miners.

November

5 • Sequestrators trying to recover the NUM's fine trace £2.7 million worth of union funds to Dublin. Meanwhile, 800 miners return to work.
6 • The Government admit that the log of the submarine which sunk the *Belgrano* is missing.
7 • Ronald Reagan is re-elected President, beating Walter Mondale, with 59 per cent of the votes cast.
12 • Nigel Lawson announces the abolition of the pound note.
20 • With the flotation of 51 per cent of British Telecom, £3,900 million worth of shares are issued.
   • The North Wales NUM decides to end its strike.
21 • Antony Newton announces that £15 is to be deducted from the supplementary benefit pay of a striking miner's dependents.

December

1   • A receiver is called in to take control of the NUM's funds.

13   • The Conservatives hold Enfield Southgate in a by-election. The Labour candidate loses his deposit.

18   • The Government announces plans to privatise the Trustees Savings Bank.

19   • The Sino-British treaty returning Hong Kong to China in 1997 is signed in Beijing.

1985

January

1   • The pound is at a record low at $1.1587.

3   • Three men are held under the Prevention of Terrorism Act in connection with Libyan bombings in London.

4   • Britain's first ever surrogate mother, Kim Cotton, gives birth to a daughter. The baby was later given to the couple who paid for her.

7   • Nine striking miners are jailed for arson, while about 1,200 miners abandon their strike.

10   • Clive Sinclair launches the battery-powered tricycle, the C5. Motoring correspondents are less than enthusiastic.

23   • The House of Lords is televised, with 300 of the 1,177 Lords present.

28   • Base rates rise (the third time since 11 January) to 14 per cent.

29   • Mrs Thatcher is snubbed when Oxford Dons do not award her an honorary degree.

February

7   • The Archbishop of Canterbury's envoy, Terry Waite, negotiates for and secures the release of four Britons from Libya.

11   • The Government faces a row when Clive Ponting is acquitted at the Old Bailey. Despite the decision, Ponting is later told he can never work for the MoD again and resigns.

    • The High Court bans mass picketing at five South Wales pits.

    • The pound falls to below $1.10, inflation rises and pressure increases on mortgages.

14   • Doctors are told that they must not give contraceptive advice to girls under 16.

19   • The Irish Government passes an emergency bill allowing the seizure of £5 million of IRA assets.

20   • The NUM votes to continue their 50-week strike. Despite the vote, 3,807 miners return to work.

25   • More miners return to work, leaving 51 per cent still striking.

27 • The pound falls to a record low of $1.0765. In the past twelve months, the pound has devalued by 27 per cent.

28 • Nine are killed and 30 injured when an IRA mortar explodes on a police station in Newry, Co Down.

March

1 • The Pentagon accepts that a nuclear war would lead to an age of 'nuclear winter'.

4 • After nearly twelve months strike action, miners vote to go back to work. Mrs Thatcher claims a 'famous victory'; Arthur Scargill denies defeat.

7 • Two IRA men are sentenced to 35 years for masterminding the 1981 bombings in London.

11 • The Government raises prescription charges to £2 per item.
• Mikhail Gorbachev becomes the Russian Communist Party leader on the death of Konstantin Chernenko. Mr Reagan proposes summit talks.

19 • Nigel Lawson's budget increases road licences, cigarettes and mortgage interest rates.

April

2 • The NUM stops its overtime ban.
• President Gorbachev accepts the US's invitation for summit talks.

8 • The NCB begins closing Ackton Hall colliery.
• 20,000 CND marchers gather at a missile base at Molesworth, Cambridgeshire.

11 • The first British baby dies of AIDS.
• The NUM accept a 10 per cent payrise package.

29 • The Government announces the introduction of computerised screening in a bid to lower number of deaths from cervical cancer.
• Opposition MPs attack the Government's proposal to abolish state earnings related pension schemes.

May

3 • The Liberal-SDP alliance make big gains in county council elections at the expense of the Tories who lose control of nine councils.

7 • The Government announces that British Gas is to be sold off within the next two years.

8 • Reagan and Gorbachev make a pledge for world peace on the 40th anniversary of VE-Day.

11 • Fifty-six fans are killed, 211 injured and 77 badly burnt in a fire at Bradford City's football ground. The chairman later admits the existence

of letters warning of the risk of fire at the ground.

20 • Four members of the RUC are killed when a 1,000lb IRA bomb explodes.

22 • The Government gives the go-ahead for a new airport to be based in London's Docklands.

• Liverpool fans rampage at Heysal Stadium in Belgium resulting in the deaths of 38 Belgian and Italian fans, and the injury of hundreds more.

28 • The European Court of Human Rights finds Britain guilty of sex discrimination over its immigration policy.

31 • English football clubs are banned from Europe by the Football Association next season.

June

2 • UEFA bans English clubs from playing in Europe 'indefinitely'.

3 • In a review of social welfare in the Commons, plans are outlined for the abolition of SERPs within fifteen years, cutbacks on housing benefits and the abolition of death grants.

5 • NACODS call off their overtime ban, ending the 15 months of industrial action in the mining industry.

6 • FIFA bans its affiliated members from any contact with England at club level.

7 • The pit whose threatened closure started the miners strike, Cortonwood, is to shut bringing job losses in Yorkshire to 10,000.

July

2 • Eduard Shevardnadze becomes Soviet Foreign Minister while Andrei Gromyko becomes Soviet President.

5 • Richard Livesey (Liberal) wins the Brecon and Radnor by-election. This defeat is the worst by-election loss for the Conservatives since the Election.

7 • Nottinghamshire miners threaten to leave the NUM.

8 • The forgers of *The Hitler Diaries* are jailed in West Germany.

• Robert Mugabe wins a landslide victory in Zimbabwe's General Election.

10 • Greenpeace's environmental ship *Rainbow Warrior*, is sunk by explosions in Auckland Harbour. One man on board is killed.

13 • Bob Geldof's Live Aid concerts in London and Philadelphia raise £50 million for famine victims in Ethiopia.

16 • The Local Goverment Bill abolishing the GLC and other metropolitan counties becomes law.

17 • British Rail announces £408 million losses, attributing £250 million of them directly to the miners' strike.

21 • President Botha imposes a state of emergency on 30 magisterial districts of South Africa to protect 'law abiding black people' against 'thuggery and violence'. The South African Council of Churches saw the move as an attempt to curb 'the tide of liberation'.

30 • The BBC, after pressure from the Home Secretary, agree not to screen an interview with Gerry Adams of Sinn Fein for their series 'Real Lives'.

31 • EEC ambassadors to Pretoria are recalled.

August

7 • Journalists strike over BBC governors' decision not to show the interview with Gerry Adams. The World Service is off the air for the first time ever.

9 • Martin Galvin, a banned American NORAID leader, defies an explusion order and is a pallbearer at the funeral of an IRA 'volunteer'.

22 • Fifty-four holiday makers are killed when a British Airtours Boeing 737's engine bursts into flames on takeoff from Manchester Airport. Other 737s are grounded.

September

5 • Lloyds of London announce worst ever underwriting losses of £188 million.

9 • Rioting breaks out between youths and police in Handsworth, Birmingham.

10 • Douglas Hurd visits Handsworth, and is pelted and jeered by crowds.

12 • Oleg Gordievsky, the KGB leader in London, defects to the West. His decision leads to a series of tit-for-tat expulsions. The score of expulsions ended at 31 each when Mrs Thatcher finally called a halt.

19 • 20,000-30,000 people are feared trapped after Mexico suffers the worst earthquake this century. The death toll later reached 2,000.

22 • The French Government finally admits their agents were responsible for the sinking of the *Rainbow Warrior*. The French Defence Minister resigns, and calls for the the head of the Secret Service to be sacked.

29 • During two days of violence in Brixton following the accidental police shooting of Cherry Groce while searching for her son, 209 people are arrested.

October

1 • Rioting breaks out in Toxteth and Peckham.

3 • Unemployment figures for September show a rise to nearly 3.5 million.

6 • PC Keith Blakelock is hacked to death as hundreds of black youths go on the rampage at the Broadwater Farm housing estate in North London.

Rioting erupted following the death of Cynthia Jarrett, whose house was earlier searched by police. By the end of the evening, 254 police officers and civilians were injured. The Home Secretary backs the introduction of the use of plastic bullets.

9 • Self-confessed IRA terrorist, Dominic McGlinchey, wins an appeal against his murder conviction.

14 • The NUT reject the latest local authority pay offer.
  • Clive Sinclair, inventor of the C5, calls in a receiver to his company TPD.
  • New regulations come into force stating that all blood donations are to be checked for the AIDS virus.

17 • Law Lords overturn the ban on giving contraceptive advice to girls under 16 without their parents' consent.

19 • Nottinghamshire and South Derbyshire miners vote to set up a breakaway union, to be called the Union of Democratic Miners.

November

15 • Treasury minister, Ian Gow resigns after the Anglo-Irish agreement is signed by Mrs Thatcher and Garret Fitzgerald giving the Republic a say in the governing of Northern Ireland.

21 • The two French agents accused of sinking the *Rainbow Warrior* are jailed for ten years each in New Zealand.
  • After their two-day Geneva summit, Presidents Gorbachev and Reagan report their successful discussions on a possible mutual 50 per cent cut in strategic nuclear arsenals, ways of exploring agreements on medium-range missiles, the importance of resolving humanitarian issues, and the prevention of incidents which might result in nuclear war. Despite their disagreement over 'Star Wars', President Reagan announces a 'fresh start' in diplomatic relations between the US and Russia, and President Gorbachev says 'the world has become a safer place'.

December

1 • The Government criticises a Church of England report on inner city deprivation.

4 • The Queen and Prince Philip join Mrs Thatcher to celebrate 10 Downing Street's 250th year as the Prime Minister's official residence.

5 • Labour hold Tyne Bridge in a by-election, with an increased majority.

10 • Two rape victims make legal history by winning financial damages from their attacker. The sum received (£17,560) was ldescribed as 'paltry'.

11 • During the first Anglo-Irish conference, 38 police are injured in clashes with Loyalists. Six days later, 13 Ulster Unionist MPs resign in order to

fight by-election campaigns based on opposition to the Agreement.

16 • The Social Services secretary decides to modify SERPS, not abolish it.

27 • Michael Heseltine, Defence Secretary, moves towards clinching the European purchase of helicopter company, Westland, in the face of a bid by a joint US/Italian venture.

1986

January

1 • Presidents Gorbachev and Reagan appear on television extending New Year's greetings to each other's countries and pledging peace.
  • US bidders for Westland arrive in Britain to campaign for their offer.

3 • A US task force heads for Libya after President Reagan accuses it of being behind terrorist attacks at Rome and Vienna airports last December.

7 • A new European bid for Westland is followed by Michael Heseltine's resignation after a row in Cabinet over the company's future.

13 • Leon Brittan admits he did receive a letter from British Aerospace concerning Westland.

20 • The Channel Tunnel is given the go-ahead at a cost of £5 billion. It will be 31 miles long, cost about £50 per car to use it, and will be operational in 1993.

24 • Leon Brittan resigns as Trade and Industry Secretary over the leaking of a letter berrating Michael Heseltine's actions while Defence Secretary.

28 • The US's troubled Shuttle programme suffers a setback when *Challenger* explodes within seconds of lift-off killing all on board.

February

2 • Newspaper magnate, Rupert Murdoch, tells his workers that he will not accept any unions at his new Wapping plant.
  • The Government publishes a White Paper proposing the privatisation of the water industry.

10 • The European bid for Westland Helicopters fails.
  • SOGAT '82 is fined £25,000 and has its assets siezed after defying a High Court injunction against picketing.

12 • A police file on Derek Hatton, deputy leader of Liverpool City Council, is handed to the Director of Public Prosecutions.
  • Police and pickets clash outside Rupert Murdoch's printing plant at Wapping.

25 • President Marcos of the Phillipines is overthrown and flees the country. Cory Acquino, wife of the assassinated opposition leader, replaces him.

28 • Sweden's Prime Minister, Olaf Palme, is assassinated.

March

2 • The Queen signs the Australia Bill which formally severs the country's last constitutional ties with Britain.

3 • Riot police take to the streets of Northern Ireland after mass protests against the Anglo-Irish agreement.

4 • Kurt Waldheim, Austria's presidential candidate, is accused of having been a member of Hitler's SS.

7 • After 229 days and 757 deaths, the state of emergency in South Africa is suspended.
 • Derek Hatton and 15 others are formally accused by the Labour Party of being members of Militant.

10 • Doctors attack a proposed further 20p increase to prescription charges. Since 1979, charges have increased 11-fold.

12 • Evelyn Glenholmes is arrested in Ireland on suspicion of involvement in the Brighton bombing.

19 • The Duke of York announces his engagement to Sarah Ferguson.

24 • An administrative blunder in Britain allows Evelyn Glenholmes to escape extradition to face terrorist charges. She walks free from a Dublin court to the fury of both British and Irish authorities.

25 • The dispute between the US and Libya heats up as US war planes inflict casualties. President Gadaffi vows to turn the Med into 'a sea of blood'.

29 • The world's first test-tube quins are born.

31 • Hampton Court Palace is seriously damaged by fire.

April

4 • In order to try to settle his dispute, Rupert Murdoch offers print unions the Gray's Inn Road printing plant and a compensation package.

9 • Mrs Thatcher meets two Ulster Unionist leaders amid speculation that concessions will be made over the Anglo-Irish agreement.

11 • Labour win the Fulham by-election from the Conservatives.
 • Plans for Sunday trading are dropped by the Government after pressure from Conservative rebels.

17 • Extremist Arab groups in Lebanon kill three British hostages, kidnap a television journalist and attack the British Ambassador's Beirut residence in retaliation for British-based US Air Force attacks on Libya.

21 • The EEC tighten sanctions against Libya; while Britain expels 21 Libyan nationals.

24 • The Duchess of Windsor dies in Paris. Her body is later brought to Britain and laid to rest at Frogmore, alongside her husband.
 • The Government drops plans to sell Land Rover to an American buyer.

28 • News reaches the West of a fire and a massive radioactive leak at a power plant in Chernobyl. Anger mounts that the Russians did not admit to the accident until four days after the event.

May
1 • Prison officers agree to go back to work after damage to prisons.
3 • In the worst violence yet in the dispute at Wapping, 175 police and 150 demonstrators are injured.
6 • The Labour Party make large gains in local elections.
10 • Britain expels three Syrian diplomats when Syria refuses to let them be questioned over the El Al bomb. The next day three British diplomats are expelled from Damascus in retaliation.
14 • As fears of a melt-down at the nuclear reactor at Chernobyl persist, President Gorbachev admits that 92,000 people have been evacuated, nine people have died and 299 have been injured. (The final death toll reached 21.)
21 • Kenneth Baker takes over from Sir Keith Joseph as Education Secretary.

June
5 • David Steel tells David Owen that the Alliance party must establish a joint nuclear policy if it is to stand any chance of winning the next General Election.
6 • Chief Constable of West Yorkshire, Colin Sampson, takes over the inquiry into the RUC's 'shoot to kill' policy from John Stalker, who is later suspended from duty for allegedly consorting with 'known criminals'.
 • Kurt Waldheim is elected President of Austria to worldwide concern.
12 • Derek Hatton is expelled from the Labour Party.
 • The Government confirms that the Northern Ireland Assembly, set up in 1982, is to be dissolved.
23 • IRA member and Brighton bomber, Patrick Magee, is sent to prison with eight life sentences.
 • Ian Paisley is forcibly ejected from the Irish Assembly as it is dissolved.
27 • In an attempt to make the Republic more acceptable to northern Protestants, Garret FitzGerald proposes that divorce becomes legal, but this is rejected by the Irish people in a referendum.

July
12 • One hundred people are injured in clashes between Catholics and Protestants in Northern Ireland during the Orange Day marches.
13 • Eduard Shevardnadze, arrives in Britain to discuss arms limitations.

15 • President Reagan agrees to Salt 2 talks in Geneva.

21 • A report states that 20 per cent of babies are born out of wedlock.

22 • Corporal punishment in schools is banned after a one-vote majority in the House of Commons.

23 • The Duke of York marries Sarah Ferguson.

30 • Divers locate the wreckage of the *Titanic* at the bottom of the Atlantic.

August

1 • The US Senate votes for stricter sanctions against South Africa.

4 • Britain remains isolated in its stance on South Africa, when Mrs Thatcher will only submit to voluntary sanctions at a Commonwealth Summit Meeting in London.

22 • John Stalker, Deputy Chief Constable of Greater Manchester, is reinstated after an investigation clears him of dealing with 'known criminals'.

September

8 • The Labour Party announces plans to de-privatise British Telecom and other privatised industries.

9 • British soccer fans are formally accused of the manslaughter of those who died at Heysal at a London Crown Court.

11 • Panic breaks out in Wall Street following the biggest share price drop since the 1929 Great Crash.

21 • Prince Charles says on television that he regularly talks to his plants.
• The Liberal Party Assembly at Eastbourne vote against their leadership and to scrap Britain's nuclear deterrent.

24 • Four million people apply for shares in the Trustee Savings Bank. It is Britain's most population flotation.

26 • David Steel, in defiant mood, vows to keep the nuclear deterrent.

28 • Neil Kinnock pledges to close down USAF bases in Britain.

October

1 • The Labour Party announce plans to phase out nuclear power in a matter of decades rather than months. However, the Labour Conference votes in favour of a non-nuclear defence policy.

2 • The US Senate overrides President Reagan's veto of sanctions against South Africa.

12 • The Queen and Prince Philip visit China. This is the first visit to China by a British monarch. The Prince causes diplomatic embarrassment when he tells English students they will become 'slitty eyed' if they remain in China too long.

13 • Superpower Summit talks in Reykjavik break down when President Gorbachev insists that America restricts its Star Wars project before any scaling down of nuclear weaponry can take place.

22 • American companies pull out of South Africa after the Senate votes to impose sanctions.

24 • Syrian Nezar Hindawi is jailed for 45 years for attempting to blow up an El Al flight on 17 April by using his pregnant girlfriend as a human timebomb. Britain breaks off diplomatic relations with Syria.

26 • Jeffrey Archer resigns as Tory Party Deputy Chairman when a newspaper alleges he paid a prostitute to leave the country.

27 • The much publicised Stock Exchange 'Big Bang' was more like a fizz when the computer dealing system failed and staff were once more forced to take to the floor.

November

4 • The Democrats win control of the Senate.

6 • Nigel Lawson announces an increase of £4.6 billion in public spending in his Autumn Statement.

• Forty-five people die after a Chinook helicopter crashes in the North Sea. This is the worst civilian helicopter crash to date, with only two of the passengers and crew surviving.

21 • The Government launches a £20 million campaign to educate people on the threat of AIDS as British victims reach 512.

23 • Barclays announce they are to 'disinvest' in South Africa.

25 • President Reagan's national security adviser, Vice Admiral Poindexter, resigns, and Lt Col Oliver North is sacked over Irangate.

26 • More than 250,000 British Gas share application forms are completed.

28 • Kenneth Baker publishes a bill giving him ultimate power in determining teachers' pay.

December

1 • Guinness shares plunged by over £300 million as the Department of Trade announces an investigation into possible 'misconduct' relating to the recent takeover of Distillers.

9 • The NSPCC reports that child abuse has doubled in the last year.

11 • South Africa introduces further sweeping reporting restrictions for television, radio and newspapers.

16 • Myra Hindley returns to Saddleworth Moor to try to identify the location of buried bodies.

18 • Miners wife Davina Thompson receives the world's first triple organ

transplant (heart, lungs and liver).

19 • John Stalker resigns from the police force.

• The Government wins its case to buy US AWACS spy planes to replace GEC Nimrods.

20 • A Gallup poll puts the Conservatives 8.5 per cent ahead of Labour.

29 • Harold Macmillan dies.

1987

January

1 • Thousands of Chinese students march on Tiananmen Square in Beijing demanding democracy.

9 • Guinness Chief Executive, Ernest Saunders, resigns as the DTI investigate the Distillers takeover.

18 • James Anderton, Chief Constable of Manchester, says he believes God is using him as a prophet.

21 • Fears mount that Terry Waite has been kidnapped on his way to meet with hostages.

24 • 162 police officers are injured as 12,000 demonstrate outside News International's Wapping plant.

29 • Mikhail Gorbachev addresses the Communist Party central policy-making committee, saying that voters should have a choice of candidates in local elections and telling Party members they had to shoulder responsibility for the social and economic stagnation in Russia over the past 20 years.

• The BBC's Director General, Alasdair Milne, resigns.

February

2 • Terry Waite is reported to the 'under arrest' in Beirut.

• Police raid the BBC's office in Glasgow and remove material allegedly gathered for a banned series on Britain's 'Secret Society' relating to a top secret project – the Zircon spy satellite. The Government are considering legal action to stop the New Statesman publishing extracts from a leaked document on Zircon.

5 • SOGAT end their year-long picketing outside News International's Wapping plant after they are threatened with fines and sequestration.

14 • Mrs Thatcher's son, Mark, weds the daughter of a Texan millionaire.

18 • Charles Haughey becomes Irish Prime Minister again after Garret FitzGerald's coalition government is defeated in the Election. FitzGerald pledges his support to Haughey in furthering the work of the Anglo-Irish agreement.

24 • Leading Nazi hunters say that there are six war criminals in Britain.

26 • Rosie Barnes wins the Greenwich by-election for the SDP/Liberal Alliance from Labour.
   • Michael Checkland is appointed Director General of the BBC.
   • In the US, the Tower Report says that President Reagan was unaware of the intricacies of the Iran arms deal, and therefore did not deliberately mislead the American people.
28 • The Archbishop of Canterbury ordains fifteen women deacons.

March
2 • Kenneth Baker moves to impose a settlement for teachers dispute.
3 • Prescription charges rise another 20p, to £2.40.
   • President Reagan accepts full responsibility for money diverted to the Contra Rebels in Nicaragua during Irangate.
6 • 200 are feared drowned outside Zeebrugge when the Townsend Thoresen ferry, *Herald of Free Enterprise*, rolls over as she sails with her bow doors open.
10 • The Vatican denounces the idea of test tube babies.
12 • Sizewell B nuclear processing plant in Suffolk gets the go-ahead from the Government.
   • Forty-seven Labour councillors from Liverpool City Council are suspended for five years for refusing to set a rate for Liverpool in 1985. The running of the Council is taken over by the Liberal Alliance.
13 • Mathew Taylor wins the Truro by-election for the Liberals following the death of David Penhaligon.
19 • Winston Silcott, and two others are given life sentences for the murder of PC Blakelock during the Tottenham riots.
26 • The EEC agree to sell off the 'butter mountain' to the Russians at 6p a pound.
27 • Neil Kinnock visits the US and meets with President Reagan. It is not thought the meeting was a great success with critics calling it 'frosty'.

April
5 • Two cousins of the Queen Mother are discovered to have been in a Surrey mental institution since 1941.
7 • Fifty more bodies found when the *Herald of Free Enterprise* refloated.
9 • The Government orders an inquiry into the £650 million purchase of Harrods by the Al-Fayed brothers.
14 • President Reagan invites President Gorbachev to a third Summit meeting in Washington.
16 • Conservative MP Harvey Proctor is charged with gross indecency.

25 • In Belfast, a senior Ulster judge, Sir Maurice Gibson, and his wife are killed by bomb.

30 • The sterilisation of a mentally sub-normal 17-year-old girl is approved by the Law Lords.

May

4 • The Government launches a new Aids awareness campaign.

6 • Inquiry clears MI5 of plotting the downfall of the Wilson Government.

7 • In local elections, Labour wins back Liverpool City Council from the Alliance, but fails to make significant gains.

8 • Eight IRA activists die when an attempt to attack an RUC post in Northern Ireland is foiled.

• US presidential hopeful, Gary Hart, stands down when it is alleged he had an extra-marital affair with model Donna Rice.

11 • Mrs Thatcher announces the date for the next General Election – 11 June.

• Klaus Barbie is put on trial in Lyons for alleged war crimes.

17 • An American frigate, *USS Stark*, is hit by Iraqi Exocet missiles in the Gulf. Thirty-seven crewmen die.

24 • Neil Kinnock is attacked for his views on a nuclear free Britain. The Conservatives lead in the opinion polls by 12 per cent.

29 • A West German, Mathias Rust, lands a light airplane in Red Square.

June

3 • The Militant Tendency wins control of the Civil and Public Services Association.

11 • Mrs Thatcher wins historic third term as PM with majority of 102.

12 • The Queen revives the title 'Princess Royal' for Princess Anne.

18 • Unemployment drops to below three million.

21 • For first time in decades, Soviets vote in local government elections.

July

1 • The body of Pauline Read, a victim of the Moors murderers, is found.

3 • Klaus Barbie is found guilty of war crimes in a Lyons court, and is sentenced to life imprisonment.

12 • *The Sunday Times* is accused of contempt of court after publishing extracts of ex-spy Peter Wright's memoirs – *Spycatcher.*

16 • British Airways announces takeover of British Caledonian for £237m.

20 • The UN Security Council tells Iran and Iraq to bring about a ceasefire or face an international arms embargo.

21 • America hoists the US flag on Kuwaiti tankers in the Gulf.

22 • The Soviets offer to dismantle medium and short-range nuclear weapons in the Asian parts of the Soviet Union.

24 • Jeffrey Archer wins £500,000 damages when he wins his libel suit against the *Daily Star* who alleged he had slept with prostitute Monica Coghlan.
  • Kenneth Baker unveils plans for national testing for children in English, Mathematics and Science.
  • US tanker, *Bridgton*, is holed by a mine in the Gulf.

31 • Mrs Thatcher refuses to help President Reagan by sending British minesweepers to the Gulf to aid Kuwaiti tankers against Iranian attack. This decision is later reversed.

August

4 • Moors murderer Ian Brady admits to five more killings.

5 • The British spy satellite project, Zircon, is abandoned at a cost of £70 million.

8 • David Owen resigns as leader of the SDP after his members vote to merge with the Liberal party against his wishes.

10 • Latest figures state that one person a day is dying of Aids.

14 • The Home Secretary, Douglas Hurd, orders a police investigation into the convictions of the 'Guildford Four'.

17 • Rudolf Hess commits suicide at Spandau Prison.

18 • Journalist, Charles Glass, escapes from his captors in Beirut.

19 • Michael Ryan commits suicide in Hungerford after an orgy of violence which left 15 victims dead and 16 wounded. The Government promises a review of the firearms laws.

27 • Head teachers warn Kenneth Baker of a possible 'revolt' among teaching staff over the national curriculum and 'opting out'.

29 • Robert Maclennan MP is appointed leader of the SDP.

30 • David Owen forms a 'breakaway' SDP.

September

2 • Mathias Rust's peace mission to Red Square ends with a four-year sentence to a Labour camp for violating Soviet airspace.

11 • The Government announces plans to abolish ILEA.

17 • America celebrates the bicentennary of her constitution.

23 • The *Spycatcher* row continues when the Government loses a court appeal to stop the publication of the book in Australia. Mrs Thatcher threatens to take the case to the Australian High Court.

28 • At the Labour Party conference, Neil Kinnock receives a mandate to review all Labour Party policies.

30 • Former Conservative MP, Keith Best, is jailed for four months for multiple Telecom share applications. His sentence is later quashed.

October

8 • Sir Jack Lyons and Heron boss, Gerald Ronson, are charged in relation to the Guinness case.

9 • Mrs Thatcher announces at the Tory Party Conference that she wants at least seven more years as Prime Minister.

14 • The first commercial flight leaves the City of London's new Dockland's airport.

16 • Britain is taken by surprise as fierce storms lash many parts of England in some of the worst gales to hit the British mainland this century.

19 • Black Monday: £50 billion is wiped off share values as the Dow Jones crashes. The crash is nearly double that which occurred on the worst day of trading during the Wall Street crash in 1929.

23 • Britain's most popular jockey, Lester Piggott, jailed for three years for tax evasion.

November

2 • Peter Brook, the Paymaster General, succeeds Norman Tebbit as chairman of the Conservative party.

8 • Eleven people are murdered and 61 are injured by the IRA as they gather for Remembrance Day in Enniskillen, Co Fermanagh, Northern Ireland.

9 • The Government announces plans to abolish free dental screening.

11 • In Russia, Boris Yeltzin is sacked from his post as Moscow's Communist party leader after attacking the Soviet leader over the slowness of political and social reforms.

12 • The term 'Yuppy' is coined in a report published by McCann Erichson, saying that Britain's under-25s are mainly concerned with consumption and material goods, rather than compassion and heavenly reward.

17 • The Government announces plans to replace the rates with a Community Charge (popularly dubbed the 'Poll Tax') from April 1990.

18 • Thirteen die and 20 are seriously injured during a fire at King's Cross underground station in London.

24 • The Government announces plans to abolish free eye testing.

December

3 • Crockford's, the Church of England Directory, publishes an anonymous preface, severely attacking the Archbishop of Canterbury. (Four days later, Dr Gareth Bennet, the canon and Oxford don who continually denied he was the author of the preface, commits suicide.)

- The Government wins a blanket ban on broadcasting reports on the security services.

8   • An American-Soviet agreement is signed in Washington abolishing medium and short-range nuclear weapons.

13   • The Chief Constable of Greater Manchester, James Anderton, calls for the outlawing of homosexuality and the flogging of criminals.

16   • The Goverment promises a further £100 million top up for the NHS in order to try and avert a financial crisis.

21   • The British media win the right to publish extracts of the controversial book *Spycatcher* despite the Government's efforts to prevent publication.

- British Airways takes control of British Midland after £250 million bid.

28   • The Bishop of Ripon, David Young, becomes the first Anglican bishop to ban homosexual clergy from his ministry.

1988

January

3   • Mrs Thatcher becomes the longest continuously serving Prime Minister this century, with nearly nine years in office.

4   • Sir Robin Butler succeeds Sir Robert Armstrong as Cabinet Secretary.

10   • Lord Whitelaw, 69, resigns as Leader of the House of Lords and Lord President of the Council because of ill health.

22   • David Steel announces he will not stand for leadership of the SDP-Liberal Alliance.

28   • The Court of Appeal rejects an appeal by the six Irishmen accused of the Birmingham pub bombings in 1974.

29   • Junior health minister, Edwina Currie, says that people should forego holidays to pay for private health care.

31   • The British Medical Association accuses the Government of deliberately running down the NHS.

February

2   • Five female Gay Rights activists abseil into the Chamber of the House of Lords, protesting over Clause 28 of the Local Government Bill preventing councils funding work which could be interpreted as 'promoting' homosexuality.

5   • John Stalker claims he was sacked with Cabinet approval during his investigations into the RUC's 'shoot to kill' policy in Northern Ireland.

8   • President Gorbachev announces he is willing to remove all Soviet troops from Afghanistan.

9 • MPs vote to allow cameras into the House of Commons in an experiment to televise the proceedings.

16 • TV-AM dismisses 229 striking technicians.

19 • The Prime Minister announces plans for a shake up of the Civil Service, including decentralising 565,000 jobs from London.

24 • Cecil Parkinson announces plans to privatise the CEGB in 1990.

March

2 • The Liberals and the SDP vote to create a new party – the Social and Liberal Democrats (SLD).

6 • Three IRA members are shot dead in Gibraltar.

11 • The English pound note ceases to be legal tender after midnight.

15 • Nigel Lawson's budget cut 2p off the standard rate of income tax to 25p in the pound as he had pledged at the last Election.

16 • At the funeral of the three IRA members shot dead in Gibraltar, the mourners come under gun and grenade attack.

17 • Ford drop plans to create 1,000 jobs by investing £40 million to create an electronics factory in Dundee when unions refuse to create a single union deal.

• The Government cuts base rate interest by 0.5 per cent to 8.5 per cent as the pound soars.

19 • Two undercover soldiers are murdered by a mob attending an IRA funeral in Belfast.

23 • Tony Benn announces he will contest Neil Kinnock for leadership of the Labour Party at the Annual Conference in October. Eric Heffer will contest the post of deputy leader.

April

3 • The Bishop of Durham attacks the Government for not helping the poor.

5 • The Government announces plans to phase out the traditional British passport, and replace it with a European passport.

12 • One of the IRA's most wanted men, Dessie O'Hare, known as the Border Fox, is sentenced to 40 years imprisonment for terrorist activities.

18 • Labour MP, Ron Brown, causes £1,000 worth of damage when he throws the mace to the ground in the Commons Chamber.

• Thirty-eight Conservative backbenchers vote against a flat-rate Poll Tax.

20 • London Underground announce £30 million safety improvements following the King's Cross disaster.

21 • The Government announces plans for a 15 per cent pay rise for nurses, introduced via a 'banding' system.

28 • The Foreign Secretary, Geoffrey Howe, fails in his bid to ban a Thames Television documentary on the killing of three unarmed IRA personnel by the SAS in Gibraltar entitled 'Death on the Rock'. He claimed it was 'trial by television'.

May

1 • Three off-duty servicemen are murdered by an IRA 'hit squad' in the Netherlands.

5 • Mrs Thatcher fails to stop the broadcasting of a BBC Belfast documentary, 'Spotlight', on the Gibraltar killings.
   • David Alton's Private Member's Bill, attempting to cut the time limit of abortions to 18 weeks, was talked out in the Commons.

9 • Francois Mitterand re-elected French President.
   • Neil Kinnock says he would accept the principle of protection from a US nuclear umbrella.

11 • David Steel says he will not stand for the leadership of the new, merged SLD.
   • 'The Third Man', Kim Philby, dies in Moscow.

13 • Geoffrey Howe says that Britain should join the ERM.

15 • The Soviet Union begin withdrawing their troops from Afghanistan.

24 • In an attempt to monitor the spread of AIDS, one in six pregnant women will be asked to undergo voluntary AIDS testing.

31 • The BBC screen 'Tumbledown', a controversial play based on a soldier's experiences during the Falklands War.

June

1 • The Government is left with a legal bill of more than £1,326,000 when it fails to win its three-year battle to prevent the publication of *Spycatcher*. However, it vows to continue the fight saying it lost on a 'technicality'.

3 • Douglas Hurd, the Home Secretary, rejects EEC plans for the uncontrolled movement of people as well as goods throughout the whole of the Community from 1992.

10 • Michael Meacher, Labour MP, loses his libel case against the Observer.

11 • Thousands of music fans and anti-apartheid campaigners pack Wembley Stadium for concert to celebrate Nelson Mandela's 70th birthday.

13 • A Dublic court refuses to extradite Patrick McVeigh, an IRA suspect, on the grounds that his identity was not proven.

15 • The IRA plant a bomb under an army vehicle which explodes during a civilian and serviceman 'fun run' in Lisburn. Five people die, and ten are injured.

17 • Neil Kinnock warns the Labour Party that they must accept change if they are ever to gain power.

20 • Neil Kinnock reaffirms Labour's commitment to a non-nuclear defence policy. This latest statement contradicts his earlier, softened approach towards nuclear weapons and leaves his critics believing that Labour's policy is still unclear.

23 • Mrs Thatcher quashes idea of Britain becoming part of 'united states of Europe' by joining a European central banking system.

27 • Latest UK trade figures show a £1.2 billion deficit in May, sparking fears that the Chancellor will have to raise interest rates again to save the pound. Critics blame Nigel Lawson's cuts in income tax rates during the budget for the slide of the pound, a consumer boom resulting in increased imports, and high inflation.

29 • The Government publishes its proposals for amending the Official Secrets Act.

July

3 • US warplanes shoots down an Iranian civilian airbus in the Straits of Hormuz, killing all 28 people on board.

5 • An Irish priest, Patrick Ryan, is arrested in Brussels for alleged IRA involvement.

6 • An oil rig in the North Sea, the Piper Alpha, explodes with the loss of 167 lives.

11 • The figures for known AIDS virus carriers in Britain rise to 8,500.

14 • The Conservatives narrowly hold the Kensington by-election but with a majority slashed 815. The SDP only just save their deposit.

17 • Neil Kinnock's visit to Zimbabwe marred when he and his wife are held at gunpoint by soldiers on the Mozambique/Zimbabwe border.

18 • Bank interest rates are raised to 10.5 per cent.

19 • Government proposals to abolish free eye tests are defeated in the House of Lords.

20 • Nicholas Ridley, Environment Secretary, announces plans to privatise ten water authorities in England and Wales.

21 • Building society mortgage lending rates go up by nearly 2 per cent to 11.5 per cent.

22 • Leon Brittan succeeds Lord Cockfield as Britain's Senior EEC Commissioner.

23 • The IRA blow up a family of three with a car bomb intended for a judge in Belfast.

25 • In a Cabinet reshuffle, Mrs Thatcher announces that the Department of Health and Social Security is to be split into two. Kenneth Clarke takes

Health, while John Moore takes Social Security.

27 • The trade deficit for June is £1,020 million.

• British Telecom's monopoly is broken with the opening of Mercury's first telephone boxes at London's Waterloo Station.

29 • Paddy Ashdown becomes the new leader of the SLD.

• The Education Act comes into being for schools in England and Wales, introducing a national curriculum for state schools, regular testing, and the ability for schools to 'opt out' of local education authority control.

August

1 • An IRA bomb explodes inside an army barracks at Mill Hill in North London with the death of one soldier and the injury of nine others.

2 • British Rail comes under attack from the Central Transport Consultative Committee for dirty trains, overcrowding and inflated fares.

5 • Prison Governors met with Home Office officials to warn about serious conditions in British prisons, which has led to a series of riots.

20 • Eight soldiers die and 27 are injured when an IRA car bomb blows up a coach near Ballygawley, Co Tyrone.

22 • New pub licencing laws come into force.

25 • The City panics with the publication of the latest monthly trade deficit figures – £2.2 billion. Another rise in interest rates follows, (from 11 to 12 per cent). Nigel Lawson now accepts that the economy is going into decline.

26 • First reports arise of seals dying because of toxic waste in the North Sea.

30 • Junior environment minister, Virginia Bottomley, refuses permission for the *Karin B* to dock in Britain and unload its 2,000-ton cargo of toxic waste. The ship had already been turned away from other European ports. Environmentalists see it as a triumph for their campaign to stop British companies cashing in on the disposal of toxic waste.

September

1 • A report says that the cost of Europe's farming policy to every British consumer is £13 per week in taxes and higher food prices.

5 • The TUC expels the electricians union, the EETPU, at their annual conference in Bournemouth.

6 • The inquest into the killing of three unarmed IRA members opens in Gibraltar.

20 • Mrs Thatcher addresses a meeting of the EEC, expressing her opinion that she is unwilling for Britain to become part of a 'United States of Europe' where many decisions concerning Britain would be made

outside of Westminster.
- The mortgage rate rises to 12.75 per cent.

26 • Members of the Social and Liberal Democrat Party become 'Democrats' at their annual conference.

30 The Gibraltar inquest reaches a verdict of 'lawful killing'.

October

2 • Neil Kinnock and Roy Hattersley are re-elected as leader and deputy leader of the Labour Party at the party's annual conference in Blackpool.

4 • A report states that 9 million people in Britain earn less than the European Commission's estimated minimum wage.

6 • Trade and Industry Secretary, Lord Young, announces plans to privatise British Steel.
- House price figures show an increase of 34 per cent in the last year.
- Neil Kinnock is defeated in his bid to change Labour's stance on unilateral nuclear disarmament at the Party Conference.

9 • Labour's shadow chancellor, John Smith, suffers a heart attack.
- David Mellor, Health Minister, warns of the possible spread of AIDS by one in four active homosexuals.

11 • The Kings Cross inquiry passes a verdict of 'accidental death' on the 31 people who perished in the fire.
- Ian Paisley interrupts the Pope's speech to the European Parliament, calling him 'the Antichrist'. Mr Paisley is ejected from the Chamber.
- Cecil Parkinson announces at the Tory Party conference that the Government intends to privatise the coal industry.

13 • The Government's final bid to ban *Spycatcher* is defeated when the Law Lords allow the British press to publish extracts.

14 • Conservatives chant 'ten more years' to Mrs Thatcher at their Party Conference in Brighton.

17 • Members of Trades Unions at GCHQ are sacked by the Government.

19 • The Home Secretary bans the broadcasting of interviews with members of paramilitary organisations.

27 • The Government increases pensions by 5.9 per cent, but refuses to raise child benefit.

November

7 • The Government publishes White Paper on Broadcasting, containing most radical proposals since the introduction of commercial television.

9 • Government White Paper proposes supplementing existing student grants with a scheme for 'top up' loans, which are to be repaid at a later date.

10 • The Govan by-election is lost by Labour to the Scottish National Party on a swing of 33 per cent.
25 • The Belgian authorities turn down an appeal by Britain to extradite Irish priest, Patrick Ryan, wanted in connection with IRA terrorist activities. Instead, he is put on a plane to Dublin.
 • Bank interest rates rise again to 13 per cent. Britain's October trade deficit stands at £2.4 billion.

December

4 • Applications for shares in British Steel are 3.3 times oversubscribed.
 • Junior health minister, Edwina Currie, causes an outcry when she says that most of Britain's eggs contain the salmonella virus.
5 • The Post Office announces that their monopoly on selling stamps is to end.
7 • Mr Gorbachev tells the United Nations he intends to substantially reduce Soviet forces, and reduce the number of troops and tanks in Eastern Europe.
9 • British egg producers begin to slaughter their flocks as egg sales slump.
12 • A train derails outside London's Clapham Junction station, killing 33 people.
15 • The Conservatives hold the Epping Forest by-election, but with a reduced majority.
16 • Edwina Currie resigns in face of the storm created by her comments on Britain's egg production.
18 • Neil Kinnock agrees that there should be electoral reform, but that proportional representation is not the answer.
21 • In Britain's worst air disaster, Pan Am Flight 103 flying from London's Heathrow Airport to New York explodes over the Scottish village of Lockerbie, killing all 258 people on board and 17 villagers.
 • The police discover an IRA bomb factory in a flat in Clapham, South London.
29 • Bank mortgage rates rise to 13.75 per cent.
 • Shelter's annual report claims that the number of homeless has doubled since Mrs Thatcher took power.

1989
January

4 • A leaked Government paper on the NHS says that hospitals will be urged to 'opt out' of local health authorities.
5 • Paul Channon, Secretary of State for Transport, says that airport security

will be reviewed following the Lockerbie bombing.

8 • A Boeing 737 crashes into the verge of the M1 just outside Kegworth,
killing 44 and injuring 82.

• Russia announces plans to dismantle its chemical weapons.

9 • University lecturers boycott exams in a protest over low pay.

13 • Foreign Office Minister, William Waldegrave, meets Yasser Arafat in what
is the Government's first official meeting with the PLO.

16 • The appeal court orders an investigation into the conviction of the
'Guildford Four'.

17 • The Government's 'Football Spectators Bill' is published proposing that
football fans carry ID cards. The football organisations unite in their
opposition to it.

21 • Kenneth Clark announces plans for reforms to the health service,
including provision for hospitals to 'opt out'.

22 • Protesters march through Maidstone objecting to British Rail's plans for a
high speed Channel Tunnel rail link through Kent.

24 • Allegations into malpractice by the West Midlands police force are
investigated by the Serious Crimes Squad.

26 • Thames Television is cleared of prejudging the trial of those accused of
killing IRA members in Gibraltar by screening their documentary 'Death
on the Rock'.

February

2 • President P W Botha resigns as leader of the South African National
Party, and is replaced by Mr F. W. de Klerk.

• Edward Heath blames a 'corrupt' press office at Downing Street for
recent Government leaks.

5 • Britain's first satellite television station, Sky, is launched amid a shortage
of receiver dishes.

10 • Pregnant women are advised not to eat certain foods which may contain
the listeria virus.

14 • The Ayatolla Khomeini orders the death of British writer, Salman
Rushdie, for his 'blasphemous' book, *The Satanic Verses.*

15 • The last Soviet soldier leaves Afghanistan after 9 years of
occupation of the country.

• Unemployment falls below two million.

20 • The Clapham rail crash inquiry begins.

• One man is slightly injured when three IRA bombs explode at the
Parachute Regiment barracks in Market Drayton.

22 • The Official Secrets Bill is passed in the Commons.

- Britain recalls its envoys to Teheran, without officially severing diplomatic relations. The move followed Britain's expulsion of Iranian diplomats from Britain as a result of Ayatolla Khomeini's death threat to Salman Rushdie.
23 • Relatives of Lockerbie victims call for the resignation of Paul Channon when it is revealed that the Department of Trade and Industry ignored a warning about a possible bombing campaign sent from the US Federal Aviation Authority.
26 • Opinion poll shows Labour one point ahead of the Conservatives. Pollsters identify the Government's stance on NHS reforms for the change in public support.

March
1 • Latest trade figures show a deficit for January of £1.7 billion.
3 • Mrs Thatcher announces 'we have become a grandmother'.
4 • Four die and more than 80 are injured in a train crash near Purley, London.
6 • Two die and 61 are injured when two trains collide outside Bellgrove near Glasgow.
7 • Iran breaks off relations with Britain over the *Satanic Verses* affair.
  • The police find a cache of Semtex near the location for a Conservative Party conference in Scarborough.
14 • The Chancellor, Nigel Lawson, delivers a rather subdued Budget with the emphasis placed on reducing inflation by maintaining high interest rates. The only real concession was a cut in tax for unleaded petrol.
16 • Latest Government figures for show an increase in violent and sex-related crimes during 1988.
21 • The IRA ambush and murder two senior RUC officers.
26 • The Soviet Union holds its first ever multi-candidate elections.
30 • The Home Office publishes a paper saying that parents will be liable for prosecution for criminal damage committed by their children.
31 • The British Medical Association publish and distribute leaflets attacking the Governments NHS reforms. The Government dismisses them as 'alarmist'.

April
3 • The new television breakfast service, Channel Four Daily, goes on the air.
4 • Neil Kinnock launches Labour's campaign against the Poll Tax.
5 • Sir Leon Brittan reveals the sources of the leaked letter over the Westland

affair as the Prime Minister's private secretary and press officer. The letter led to the resignation of both himself and Michael Heseltine, whose reputation it was designed to damage.

6 • Norman Fowler, Employment Secretary, announces the abolition of the 42-year old National Dock Labour Scheme.

• Latest figures suggest the cost of home-ownership has risen by 62.5 per cent in the last year.

15 • Ninety-five supporters are crushed to death and 170 are injured after fans surge into an enclosure at Hillsborough football ground in Britain's worst ever sporting disaster.

17 • Nigel Lawson rejects plans for Britain to enter into a European monetary system.

18 • With the prospect of water privatisation nearing, the Government is warned to purify its product to meet EEC standards or face the European Court.

25 • BBC staff strike over pay.

• President Gorbachev 'pensions off' 110 former Soviet Politburo members left over from the old regime. All were opposed to his reforms.

26 • Babyfood manufacturers, Heinz, are held to ransom and products are removed from shelves after they are found to be spiked with glass.

28 • Fourteen Liverpool supporters receive three-year jail terms from a Belgian court for their part in the Heysal Stadium riot.

May

1 • Inmates at Risley remand centre climb out onto the roof and begin three days of protests over conditions.

3 • Mrs Thatcher celebrates a decade as Prime Minister. The Opposition declare a national day of mourning.

5 • Labour win the Vale of Glamorgan by-election, a seat previously held by the Conservatives for 38 years.

• Britain invites three South African envoys to leave the country within a week after it is discovered that South Africa had been willing to exchange British defence secrets for arms with Ulster loyalists.

11 • A row breaks out between John Moore, the Secretary of State for Social Security, and Chris Pond, the Director of the Low Pay Unit which claims that more than 30 per cent of the population lives at or below the poverty line. Mr Moore rebuffs his critics, saying they would 'find poverty in paradise'.

12 • BBC workers vote for a series of lightning strikes to support their 16 per cent pay claim.

- Kenneth Baker decides that the promotion of foreign languages for the under-16s would be too expensive.
14 • Interest rates rise to 14 per cent.
16 • Divisions within the Government over Britain's entry (or not) into the EMS become more apparent when Sir Geoffrey Howe says that Britain will join 'when the time is right'.
17 • The British Medical Association vote to reject the Government's NHS reforms.
- The British Government rejects the EC's Social Charter designed to guarantee workers' rights.
18 • Neil Kinnock unveils Labour's 'new look Labour Party' policy document.
19 • Mrs Thatcher blames Nigel Lawson for inflation at 8 per cent.
22 • The pound falls to $1.58.

June
1 • Alex Murphy and Henry Maguire, are sentenced to life imprisonment for the murders of two army corporals at a Belfast funeral.
- University lecturers accept a 6 per cent pay offer and end their industrial action.
4 • Chinese troops fire on students marching for democracy in Tiananmen Square. An estimated 2,600 are killed, with thousands more injured.
5 • Britain refuses residency to 3.25 million Hong Kong Chinese who currently hold British passports.
12 • The Chancellor says that Britain will not join the EMS before 1990.
15 • In the European Elections, Labour wins 45, and the Conservatives 32, of the 78 British seats. Some Conservatives blame Mrs Thatcher for a lacklustre election campaign. The Greens won a surprise 15 per cent of the total vote, with the Lib Dems registering only 6 per cent.
22 • House of Lords overturn Government's decision to freeze child benefit.
23 • Michael Heseltine and Leon Brittan call on Mrs Thatcher to pledge Britain's entry into the EMS at the Madrid Summit.

July
2 • A British serviceman and his family are killed by an IRA car bomb in West Germany.
3 • Sir Geoffrey Howe heckled and booed during a visit to Hong Kong because of the Government's refusal to allow entry to Hong Kong's British passport holders.
7 • Nicholas Ridley, Environment Secretary, gives the go-ahead for the construction of a new town, Foxley Wood, in Hampshire.

19 • The Government publishes plans for a radical shake up of the legal profession.

20 • GPs reject the Government's new contracts offer.

24 • In a Cabinet reshuffle, Sir Geoffrey Howe becomes leader of the House of Commons and deputy prime minister after refusing a post later offered to Doublas Hurd (Home Secretary). Howe is replaced as Foreign Secretary by John Major.

29 • Britain is in the grip of a heatwave with the London Weather Centre declaring it the hottest summer for a century.

August

1 • Cruise missiles from Greenham Common loaded onto an aircraft carrier to be transported back to America.

2 • The Midland Bank blames third world debtors for half-year losses of £500 million.

• Argentina lifts its trade embargo with Britain.

4 • The South Yorkshire police force is blamed for the Hillsborough football ground tragedy.

10 • The Government is warned by the Social Services Select Committee that their timetable for NHS reform could jeopardise the standard of health care to patients.

20 • Fifty-one people die when their pleasure boat on the Thames, the Marchioness, collides with a dredger and sinks.

23 • Britain's latest monthly trade figures show a deficit of £2.06 billion.

25 • The first pictures of Neptune are beamed back to Earth from Voyager 2.

30 • Claims that security forces in Northern Ireland regularly leak the names of IRA suspects are made by paramilitary organisations.

September

1 • Ten water companies in England and Wales are privatised.

9 • David Owen is twice as popular as Paddy Ashdown, says opinion poll.

13 • Ambulance staff ban overtime over a 6.6 per cent pay offer and a refusal by the Government to take talks to arbitration.

15 • Paddy Ashdown, at the SLD party conference in Brighton, repeats his aim for the SLD to replace Labour as the main Opposition party.

20 • Latest figures from Scotland show that nearly 300,000 people in Strathclyde have refused to pay the Poll Tax.

21 • The Government admits a serious shortage of qualified teachers.

22 • An IRA bomb kills 10 and injures 22 bandsmen at the Royal Marines School of Music in Deal, Kent.

27 • David Owen admits to his supporters at the SDP conference in
Scarborough that the Party is no longer a national force.
29 • The Government postpones the £15 billion electricity privatisation
because of difficulties in determining a new structure for the industry.

October

2 • Eurotunnel announce that they need a further £1.5 billion to complete
the Channel Tunnel project.
5 • Interest rates rise to 15 per cent.
9 • The pound slides steeply, wiping £6.54 billion off share values.
16 • A report published by the Equal Opportunities Commission states that
female white-collar workers earn less than half that of their male
counterparts.
19 • The 'Guildford Four' are released after 14 years in jail pending an inquiry
into their conviction in 1975 which the court says was based on
'fabricated evidence'.
23 • Ambulance workers begin a 'work to rule' over their pay claim.
24 • In a televised interview, Nigel Lawson demands thatSir Alan Walters
stops publicly undermining his position as Chancellor.
26 • Nigel Lawson resigns as Chancellor of the Exchequer. He is replaced as
Chancellor by John Major, and Douglas Hurd becomes Foreign Secretary.
31 • Nigel Lawson publicly humiliates Mrs Thatcher in the House of
Commons when he described the events leading up to his resignation as
Chancellor.

November

1 • Three women join Labour's shadow cabinet: Ann Clwyd, Margaret
Beckett and Joan Lester.
3 • The prospectus for water privitisation is issued.
• The new Northern Ireland Secretary, Peter Brooke, causes controversy by
suggesting that the Government should talk with Sinn Fein, the political
wing of the IRA – provided the IRA first renounces the use of terrorism.
7 • The Church of England votes in favour of measures to allow the
ordination of women priests.
• Labour MP, Paul Boateng, becomes the House of Commons' first black
front bencher.
8 • The Army are called in to help deal with emergency ambulance calls.
• The entire East German Politburo resigns. Hans Modrow, a moderate, is
appointed Prime Minister.
9 • East Germans are allowed to pass freely into West Germany for the first

time in almost 30 years as the Berlin Wall begins to be chipped away by elated East and West Germans.

- Energy Secretary John Wakeham says that nuclear power stations will not be privatised.

21 • Televised proceedings of the House of Commons begin.
- Ambulance staff ban the attendance of all but emergency call-outs.

22 • The NHS reform bill is published.

23 • In Czechosolovakia, all the country's Communist leaders resign.
- Sir Anthony Meyer challenges Mrs Thatcher for the leadership of the Conservative Party.

27 • The pound reaches its lowest point for three years against the German mark.

28 • Most British newspapers agree to publish a Code of Practice.

30 • A row erupts in the Commons following a National Audit Office report into the sale of Rover to British Aerospace. British Aerospace is said to have received 'inducements' of £38 million from the Government.

December

5 • Mrs Thatcher defeats Sir Anthony Meyer in the leadership ballot.

6 • The Government's privitisation of water is 5.7 times oversubscribed.

7 • The Broadcasting Bill is published.

9 • At the EC Summit in Strasbourg, Mrs Thatcher again dissents on Britain joining the EMS and implementing the Social Charter.

10 • A new government is sworn in in Czechoslovakia, the majority being non-Communist.

12 • MPs vote to prosecute alleged war criminals residing in Britain.

20 • Banks say that the Government's plans for student loans are unworkable and refuse to implement them.

19 • West German Chancellor, Helmut Kohl, pays an official visit to East Germany and talks of unification.

20 • US troops invade Panama, and within days capture Manuel Noriega and install a new government.

22 • Divisions surface within the Conservative Party when plans are announced to allow 225,000 Hong Kong immigrants to reside in Britain.

25 • The Ceaucescus are executed. The National Salvation Front takes over in Romania and vows to abandon Communism.

1990
January

3 • Employment Secretary, Norman Fowler, resigns.

15 • Soviet government declares state of emergency in Nagorno-Karabakh.

18 • Former boxing champion, Terry Marsh, charged with attempted murder of Frank Warren, his former manager.

23 • Metropolitan Police become first force to scrap height requirements.

25 • Winds of up to 110 mph sweep across Britain killing 47 people.

29 • Government shelves plans for compulsory identity cards for football supporters.

February

2 • President de Klerk announces lifting of 30-year ban on South Africa's Communist Party, the African National Congress and other anti-apartheid organisations.

7 • Soviet Central Committee votes to end Communist Party's monopoly of power.

11 • Nelson Mandela released after more than 27 years in prison.

15 • Perrier withdraw all bottles from sale following discovery of traces of benzene in some supplies.

19 • Over 7,000 Romanian miners drafted into Bucharest to counter anti-government demonstrations.

26 • More gales sweep across Britain, killing 18 people.

March

4 • Welsh Secretary, Peter Walker, announces he will resign in May.

9 • NUM Executive agrees to independent enquiry into allegations of Libyan funding for the 1984 Miners Strike and that Arthur Scargill used some of this money to pay off his mortgage.

11 • Lithuania becomes first Soviet republic to declare independence from the Union.

14 • Mikhail Gorbachev elected to new executive post of President of the USSR.

18 • East Germany holds first free elections, and the Alliance for Germany wins 48 per cent of the vote.

• Recorded temperature of 22°C makes this the hottest March for 25 years.

22 • Labour win Mid-Staffordshire from the Conservatives in their best by-election performance for half a century.

23 • Duchess of York gives birth to her second daughter, Eugenie.

25 • Dr Runcie announces he will retire as Archbishop of Canterbury in January 1991.

31 • Serious rioting follows a mass rally against the Poll Tax in Trafalgar Square. 341 people arrested.

April

1 • Inmates seize control of Manchester's Strangeways prison. Prison officers stormed the buildings 24 days later.

2 • Britain's second biggest earthquake in 100 hundred years registers 5.2 on the Richter Scale.

11 • Customs officers in Middlesbrough impound steel cylinders bound for Iraq. It was later announced that they formed part of a 140-ton 'supergun'.

18 • Soviet government cuts off oil supplies to Lithuania.

22 • Greek authorities arrest British driver when customs officials find his lorry is carrying parts for Iraqi 'supergun'.

24 • Great Train Robber, Charles Wilson, shot dead at his home in Spain.

May

3 • First local elections in England and Wales following introduction of the Poll Tax give Conservatives some gains in London but a bad drubbing virtually everywhere else.

4 • Latvian Parliament votes to secede from USSR, as does Estonia next day.

6 • New 071 and 081 dialling codes introduced in London.

14 • Seven civilians injured by IRA bomb explosion outside army buildings in Eltham, south east London.

15 • Van Gogh's 'Portrait of Dr Gachet' becomes most expensive painting in the world when it is sold in New York for £49.7 million.

16 • Army sergeant killed and another badly injured by IRA bomb outside Army Careers office in Wembley, north London.

20 • National Salvation Front win Romania's first free elections for more than 50 years.

27 • IRA shoot dead two Australian tourists in the Netherlands after mistaking them for off-duty British servicemen.

29 • Boris Yeltsin elected President of Russian Federation.

June

1 • IRA gunmen kill off-duty soldier at Lichfield railway station.

3 • David Owen's SDP formally disbanded.

4 • House of Lords rejects Government's War Crimes Bill.

8 • Civic Forum win Czechoslovakia's first free elections since the war.

9 • 17 civilians injured by IRA bomb at headquarters of Honourable Artillery Company in London.

12 • Russian Parliament votes that the republic has the right to secede from the USSR.

14 • Home Secretary, David Waddington, refers Maguire family cases to Court of Appeal because their convictions for running an IRA bomb factory cannot be upheld.

15 • Barbara Castle made a Life Peer.

16 • Belgian police capture three IRA suspects in woods near Hoogstraten.

25 • IRA bomb explodes at Carlton Club in London.

30 • Deutschmark becomes legal tender in East Germany.

July

2 • Uefa lifts ban on all English clubs, except Liverpool, playing in Europe.

6 • NATO leaders issue London Declaration, formally ending the Cold War.

12 • Boris Yeltsin resigns from the Soviet Communist Party.

14 • Nicholas Ridley resigns from Cabinet following *Spectator* interview in which he claims Germans were aiming to 'take over the whole of Europe'.

19 • NUM announce they will sue Arthur Scargill and Peter Heathfield to recover money raised by foreign miners in support of British miners during the 1984 strike.

24 • Three policemen and a nun killed by IRA bomb near Armagh.

25 • Announcement that George Carey, Bishop of Bath and Wells, will succeed Robert Runcie as Archbishop of Canterbury.

30 • Conservative MP, Ian Gow, killed by IRA car bomb outside his home.

August

2 • Iraqi forces invade Kuwait and mass along the border with Saudi Arabia.

4 • Queen Mother's 90th birthday.

5 • EEC, US and Japan ban imports of Iraqi and Kuwaiti oil. ANC announces suspension of its armed struggle against South African government.

• Pakistan premier, Benazir Bhutto, dismissed from office by the President.

7 • US Government begins sending forces to Saudi Arabia.

10 • Arab leaders vote to send troops to Saudi Arabia.

19 • Iraq rounds up foreigners to use as a 'human shield' at key installations.

24 • Beirut hostage, Brian Keenan, is released.

• Embassies in Kuwait City which had refused Iraqi orders to close are surrounded by troops and essential services cut.

25 • UN Security Council vote unanimously to authorise naval blockade of Iraq under UN supervision.

27 • Ernest Saunders, Gerald Ronson, Anthony Parnes and Sir Jack Lyons found guilty of breaking the law during the Guinness takeover of the Distillers Group.

31 • South Africa's governing National Party announces that it will, in future, open its membership to people of all races.

September

2 • 200 British women and children allowed to leave Baghdad by plane.

6 • A further 247 British women and children fly out of Iraq after 500-mile drive from Kuwait.

9 • Joint statement from Presidents Bush and Gorbachev calls for unconditional Iraqi withdrawal from Kuwait.

13 • NUM officials agree to drop legal action in return for payment of £742,000 from funds of International Miners Organisation in Paris.

18 • Air Chief Marshal Sir Peter Terry seriously wounded by the IRA at his home in Stafford.

• IOC announce that 1996 Olympics will be held in Atalanta, Georgia.

20 • Polly Peck Chairman, Asil Nadir, questioned by Fraud Squad. Shares in the company suspended.

21 • Nicu Ceausescu sentenced to 20 years imprisonment for his role in trying to suppress Romanian uprising.

25 • UN Security Council imposes air blockade on Iraq.

October

2 • Germany celebrates reunification.

8 • Britain joins European Exchange Rate Mechanism and interest rates fall.

12 • Inflation rises to 10.9 per cent, the highest figure for eight years.

15 • President Gorbachev awarded the Nobel Peace Prize.

18 • Lib Dems overturn 17,000 majority to take Eastbourne from the Conservatives in by-election.

23 • Edward Heath returns from Baghdad with 37 British hostages.

24 • Six soldiers and one civilian killed when IRA force two 'human bombs' to drive to army checkpoints in Northern Ireland.

28 • At Rome Summit, EEC leaders agree timetable for monetary union which Mrs Thatcher denounces as 'cloud cuckoo land'.

30 • Mrs Thatcher savages Jacques Delors in Commons exchanges on Rome Summit.

November

1 • Sir Geoffrey Howe resigns from Government over Mrs Thatcher's European policy, saying: 'I believe I can no longer serve with honour'.

2 • Michael Heseltine sends letter to his constituency party stating that the Conservatives were facing a crisis. He says later that there are no

'foreseeable' circumstances in which he would challenge Mrs Thatcher.
- Sky and BSB announce merger.
6 • Trying to calm party nerves, Mrs Thatcher speeds up timetable for annual leadership contest. The first ballot is to coincide with the World Summit in Paris.
7 • Terry Marsh acquitted of attempted murder of Frank Warren.
8 • President Bush announces he has ordered three additional aircraft carriers and 100,000 extra troops to the Gulf.
9 • Ireland elects Mary Robinson its first woman President.
10 • IRA ambush and kill four men in County Armagh.
11 • Mrs Thatcher says she will hit any leadership challengers 'all round the ground'.
13 • With Mrs Thatcher listening, Sir Geoffrey Howe stuns a packed House of Commons with his 19-minute resignation speech, explicitly attacking her and inviting others 'to consider their own response'.
14 • Claiming support from 100 MPs, Michael Heseltine launches his leadership challenge.
15 • Unemployment increases to 1.7 million after the biggest monthly rise since 1986.
18 • Mrs Thatcher leaves Britain for the Paris Summit.
- Saddam Hussein announces intention to phase release of all 2,000 foreign hostages after Christmas.
19 • Paris Summit agrees non-aggression treaty and reduction of conventional weapons in Europe by nearly one-third.
20 • First round of Conservative leadership contest results in 204 votes for Mrs Thatcher and 152 for Michael Heseltine. As this leaves Mrs Thatcher 4 votes short of the required majority, a second ballot is required.
21 • Returning to London, Mrs Thatcher declares: 'I fight on, I fight to win'. But support slips away from her. Cabinet Ministers, summoned to her room in the Commons, tell her she cannot win.
22 • Mrs Thatcher withdraws from second ballot and John Major, Chancellor of the Exchequer, and Douglas Hurd, Foreign Secretary, enter the contest.
27 • Second ballot results in 185 votes for John Major, 131 for Michael Heseltine and 56 for Douglas Hurd. Mr Major is 2 votes short of an overall majority but the other two candidates concede defeat and he becomes, at 47, the youngest Prime Minister this century.

December
1 • British and French engineers shake hands and exchange flags as the two

halves of the Channel Tunnel are linked.

  • Conservatives select John Taylor, the first black parliamentary candidate for a seat they already hold.

2 • Helmut Kohl becomes first Chancellor of a united Germany.

6 • Saddam Hussein orders release of foreign hostages in Iraq and Kuwait.

7 • Landslide victory for Lech Walesa in first free Presidential election in Poland.

  • Queen awards Mrs Thatcher the Order of Merit and Denis Thatcher becomes an hereditary baronet.

8 • Blizzards sweep across north and west Britain, killing ten people and cutting power supplies to millions of homes.

12 • President Bush lifts US trade ban to help overcome food shortages in USSR.

13 • Unemployment increases by 57,600, the biggest increase for nine years.

20 • Eduard Shevardnadze resigns as Soviet Foreign Minister.

25 • Soviet Parliament approves new powers for President Gorbachev.

  • Ex-King Michael of Romania expelled from the country only hours after returning for the first time in 43 years.

1991

January

6 • Fierce storms sweep across Britain and Ireland leaving 30 dead.

13 • Soviet troops fire on Lithuanian civilians outside television building in Vilnius, killing 14.

16 • US air attack on Baghdad begins Gulf War.

18 • Iraq launches Scud missile attack on Israel.

25 • Iraqis begin pumping millions of gallons of oil into the Gulf.

29 • Iraqi land forces invade Saudi Arabia.

February

1 • South African President de Klerk announces abolition of remaining apartheid laws.

7 • IRA mortar attack on 10 Downing Street during Cabinet meeting which resumes in the basement.

9 • In Lithuania's independence referendum, 90 per cent vote for an independent republic.

18 • One person killed and 43 injured when IRA bomb explodes at London's Victoria station during morning rush hour.

21 • Soviet/Iraq peace plan rejected by Allies.

22 • Iraqi troops fire hundreds of oil wells in Kuwait.

24 • Allied land offensive begins against Iraqi forces occupying Kuwait.
25 • Saddam Hussein orders his troops out of Kuwait.
28 • Midnight ceasefire in Iraq and Kuwait.

March

3 • Allied and Iraqi military leaders meet in occupied Iraq to agree terms for permanent ceasefire.
   • Shias in southern Iraq revolt against Hussein regime but are suppressed.
4 • Eleven Allied POWs released by Iraqis.
7 • Conservatives lose Ribble Valley by-election to the Liberal Democrats.
14 • Court of Appeal quashes Birmingham Six convictions after they have served nearly 16 years in prison.
17 • People of the Soviet Union vote in referendum to preservie the Union.
19 • VAT raised to 17.5 per cent specifically to finance the Government's cut of £140 per head in this year's Poll Tax.

April

3 • UN Security Council tells Iraq to destroy its stockpiles of weapons and pay war reparations to Kuwait.
4 • Children taken into care in Orkneys after allegations of abuse, returned home after social worker procedures judged 'fundamentally flawed'.
7 • Parachute drops of supplies to Kurdish refugees in mountains along border with Turkey.
17 • US troops move into Iraq to establish centres for Kurdish refugees.
19 • Dr George Carey becomes the 103rd Archbishop of Canterbury.
23 • Government announces that Poll Tax will be replaced by a council tax, based on capital value of property.
30 • Over 100,000 people die in Bangladesh cyclone.

May

14 • Winnie Mandela sentenced to six years' imprisonment for part in kidnapping and assault on four black youths.
16 • Labour wins Monmouth by-election from Conservatives after a controversial campaign on the NHS.
18 • Helen Sharman becomes the first Briton in space when she accompanies Soviet Soyuz rocket.
   • Six-year-old Bradford girl badly injured in attack by pit bull terrier.
20 • Government announces further education reforms, including the abolition of distinctions between polytechnics and universities.
   • During state visit to the United States the Queen confers honorary

knighthood on the Gulf Allied Commander, General Norman Schwarzkopf.

21 • Rajiv Gandhi, former Indian Premier, assassinated by a bomb at an election campaign meeting.
• Ban on import to Britain of pit bull terriers and Japanese tosa dogs.
• Ethiopia's President Mengistu flees to Zimbabwe following advance of rebel forces on capital.

28 • Addis Ababa falls to forces of the People's Revolutionary Democratic Front.

30 • Inquiry report condemns practice of 'pindown' used in four Staffordshire Social Services homes.
• George Walker removed as chief executive of Brent Walker group.

June

3 • Prince William has operation following accidental blow to head from golf club at his school.

13 • The people of Leningrad vote to change its name back to St Petersburg.

25 • Croatia and Slovenia declare independence from the Yugoslav republic.

26 • The two men, Pottle and Randle, who admitted helping master spy George Blake to escape from prison 25 years earlier, are acquitted at Old Bailey trial.

27 • Yugoslav tanks move into Slovenia.

28 • Mrs Thatcher announces she will not stand at the next election.

July

2 • John Birt appointed to take over as BBC director general from 1993.

4 • Labour holds Liverpool Walton by-election in face of direct challenge by Militant candidate, standing as 'Real Labour'.

5 • The Bank of Credit and Commerce International (BCCI) closes after discovery of widespread fraud.
• A Dutch court acquits four IRA suspects of the murder of two tourists in Roermond.

7 • Two IRA suspects break out of Brixton prison, shooting a car driver before stealing his vehicle for their getaway.

10 • The International Cricket Commission readmits South Africa to full membership.

18 • Extensive flooding across China kills at least 1,700 people.

22 • John Major launches his Citizen's Charter, promising increased quality and value for money in public services.

23 • Defence Secretary Tom King announces that 22 regiments will merge in

the biggest armed forces restructuring this century.

29 • Two founders of BCCI indicted in New York on charges of defrauding depositors of some $5 billion.

31 • At the end of their Moscow Summit, Presidents Bush and Gorbachev sign the Strategic Arms Reduction Treaty.

August

8 • John McCarthy freed after more than five years captivity in Beirut.

19 • Soviet coup in which eight-man junta take control announcing that president Gorbachev had been relieved of his duties due to ill-health.

• Boris Yeltsin announces that he is taking control of Russia.

20 • Soviet troops clash with Yeltsin supporters in Moscow, killing three.

• Russian troops defect to Yeltsin as coup collapses.

21 • President Gorbachev flies back to Moscow to resume his Presidency.

• Estonia and Latvia declare independence.

23 • President Gorbachev publicly humiliated by Boris Yeltsin in Russian Parliament when the latter insists that Gorbachev reads out the minutes of a Soviet cabinet meeting.

27 • Moldavia becomes eighth Soviet republic to secede from the Union.

• EEC recognises independence of Estonia, Latvia and Lithuania.

28 • Soviet government formally dismissed and the ruling body of the KGB disbanded.

September

2 • The United States formally recognises the independence of the three Baltic republics.

9 • Serious rioting and arson in Tyneside.

12 • Unemployment rises to 2.4 million, the highest figure for three years.

25 • Beirut hostage, Jackie Mann, flies home to Britain.

• Sir Roland Smith resigns as Chairman of British Aerospace and is replaced by Sir Graham Day.

27 • President Bush announces extensive cuts in nuclear arms.

October

1 • Soviet Union announces plans to cut its armed forces by almost half in response to US proposals to cut its nuclear weapons.

3 • Director of Public Prosecutions, Sir Allen Green, resigns after police report him for kerb-crawling in notorious Kings Cross area.

9 • Transport Secretary Malcolm Rifkind rejects British rail's preferred south London route for the Channel tunnel high speed link in favour of a route through east London.

15 • Senate confirms Judge Clarence Thomas confirmed as member of US Supreme Court by 52 votes to 48 after damaging allegations of sexual harassment against him from former work colleague, Professor Anita Hill.

16 • Thames, TVS, TSW and TV-AM all lose their television franchises.

21 • US hostage, Jesse Turner, freed after five years captivity in Beirut.

22 • Polly Peck chairman, Asil Nadir, charged on 58 counts of theft amounting to £130 million.

23 • House of Lords makes historic ruling that marital rape is illegal.
   • Polly Peck adminstrators issue Asil Nadir with writs for £1 billion.

25 • Dr Malcolm Smith wins £150,000 slander damages against former medical partner who alleged he sexually harassed her.

28 • *Daily Mirror* foreign editor, Nick Davies, accused of working for Israeli secret service Mossad, dismissed.

30 • Joyriders kill 12-year-old girl in Liverpool, the twelfth person to die in such incidents in under two months.

November

3 • Israeli and Palestinian delegates in Madrid hold their first face-to-face talks since the 1967 War.
   • The ancient city of Dubrovnik shelled by Serbian forces.

4 • Imelda Marcos returns to the Phillipines after six years exile.

5 • Robert Maxwell dies at sea after disappearing overboard from his yacht off the Canary Islands. Shares in Maxwell Communications and Mirror Group Newspapers suspended on the Stock Exchange.

7 • Three by-elections on one day: Labour wins Langbaurgh from the Conservatives and holds Hemsworth and the Lib Dems win Kincardine & Deeside from the Conservatives.

10 • Robert Maxwell buried on the Mount of Olives in Israel.

15 • Two members of IRA killed by their own bomb in St Albans.

18 • Terry Waite and Tom Sutherland released by Beirut kidnappers.

19 • Eduard Shevardnadze reappointed Soviet foreign minister 11 months after he resigned the post.

24 • British engineer Ian Richter, held in Iraq for over five years on spying charges, is released.
   • Freddie Mercury dies of Aids.

25 • Appeal Court clears Winston Silcott of PC Blakelock murder because of fabricated police evidence.

26 • Three supermarket chains defy the law by announcing plans to open on Sundays up to Christmas.

- Polly Peck's founder, Asil Nadir, declared bankrupt.
29 • Home Secretary, Kenneth Baker, is first government minister found guilty of contempt of court after deporting teacher from Zaire.

December
1 • IRA fire bombs explode in several London stores.
2 • Ukraine votes to become an independent state.
- American hostage, Joseph Cicippio, released in Beirut.
3 • Disclosures that private Maxwell companies were funded by unauthorised loans from the Mirror pension fund leads to Kevin and Ian Maxwell surrendering executive control of the family's publishing and media empire.
4 • The last American hostage in Beirut, Terry Anderson, is released.
- Serious Fraud Squad begin investigation into £526 million found missing from Maxwell company pension funds.
5 • *Daily Mirror* put up for sale.
8 • End of USSR looms as leaders of Belorussia, Russia and the Ukraine announce the formation of a new commonwealth of independent states.
10 • Historic treaty on political and economic union signed by EEC leaders in Maastricht. Britain secures its own opt-out from single currency and the social charter.
11 • William Kennedy Smith cleared of rape charge by Palm Beach jury.
13 • Five Soviet republics announce they will join new commonwealth.
- Over 60 people injured by IRA bomb planted at a police station in County Armagh.

CHAPTER THREE

THE MARGINALS

In this chapter we offer a few examples of the marginal seats which mark the battle lines for the general election. They range from the highly vulnerable seats to those which only a major change in voting opinion could possibly shift.

Ayr

1983	result	%	1987	result	%
Con	21,325	42.8	Con	20,942	39.4
Lab	13,338	26.7	Lab	20,760	39.1
Lib	12,740	25.6	Lib	7,859	14.8
SNP	2,431	4.9	SNP	3,548	6.7
Majority	7,987	16.1		182	0.3
Turnout		76.7			79.9

This seat did not even feature in the list of marginals in the ITN 1987 Election Factbook. Held by George Younger, formerly both Secretary of State for Scotland and for Defence, ever since 1964, he came within a whisker of being the biggest casualty of the election. Ayr had never been a rock-solid Conservative seat but the addition of Troon in the 1983 boundary changes was thought to make it safer. With George Younger's retirement this must be Labour's best chance, with their candidate Alastair Osborne, to take the seat for the past quarter century. They could well be helped by the Government's decision to break the local Prestwick Airport's monopoly on international flights from Scotland. In the May 1990 Regional Council elections, Labour won the seat narrowly. However, Conservative Phil Gallie will be encouraged by his party's recovery in Scotland since Mrs Thatcher's resignation and will hope that 1987 marked rock bottom in their post-war electoral fortunes. But his support for trust status for the local hospital may cost him crucial votes.

Barrow & Furness

1983	result	%	1987	result	%
Con	22,284	43.6	Con	25,432	46.5
Lab	17,707	34.7	Lab	21,504	39.3
SDP	11,079	21.7	SDP	7,799	14.2
Majority	4,577	8.9		3,928	7.2
Turnout		75.2		79.0	

One of the most spectacular signs of Labour's disastrous fortunes in the 1983 general election was their loss of this seat which they had held since 1945. Labour's non-nuclear defence policy ripped apart its vote in a town dominated by theVickers shipbuilding yard where the Trident nuclear submarine was being built. Perched on the southern edge of the Lake District, it is an industrial town set in rural, tourist Cumbria which has been building ships since the 1870s. In 1986, the Vickers yard was privatised and became VSEL. More than 80 per cent of the employees brought shares in it. Doubtless, the Conservative victor of 1983, former Manchester Councillor Cecil Franks, will see that as a reason why his majority fell only slightly in 1987. However, with Labour's abandonment of unilateral nuclear disarmament, and the announcement in March last year that VSEL were looking to reduce their workforce from 12,500 to between 7-9,000 by 1995, he would appear to be very vulnerable this time. Yet the May 1991 local elections showed a 5 per cent swing to the Conservatives since the 1987 general election. Labour's John Hutton should win but it will be a tight contest.

Basildon

1983	result	%	1987	result	%
Con	17,516	38.7	Con	21,858	43.5
Lab	16,137	35.6	Lab	19,209	38.3
SDP	11,634	25.7	Lib	9,139	18.2
Majority	1,379	3.1		2,649	5.2
Turnout		69.0			73.8

The 1983 boundary changes seemed set to turn the new Basildon seat into a good Labour prospect. Much of its Conservative territory had moved to Billericay, along with its previous MP,Harvey Proctor. But David Amess won the seat for the Conservatives by a narrow majority (thus enabling him to celebrate his marriage three months later in a reception in the House of Commons); and he saw his vote improve and his majority increase in 1987. Labour's recovery among skilled workers and the sizeable 1987 Alliance vote waiting to be squeezed should make this a strong prospect for switching this time. Labour's John Potter will have been encouraged by the near 6 per cent swing to them in the May 1991 local elections, compared with the 1987 general election. Also, by the ICM poll across Essex last autumn which showed a significant revival in their fortunes in the county. Basildon normally declares fairly early on election night and its result in 1987 certainly showed that the Conservatives were on course for another big victory in 1987. Everyone will be watching it closely next time as an important indicator of the outcome.

Batley & Spen

1983	result	%	1987	result	%
Con	21,433	39.6	Con	25,512	43.4
Lab	20,563	38.0	Lab	24,150	41.1
SDP	11,678	21.5	SDP	8,372	14.3
Ecology	493	0.9	Other	689	1.2
Majority	870	1.6		1,362	2.3
Turnout		73.4			79.0

 But for Labour's post-War electoral low in 1983 they would have won this seat easily. It was created out of a marginal area from the old Brighouse & Spenborough constituency and strong Labour wards from the old Batley & Morley seat. Elizabeth Peacock, a former North Yorkshire County Councillor, looked to have a hard job holding the seat in 1987 against Ken Woolmer, the former Labour MP for Batley & Morley. However, Labour's recovery last time was not as great as the increase in the Conservative vote. Things will not be so easy for her this time. The May 1991 local elections saw Labour with an 8 per cent lead in the constituency which seems to suggest that their candidate, Eunice Durkin, will be buying a season ticket to London later this year.

Birmingham, Northfield

1983	result	%	1987	result	%
Con	22,596	42.7	Con	24,024	45.1
Lab	19,836	37.5	Lab	20,889	39.3
Lib	10,045	19.0	SDP	8,319	15.6
Other	420	0.8			
Majority	2,760	5.2		3,135	5.8
Turnout		71.2			72.6

This is a classic bellweather seat and what happens here this time will tell us a lot about the outcome of the general election. In 1979 it provided one of the most astonishing results of the election. Conservative Jocelyn Cadbury destroyed a Labour majority of more than 10,000, as car workers from the Longbridge plant in the constituency and their wives turned against Labour. In 1982 Mr Cadbury committed suicide and in the subsequent by-election Labour's John Spellar (an official in the Electricians Union) just scraped home with a wafer-thin majority of 289 votes. Labour's feeble performance was a pointer to their failure in the subsequent (1983) general election. John Spellar was then

defeated by Conservative Roger King, founder of a motor accessory business.
Mr Spellar is now standing in the safe Labour seat of Warley West and the
Labour candidate is Richard Burden. Mr King strongly supported a November
1991 general election. This was not surprising given the results of the May local
elections in the constituency which showed a near 4 per cent swing to the
Conservatives compared with the 1987 general election. Mr King said at the
time that John Major should go to the country because political
prospects for 1992 were far less certain. It will be small consolation to be
proved right if he loses his seat in the process.

Birmingham, Yardley

1983	result	%	1987	result	%
Con	17,986	43.2	Con	17,931	42.6
Lab	15,141	36.3	Lab	15,409	36.6
SDP	8,109	19.5	Lib	8,734	20.8
Other	415	1.0			
Majority	2,845	6.9		2,522	6.0
Turnout		72.2			73.9

In every general election since 1959 this constituency has been won by
whichever party went on to form the Government. Situated on the south-
eastern edge of Birmingham it is a mixture of council and private housing, with
a mainly skilled, working class population. Indeed, Yardley is one of the most
working class Conservative seats in the country. However, its role as a Con/Lab
barometer seat is increasingly jeopardised by very strong Lib Dem performances
in the annual local elections. In May 1991, the Conservative share of the vote
fell to 19.6 per cent, with Labour also down at 22.2 per cent whilst the Lib Dem
share in the constituency was 56.6 per cent. The Lib Dems have been knocking
at the door of this constituency for some years now but have always been
defeated by the weak general election performance of centre parties in theWest
Midlands conurbation. Labour's Estelle Morris needs to squeeze their 1987 vote
if she is to take the seat but her task is tougher than the figures suggest.

Cambridge

1983	result	%	1987	result	%
Con	20,931	41.5	Con	21,624	40.0
SDP	14,963	29.7	SDP	16,564	30.6
Lab	14,240	28.2	Lab	15,319	28.3
Other	286	0.6	Other	597	1.1

1983	result	%	1987	result	%
Majority	5,968	11.8		5,060	9.4
Turnout		75.2			78.0

Cambridge has resisted Labour's blandishments at a Westminster level for a long time (although the City Council is currently Labour-controlled). They won it narrowly for the first time in 1945 but the Conservatives took it back in 1950 and held it until Labour's 1966 landslide. However, Labour's local reign was short-lived as the Conservatives won it back in a by-election in 1967. Since then it has remained with them. Robert Rhodes James held the seat in a 1976 by-election. A Tory 'wet', he has been at odds with the Government over its Higher Education policies and a strong opponent of its student loans scheme. He retires this time (the Conservatives have selected Mark Bishop to stand for them) and this has fuelled the hopes of his opponents. The Alliance narrowly took second place in 1983 and held it when SDP President, Shirley Williams was their 1987 candidate. In the May 1991 local elections there was a 12 per cent swing to Labour compared with the 1987 general election and their candidate, Anne Campbell, must hope to win the seat with a substantial centre vote next time. The Lib Dems take a different view and hope that they will benefit by squeezing Labour. Either way the seat is unlikely to change hands unless local voters decide to clear the log-jam in the anti-Conservative majority.

Cannock & Brentwood

1983	result	%	1987	result	%
Con	20,976	40.9	Con	24,186	44.5
Lab	18,931	37.0	Lab	21,497	39.5
SDP	11,336	22.1	Lib	8,698	16.0
Majority	2,045	3.9		2,689	5.0
Turnout		77.4			79.8

This was a Labour seat from 1945, apart from four years (1970-74) and was expected to remain so after the 1983 boundary changes. In the event, Conservative Gerald Howarth won. He inherited a seat with a strong tradition of coalmining, although most of the pits have now closed. In recent years a number of commuter villages have developed, serving the West Midlands industrial centres and the Conservatives will doubtless be looking to these new voters as proof that the seat is changing their way. However, the shock loss of the neighbouring Mid Staffordshire seat to Labour in the March 1990 by-election will also have fortified the latter in the belief that they should never have lost this constituency in the first place and it will return safely to the fold (and their candidate Tony Wright) this time.

Cardiff Central

1983	result	%		1987	result	%
Con	16,090	41.4		Con	15,241	37.1
Lib	12,638	32.6		Lab	13,255	32.3
Lab	9,387	24.2		Lib	12,062	29.3
Plaid	704	1.8		Plaid	535	1.3
Majority	3,452	8.8			1,986	4.8
Turnout		72.1				77.6

This seat has been Conservative in one guise or another for sometime now. It comprises the civic centre and the inner city housing in Cathays, with the posher suburbs up Cyncoed way. Conservative Ian Grist, sacked from the Welsh Office in John Major's first shuffle last year, has held it since 1974. The figures show what an extraordinary balancing act he has had to perform in recent years, with just over 3,000 votes dividing him from the third placed candidate in 1987. In the May 1991 local elections the Lib Dems took 38.7 per cent of the vote in the seat, with Labour taking 29.4 per cent and the Conservatives down to 21.1 per cent. But despite its local fueding, Labour will see their candidate, Jon Jones, as the principal challenger at the next election. They calculate that his opposition to the Cardiff Bay barrier will stand him in good stead locally. They will also be fortified by their two great by-election victories in Wales, the Vale of Glamorgan and Monmouth, in the belief that Cardiff will return three Labour MPs next time.

Colne Valley

1983	result	%		1987	result	%
Lib	21,139	39.8		Con	20,457	36.4
Con	17,993	33.9		Lib	18,780	33.4
Lab	13,668	25.8		Lab	16,353	29.1
Other	260	0.5		Other	614	1.1
Majority	3,146	5.9			1,677	3.0
Turnout		76.2				80.1

The seat was greatly changed as a result of the 1983 boundary revisions. It lost much of its distinctive Pennine character and gained a great slab of

Huddersfield in return. For many years prior to that it had been a Lab/Lib marginal. It returned a Labour MP as early as 1908 and has been represented by Victor Grayson and Philip Snowden. From 19450-66 it was held by Labour and then by the Liberal, Richard Wainwright, from 1966-70. Labour won it back between 1970-4, only to lose it again to Richard Wainwright between 1974-87. Mr Wainwright retired in 1987 and the seat fell to the Conservatives for the first time in its history when Graham Riddick, a former salesman with the Coca Cola company, won it. He was undoubtedly assisted by the fact that the wards which came into the seat from Huddersfield West were largely Conservative. This must be a strong candidate for change at the next election: the only question is whether Labour's John Harman or the Lib-Dem's is the most likely winners.

Darlington

1983	result	%	1987	result	%
Con	22,434	44.6	Con	24,831	46.6
Lab	18,996	37.8	Lab	22,170	41.6
SDP	8,737	17.4	Lib	6,289	11.8
Other	108	0.2			
Majority	3,438	6.8		2,661	5.0
Turnout		77.1			80.8

Whilst it is part of the strongly Labour county of Durham, the town is not typical of the area. An attractive market town, it never relied on the county's industrial staples of coal and shipbuilding and was thus able to avoid the worst consequences of their decline in the rest of the region. It developed as a result of the 19th century railway expansion. The railway workshops were run down in the 1960s but the town successfully diversified into light engineering. Its retail and service sectors also grew, until today about half of its population work in non-manual jobs. Darlington has swung between the two main parties throughout the post-War period. Labour held it between 1945-51, from 1951 to1964 it stayed Conservative; and from 1964-83 it reverted to Labour. In March 1983, Labour's Ossie O'Brien held the seat in a by-election and some argued subsequently that this saved Michael Foot from being challenged for the party leadership. The victory was illusory. Mr O'Brien served as an MP for less than three months. In the June general election he was defeated by his Conservative by-election challenger, Michael Fallon. Facing Mr O'Brien again in 1987, Mr Fallon held on. He made great play of Labour's defence and energy policies, claiming that its anti-nuclear stance would jeopardise local factories with nuclear-related orders on their books. Much has changed since then and he must now be vulnerable to Labour's Alan Milburne: the May 1991 local elections showed a swing of nearly 8 per cent to Labour since the last general election.

Derby North

1983	result	%	1987	result	%
Con	22,303	43.7	Con	26,516	48.8
Lab	18,797	36.8	Lab	20,236	37.3
Lib	9,924	19.5	Lib	7,268	13.4
Other	291	0.5			
Majority	3,506	6.9		6,280	11.5
Turnout		72.5			75.8

It fell to the Conservatives in 1983 – the first time they had won a seat in Derby since 1935. Phillip Whitehead narrowly held it in 1979 (by 214 votes) but was defeated four years later by Greg Knight, mananging director of a music publishing company. Mr Whitehead fought the seat again in 1987 but saw the Conservative majority increase substantially. The constituency is certainly no longer the perennial Labour marginal of yesteryear. It is the more middle class of the two Derby seats and Greg Knight must believe he is there to stay. The 1989 County elections encouraged him – showing a 5 per cent Conservative lead in the seat. However, his Labour opponent, Bob Laxton, will likely point to the neck and neck share of the vote in last May's local elections when six of North's eight Wards polled. He will also seek his own encouragement from last October's Press Association poll which showed the biggest regional swing to Labour since 1987 in the East Midlands. It will be a hard nut for Labour to crack, but crack it they must.

Down South

1983	result	%	1987	result	%
Unionist	20,693	40.3	SDLP	26,579	47.0
SDLP	20,145	39.2	Unionist	25,848	45.7
Sinn Fein	4,074	7.9	Sinn Fein	2,363	4.2
Other	6,417	12.6	Other	1,744	3.1
Majority	548	1.1		731	1.3
Turnout		76.7			79.4

This is a predominantly rural constituency but with some fishing. It also has a tourist industry based upon the seaside resort of Newscastle and the attractions of the Mourne Mountains and forest parks. Enoch Powell represented the seat from October 1974 until his defeat at the last election. In large part his defeat was the product of boundary changes which lost him Protestant voters and gained him Catholics (although his non-sectarian image attracted some Catholic voters throughout his tenure). But his strong anti-EEC views did not go down too well with some of the farmers in the constituency. In December 1985 all 15 Unionists resigned their seats as a protest against the Anglo-Irish Agreement. Mr Powell was reported to be unhappy about this tactic and the subsequent by-elections (January 1986) proved to be a farce. The Unionists lost one seat to the SDLP and in Down South the voting presaged troubles ahead. Although not facing a DUP candidate (as in 1983) Mr Powell's vote increased by less than 5 per cent, whilst that of his SDLP challenger, Eddie McGrady, increased by 5.7 per cent. In 1987 Mr McGrady closed in for the kill and won the seat. It remains vulnerable but Mr McGrady must have a reasonable prospect of holding it.

Elmet

1983	result	%	1987	result	%
Con	23,909	47.3	Con	25,658	46.9
Lab	16,053	31.8	Lab	20,302	37.1
SDP	10,589	20.9	SDP	8,755	16.0
Majority	7,856	15.5		5,356	9.8
Turnout		75.4			79.3

This constituency was an entirely new creation in 1983 (named after a kingdom in the Dark Ages) and contains stark contrasts within it. It drew large council tower blocks from Denis Healey's Leeds East seat and great slabs of rich agricultural land from the old, solidly Conservative, Barkston Ash seat. The Conservative, Spencer Batiste, became its first MP in 1983 but saw his majority fall by 2,500 in 1987. His strong support for the working miners during the 1984 Miners Strike did not endear him to some of his constituents who remember the area's strong mining tradition. He will not have been cheered by the results of the May 1991 local elections when the Labour share of the vote in the constituency was 45 per cent, compared with 38 per cent for the Conservatives (with the Lib Dems at 15 per cent). Wetherby, an expanding market town which has seen an influx of prosperous commuters in recent years forms the Conservative bedrock in the seat. But the battle will be won or lost elsewhere in Elmet. Labour, represented by Colin Burgon, must be hoping third time lucky to win the 'kingdom' next time.

Hampstead and Highgate

1983	result	%	1987	result	%
Con	18,366	41.2	Con	19,236	42.5
Lab	14,996	33.7	Lab	17,015	37.6
SDP	11,038	24.8	SDP	8,744	19.3
Other	156	0.3	Other	271	0.6
Majority	3,370	7.5		2,221	4.9
Turnout		66.9			71.5

Attention will inevitably focus upon this constituency during the campaign. Not only is Conservative Sir Geoffrey Finsberg retiring but Labour have selected the actress, Glenda Jackson, as their candidate. The Conservative hopeful, Oliver Letwin, may find it hard to compete with such star quality. However, he may be encouraged by the fact that Labour has only won the seat once since 1945, with Ben Whitacker as their MP 1966-70. Given the area's middle class reputation it was something of a modest triumph for Labour to see off the SDP challenge in 1983. But that reputation is itself something of a myth as there are strong Labour areas in Kilburn and West Hampstead. This time all is to play for. In the May 1990 London Borough elections there was a 6 per cent swing to Labour compared with the 1987 general election in the constituency (even though the Labour-controlled Borough of Camden in which it is situated does not enjoy the highest reputation in London). Labour must believe that Glenda Jackson has the best chance in years to grab the seat for them. The Conservatives must hope that the anti-Labour 'London effect' which saw a swing to them in the capital in 1987 will see them through again this time.

Harlow

1983	result	%	1987	result	%
Con	21,924	41.1	Con	26,017	47.2
Lab	18,250	34.2	Lab	20,140	36.6
Lib	12,891	24.2	SDP	8,915	16.2
Other	266	0.5			
Majority	3,674	6.9		5,877	10.7
Turnout		76.5			78.4

Harlow is a clear example of Labour's problem in recent years. The post-War Harlow New Town comprises the core of the seat, brimming over with skilled workers who were once Labour's bedrock support. But New Towns are no longer safe Labour territory. Few expected Labour's Stan Newens to lose in 1983, after all, he had survived a 13 per cent swing to the Conservatives in 1979 with a majority of 4,000 votes. But he was comprehensively defeated by Conservative barrister, Jerry Hayes. And Labour's gloom can only have deepened in 1987 when Mr Hayes's majority increased by more than 2,000 votes. Still, Harlow has to won if Labour is to create a majority of its own next time. Their candidate, Bill Rammell, will be banking on the significant improvement in support among skilled workers since 1987, the growth of unemployment in the South East during the latest recession; and the legacy of high mortagage rates over the last couple of years. However, Labour face an assiduous and energetic opponent in Gerry Hayes who has established his own 'incumbency effect' He will be hoping that the New Towns have drifted so far from Labour in the last 12 years that they are now beyond their reach. At least in Westminster terms, because in the May 1991 local elections Labour's share of the vote in the constituency represented a 12 per cent swing to them since the 1987 election.

Hyndburn

1983	result	%	1987	result	%
Con	19,405	42.2	Con	21,606	44.4
Lab	19,384	42.2	Lab	19,384	39.8
SDP	6,716	14.6	SDP	7,423	15.2
Other	435	1.0	Other	297	0.6
Majority	21	0.0		2,220	4.6
Turnout		77.4			80.5

The constituency is named after the Borough (in turn named after the river which flows through it northwards to the Calder) which lies between Blackburn and Burnley, the bulk of which is made up of the more popularly known town of Accrington. Situated in north-east Lancashire it comprises, in addition, a series of small, former textile towns. Predominantly a working class seat, it has one of the highest levels of owner-occupation for any constituency in the country. Labour held the seat between 1945-83: their first shock was to lose it to Ken Hargreaves by 21 votes after six recounts in 1983 (it was the last seat to be declared in that election). The second shock was to see the most marginal Conservative seat in the country increase its majority to over 2,000 in the 1987 general election. The Labour candidate then was the Leader of Liverpool Council, Keva Coombes. Some felt that he brought with him the spectre of the 'Liverpool factor' with all its association of Militant politics and Labour's civil war. This time the issues are more likely to be national than local and Labour's candidate, Greg Pope, will hope to gain most from this different focus.

Keighley

1983	result	%	1987	result	%
Con	21,370	42.6	Con	23,903	45.8
Lab	18,596	37.0	Lab	18,297	35.0
Lib	9,951	19.8	Lib	10,041	19.2
Other	302	0.6			
Majority	2,774	5.6		5,606	10.8
Turnout	78.9				79.5

Former financial journalist and MP for Brighouse & Spenborough, Gary Waller, defeated the Labour incumbent, Bob Cryer, in 1983. Keighley itself is a long established woollen textile town but its industry has declined significantly. The 1983 boundary changes brought into the seat the blue chip Conservative spa town of Ilkley which tipped the balance their way. The constituency also boasts the Brontes' home in Haworth and some very attractive parts of the Yorkshire moors. Bob Cryer went on to hold Bradford South for Labour in 1987 and, having overcome his incumbency effect in 1983, Gary Waller had built up his own by 1987. In the May 1991 local elections the Conservatives still led Labour (by about 4 per cent) in terms of the popular vote in the constituency. Keighley presents a more difficult task for Labour, post-1983, but is a seat they must win if they are sustain a serious challenge to the Conservatives next time. What happens to the 1987 Alliance vote will almost certainly hold the key to whether Gary Waller remains or is replaced by Labour's Tommy Flanagan.

Lancashire West

1983	result	%	1987	result	%
Con	25,458	46.2	Con	26,500	43.7
Lab	18,600	33.8	Lab	25,147	41.5
SDP	10,983	20.0	SDP	8,972	14.8
Majority	6,858	12.4		1,353	2.2
Turnout		74.4			79.7

A seat of considerable contrasts. Ormskirk and its surrounding countryside is pure lace curtain Conservative, whereas Skelmersdale New Town is rock solid Labour with unemployment levels to match. Ken Hind won it for the

Conservatives in 1983 with a majority of 12.4 per cent. On paper it seemed destined to settle as a fairly safe Conservative seat. But any complacency on their part was ripped apart in 1987 when Labour's Colin Pickthall turned in one of the best performances for his party anywhere in Britain. The Conservative majority was slashed to 2.2 per cent. Mr Pickthall is standing again this time and if he can marshal his vote in Skelmersdale he has a very good chance to unseat Mr Hind next time. Both men will have pondered the May 1991 local election results which gave Labour a 9.5 per cent lead in the votes cast in the constituency.

Lewisham East

1983	result	%	1987	result	%
Con	17,168	40.3	Con	19,873	45.1
Lab	15,259	35.9	Lab	15,059	34.2
SDP	9,351	22.0	SDP	9,118	20.7
Others	764	1.8			
Majority	1,909	4.4		4,814	10.9
Turnout		69.5			73.9

This is a mixed constituency, with the Conservatives strongest around Blackheath to the north and Labour strongest in the council estates to the south. Labour's Roland Moyle held the seat from 1974 but was defeated by Olympic cox Colin Moynihan in 1983. Mr Moynihan subsequently found fame as Minister of Sport and in ITV's 'Spitting Image'. In 1987 his Labour challenger was Russell Profitt, a black left-winger, employed as principal race relations officer in the London Borough of Brent – all of which were guaranteed to meet with Mr Moynihan's approval. The Conservative vote rose by nearly 3,000 whilst Labour's share fell slightly. The result here may also have been influenced by Labour's disastrous by-election loss in neighbouring Greenwich a few months earlier. Indeed, the SDP vote held up remarkably well between both elections. This time Mr Moynihan faces Bridget Prentice. He will also, doubtless, have reflected upon Labour's gain of nine Conservative seats on a swing of 5 per cent in Lewisham during the London Borough elections of May 1990. Lewisham Council has become something of a Labour party showcase, pioneeering refunds for residents in the event of Council services being unsatisfactory. This should be a fascinating contest providing an important indicator to whether Labour triumphs in London (and hence, in Britain) or is driven into the sand.

Sherwood

1983	result	%	1987	result	%
Con	21,595	41.0	Con	26,816	45.8
Lab	20,937	39.7	Lab	22,321	38.2
SDP	10,172	19.3	Lib	9,343	16.0
Majority	658	1.3		4,495	7.6
Turnout		76.3			81.4

But for the 1984 Miners Strike this would have been a most likely Labour gain in the 1987 general election. In 1983 it was a newly-created constituency and comprised the most intensively mined area in the country. It was expected to form a safe Labour seat in that year's election. But 1983 was an historic low point for Labour and saw the seat fall to local Conservative farmer, Scotsman Andrew Stewart, with a 658 vote majority. To the despair of Labour's moderate candidate, barrister William Bach, the Miners Strike saw the Nottinghamshire coalfields invaded by flying pickets from Yorkshire, violence at Ollerton Colliery and the formation of the breakaway Union of Democratic Miners. In 1987 Mr Stewart's majority rose to 4,495 whilst Labour's share of the vote fell slightly. Sherwood is firm UDM country and anger at their treatment by the NUM and their cold-shouldering by the Labour Party still runs deep. Mr Stewart's fate seems to rest on whether Neil Kinnock has really succeeded in laying the ghosts of Labour's past (including Arthur Scargill). His candidate this time is Paddy Tipping. Labour should be in with a good chance.

Southampton, Itchen

1983	result	%	1987	result	%
Con	21,937	41.4	Con	24,419	44.3
SDP	16,647	31.5	Lab	17,703	32.1
Lab	14,324	27.1	SDP	13,006	23.6
Majority	5,290	9.9		6,716	12.2
Turnout		73.2			75.8

Time was when the City of Southampton boasted one safe Labour seat and one Conservative/Labour marginal. But, since 1983, both have had Conservative MPs. Itchen (named after the river) used to be the safe Labour seat, returning the former Speaker, Horace King, to Parliament between 1955-71. Indeed, Labour held an unbroken succession from 1945 to 1983. Speaker King was succeeded by Bob Mitchell (who had represented the other Southampton seat,

Test, from 1966-70) in a 1971 by-election. Mr Mitchell switched to the SDP before the 1983 election and when it came he pushed Labour into third place but Conservative Christopher Chope won the seat. He went on to increase his majority in 1987, leaving Labour the cold comfort of pushing Mr Mitchell into third place. Mr Chope must feel fairly comfortable with his 12.2 per cent majority. However, in the May 1991 local elections the Conservatives won only two of the seven wards in the constituency. Labour has controlled the City Council since 1984 and they are one of their party's more effective local authorities nationally. It would be ironic indeed if Mr Chope, former leader of London's Wandsworth Council, was run close, in part, because his Labour opponent, John Denham, benefited from the standing of his local Council.

York

1983	result	%	1987	result	%
Con	24,309	41.3	Con	25,880	41.6
Lab	20,662	35.1	Lab	25,733	41.4
SDP	13,523	23.0	SDP	9,898	16.0
Others	352	0.6	Other	637	1.0
Majority	3,647	6.2		147	0.2
Turnout		75.1			78.4

It has the Minster, the walls, the railway and the chocolate factories. But the city's economy has diversified over the years with a strong emphasis on tourism. The constituency is highly marginal and has changed hands repeatedly since the War. Its last Labour incumbent was Alex Lyon who held it from 1966-83. He was defeated then by Conservative wine consultant, Conal Gregory, perhaps as the result of a very strong SDP performance for such a marginal seat. This time the heat is on Mr Gregory. In 1987 he saw his majority fall to 147 votes. Labour's Hugh Bayley will hope to capitalise upon his party's control of the City Council which has pioneered customer contracts with local residents on such matters as street cleaning (the title of this civic initiative reflecting the city's Cadbury connection – namely, 'Quality Street'). Mr Gregory looks an early victim to Labour's recovery since last time.

CHAPTER FOUR

PARTY PROSPECTS

Whatever its final outcome, the next election promises to be one of the most interesting in recent years. It could also result in the collapse of one of two 'iron laws' of post-war British politics. The first is that no Government has recovered to win the subsequent general election having been as far behind the Opposition in the opinion polls as the present one was in 1990. The second is that no party has achieved the size of swing from any previous election that Labour needs in order to win the next one. The only way both 'iron laws' could be preserved from terminal rust is if the election produced a hung parliament.

In this chapter we rehearse the prospects for each of the three main parties. Much could change before polling day. However, those with nerves of steel have enough evidence upon which to offer tentative judgements.

Before launching into those judgements it is worth considering what room the parties have to shift opinion their way. One of the questions in the Harris/ITN analysis exit polls for the last three general elections attempted to find out when voters made up their minds which party they would support. The overall answers to this question are set out below:

	1979	1983	1987
	%	%	%
Election day	6	8	8
Last week	12	12	10
During campaign	28	23	21
Before election	53	57	60

The most obvious point to emerge is the increase in the number of voters who decide which way they will vote before the election campaign begins.

If we apply the 1987 exit poll figures to the 31.8 million people in Britain who actually voted then, we find that some 19 million had already decided before the election, compared with about 13 million who made up their minds between the campaign beginning and polling day itself.

The Conservatives
Until the departure of Mrs Thatcher, Conservative prospects for the next election looked decidedly grim. Her departure was not the product of some

momentary loss of nerve. From the European Parliament elections in June 1989 onwards, Conservative MPs had seen Labour's fortunes ebb as theirs waned. They had witnessed 88 opinion polls with Labour's lead in double figures, the by-election losses of Mid-Staffordshire in March 1990 and Eastbourne in October; and humiliation in Bradford North in November. Underlying it all was seething discontent over the poll tax which Mrs Thatcher seemed unable to address except by throwing money at it (an Harris/ITN poll on 28 November 1990 found only 5 per cent of people who wanted the poll tax kept in its original form). In April 1990, Mrs Thatcher registered the lowest level of satisfaction for a Prime Minister since Gallup began polling in Britain in 1938. The table below sets out the league table:

Lowest percentage of respondents 'satisfied' with the Prime Minister
(Gallup series)

Winston Churchill	48%	(April 1954)
Alec Douglas-Home	42%	(December 1963)
Anthony Eden	41%	(April 1956)
Clement Attlee	37%	(September 1948)
James Callaghan	33%	(November 1976)
Neville Chamberlain	32%	(May 1940)
Edward Heath	31%	(June 1971)
Harold Macmillan	30%	(October 1957)
Harold Wilson	27%	(May 1968)
Margaret Thatcher	23%	(April 1990)

Mr Major began his premiership with an immediate advantage - he was not Mrs Thatcher. It was as if the country had changed its Government without the expense and disruption of a general election. The prospects for the Conservatives were immediately transformed and they surged ahead of Labour in the opinion polls. However, within a few weeks their lead began to diminish and might have continued to do so, except that the Gulf War broke out in January 1991. A MORI poll published in *The Sunday Times* on 27 January found Mr Major the most popular Prime Minister since Winston Churchill. Some argue that he should have called an election in March, after the Gulf War ended. The opinion polls then were hardly decisive (unlike the loss of Ribble Valley to the Lib Dems on 7 March) and he did not. The May local elections, with their loss of some 900 seats, were hardly impressive enough to trigger a June election. And this judgement seemed to be confirmed when Labour won the Monmouth by-election on 16 May. Much effort was invested in trying to make a November election possible. But Labour's highly successful Party conference and the subsequent opinion polls showing Labour leads of between 2 and 7 per cent narrowly persuaded Mr Major to support those arguing for further delay.

If the Conservatives lose the election there will be complaints of missed opportunities. The consequence of these delays has been that the party now faces an election in a recession. When, as Chancellor, Mr Major made the bold statement: 'If it isn't hurting, it isn't working' he was not planning for the pain to last up to and throughout the general election campaign. Nevertheless, the Conservatives believe they have a number of cards to play which will overcome the economic gloom. Firstly, there is Mr Major himself. Polling shows a distinct gender gap in his approval ratings, with women voters disproportionately favouring him. He is also the 'Teflon' Prime Minister who has escaped blame for the recession. The Harris/ITN poll this January found that 71 per cent of respondents blamed Mrs Thatcher for 'Britain's present economic situation' and only 25 per cent who blamed Mr Major.

Clearly the Prime Minister's personality will feature heavily in the Conservative campaign. At the heart of this decision is the belief that our elections are becoming more presidential: that, as some Conservatives argue, nobody would choose Neil Kinnock over John Major. But the evidence for such an assertion is less than clear. Just before the 1970 election, Harold Wilson's approval rating as Prime Minister was 49 per cent and that of Edward Heath, as Leader of the Opposition, was 28 per cent. Yet history tells us that Mr Heath became Prime Minister the following month. Also, the Harris/ITN exit poll in the 1987 election showed that more people thought Neil Kinnock 'came across best during the campaign' than Margaret Thatcher. But Mrs Thatcher was able to console herself with a parliamentary majority of 101 in the Commons. This is not to say that personality will count for nothing, but we have a parliamentary system, not a presidential one, and it will not decide the outcome of the election.

The second card is their belief that the national opinion polls overstate Labour's likely performance. The Conservative interpretation is that Labour will pile up votes in both safe and hopeless seats whilst underperforming in the key marginals. This may be true but it is saluatary to remember that polls in marginal seats were the disaster area of market research in the 1987 campaign.

The third card is the decline in the numbers on the electoral rolls as some voters attempt to escape the poll tax register. It is thought that this will cost Labour vital votes in a number of seats, especially in London (one estimate puts the potential loss for Labour at 15 seats).

But the outcome of the election is likely to be determined by more basic political factors. The Conservatives have viewed the 1980s as their decade. It was a period which some of them claim has changed British society out of all recognition from the previous post-war decades. They believe that, along with the increases in home ownership, share ownership and self-employment has come a fundamental realignment in political allegiance which is of irreversible benefit to the Conservatives. They point to their electoral advance across most of England (where 80 per cent of all Westminster seats are found) since 1979 and claim that the scale of that advance is too great for Labour to overcome.

However, for many Conservatives, the departure of Mrs Thatcher marked the end of the complacent belief that they had become the natural party of government. The golden years of facing an evenly-divided opposition ended at the 1989 Euro elections. They expect the next election to be the most competitive since 1974. Their main hopes now are that the voters will recoil from Labour's tax proposals; and that they will trust the Conservatives, rather than Labour, to steer the country out of its economic problems. Inevitably, the backdrop to the election will be the nation's verdict on 13 years of Conservative rule. The Conservatives hope that Mr Major's replacement of Mrs Thatcher will neutralise any mood for change.

Labour

Win or lose the next election, Neil Kinnock has already secured one of the most remarkable revivals since that of Lazarus. In the June 1983 general election the Labour Party crashed in flames: losing its deposit in one-fifth of all the seats in Britain; and finishing barely 700,000 votes ahead of the Alliance. In October 1983, Mr Kinnock inherited a battered and demoralised party, besieged in a series of urban ghettos and regional fastnesses. By the 1987 election he had restored Labour's fortunes sufficiently to mount a respectable campaign and to reassert its position as the main Opposition party. In the 1989 Euro elections they defeated the Conservatives for the first time in a nationwide vote since October 1974; and, in 1990, they achieved their highest ratings since polling began in Britain. In these circumstances it might seem a little churlish to ask: 'is this enough?' but the question is fundamental to Labour's prospects this time.

Mr Kinnock's control of his party is now absolute. The changes he has wrought on party policy have been profound. But the biggest test of all is whether he can win the next election; and it is easier for the Conservatives to lose than it is for Labour to win. The obstacles to gaining around 100 seats for a Labour majority are formidable indeed. One has only to recite some of the

constituencies they will need to win to register the scale of their task -
Blackpool North, Dover, Gravesham, Lancaster.

Looking at the 1987 election result and basing the calculations on the seats won
then it is possible to assess Labour's problem in detail:

Seats Labour needs to win to gain a majority of **one**: 97
Seats Labour needs to win to become the largest single party: 74

The figures relating to Labour as largest single party are based upon a straight
swap between themselves and the Conservatives. The actual figure could be
less if the Conservatives lost any seats to the Lib Dems or Nationalists. But, even
so, we can see why there has been such scepticism about Labour's prospects
for achieving either goal. And, if that were not enough of a problem, Labour is
also being challenged in Scotland by a resurgent SNP; and facing considerable
uncertainty in London which, in 1987, actually swung to the Conservatives.
However, Labour claim that these calculations are based upon the experience
of 1983 and 1987, when there was an unprecedented split in the anti-
Conservative vote. They claim that if they gained 40 per cent of the vote this
time that in itself (based on 1987 voting figures) would mean a switch of some
2.7 million voters to them. And neither of the two main parties has ever
managed to gain that many votes from one election to another since the war.
Thus they are less daunted than some by the scale of their task because they
believe that the 'distortion' of voting in the 1980s disguises the real possibilities
for change this time.

Labour also believe they have finally buried the long-standing claim that social
change is moving, relentlessly, against them. For years a variety of people have
argued that, as the demographic groups which make up Labour's traditional
support diminish, then so do their chances of ever winning a majority of seats
in the Commons. This view has developed into a mutation of the Marxist view
of history, recast into the historical inevitability of Conservatism. Labour argue
that the scale of their recovery since the early 1980s could not have been
achieved without large numbers of skilled workers and the middle classes
supporting them. The ultimate test of this belief will, of course, be found in the
voting behaviour of these demographic groups in key marginal seats
throughout Britain on election day.

Labour is also charged with failing to break the Government's opinion poll lead
on which party can best handle the economy. Their critics say that this is a

rather damning indictment of Labour (notwithstanding John Smith's 'prawn cocktail offensive' to reassure the City of their credentials) given the current state of the economy. However, Labour take some comfort from the fact that in September 1964, one month before they won the election, the Conservatives led them by 11 per cent in the polls on the question of which party could best cope if Britain ran into economic difficulties.

Within the Labour party there are those who criticise the leadership for not launching a crusading campaign many months ago. They argue that only by 'inspiring' voters will the party be able to conquer the great electoral mountain they have to climb in order to win this time. Whether their criticism is justified or not, Labour's stance on taxation could make this election one where there is a real argument about tax cuts versus public expenditure. It will be a real test of their assertion that the public has turned its back upon the 'greedy' Thatcherite eighties and is looking for a better alternative.

But, whatever the outcome of the election, Labour is in better heart than for many years. They believe that the result will be decided on the basis of solid, old-fashioned politics, fought by parties presenting serious alternatives which will be judged by more than 30 million of their fellow citizens. For much of the last ten years elections seemed, for Labour, to be the product of an inexorable process of political predestination. They hope that they will be the principal beneficiaries of a new age of really competitive politics.

Liberal Democrats
Paddy Ashdown enters this election with his personal standing as leader of the Lib Dems at a very high level. The December 1991 Gallup registered 58.6 per cent of respondents who thought he was proving a good leader of his party, compared with 50 per cent who were satisfied with John Major and 36 per cent satisfied with Neil Kinnock. However, as discussed earlier, our political system is parliamentary, not presidential (if it were, Mr Ashdown would, on the above figures, be set to become the next Prime Minister, and nobody is suggesting that). The party believes that a variety of indicators show they will perform well in this election. Since 1987 they have overturned two rock-solid Conservative majorities in parliamentary by-elections in England and won a highly competitive one in Scotland. In the annual local elections they have performed far better than the national opinion polls suggested. All-in-all, they believe that polling day will bring some considerable surprises for their opponents.

Shortly after he was elected leader, Paddy Ashdown stated that his intention was to replace Labour as one of the two main parties. It was a bold ambition but it hit an iceberg in June 1989 when the Lib Dems polled only 6.1 per cent of all the votes cast in the European Parliament elections. During the subsequent fourteen months the party's poll ratings averaged single figures. They have recovered from those dark days but, since 1987, they have not performed anywhere near the strength of the old Alliance parties. During the 1983-7 Parliament there were 214 published opinion polls and the Alliance scored 20 per cent or more in 184 (or 86 per cent) of them. Indeed, they registered 30 per cent or more in 41 (nearly one-in-five) reaching a high of 39 per cent in a poll in September 1985. In stark contrast, in the 325 polls between the last election and December 1991, the Lib Dems scored 20 per cent or more in only *two*, less than 10 per cent in 160 (49 per cent) and in nearly one-in-ten they scored 5 per cent or less. Nor is the relative decline in their performance limited to opinion polls. If we compare the 23 parliamentary by-elections in Britain since the last election with the 16 which occurred during the 1983-7 election we can also see the marked difference:

Parliamentary by-elections in Britain

	1983-7	1987-91	Difference
	%	%	%
Conservative	30.4	27.4	-3.0
Labour	28.4	37.7	+9.3
Alliance/Lib Dem	39.0	19.9	-19.1
Others	2.2	14.9	+12.7

All this evidence suggests that the Lib Dems are unlikely to reach the 23.1 per cent of the vote they achieved in the 1987 election. Much of the support which the Alliance soaked up from alienated Labour voters in the 1980s has clearly gone back to Labour. In this Parliament the Lib Dem by-election gains have been in solid Conservative seats - Eastbourne, Ribble Valley and Kincardine & Deeside. And this helps to explain the political tight-rope Paddy Ashdown has to walk. If the party is to retain those particular gains at this election, and make more in similar blue chip Conservative territory, they can hardly make common cause with Labour. Yet, if they appear to court the Conservatives too closely, they risk losing those voters who want a change after 13 years of Conservatism.

This is their dilemma: the forthcoming election is likely to be the roughest and most closely fought for many years and this is not the sort of climate in which people on the sidelines will prosper. They claim that they will do much better than the pre-election opinion polls suggest. But David McKie's article in the

Guardian (23 December, 1991) showed: 'party performances in the last six general elections have in almost every case been remarkably close to the average of the opinion polls in the three months before the contest'. If we take the last three months of 1991, the Lib Dem poll average was 14 per cent. One reason offered by the party for the polls understating their electoral strength is that they were the second party in 230 out of the 376 Conservative seats at the last election. Their argument goes that when people go to vote in these seats they will realise that Labour stands no chance of winning and will vote Lib Dem instead. This may be true to some extent but it is very unlikely that it would transform a 14 per cent poll figure into a vote of, say, 20 per cent.

The best prospect for the Lib Dems seems to be in concentrating on specific target seats which they might win even if their overall share of the vote declines. Such targeting has worked extremely well for them in local elections. In May 1991 they gained an extra 500 seats when their share of the vote fell by about 5 per cent. Yet will this strategy succeed if they are swept up, in terms of resources and personnel, in a national 'dog fight' seen substantially in terms of Conservative versus Labour? But, whatever its size and the number of MPs returned, the Lib Dem vote is likely to be crucial to the outcome of the election. In both the 1983 and 1987 general elections the Conservatives secured massive majorities on shares of the vote smaller than their vote in 1964 when they were defeated. This was because the third party vote in the 1980s was the highest for sixty years and the consequent division of the opposition vote reaped enormous rewards for the Conservatives. Not unnaturally the Conservatives hope to benefit again, but the entrails are not as propitious as in the past. Labour hopes that the Lib Dems will have a disproportionate number of alienated Conservatives among their supporters this time. Mr Ashdown's greatest influence upon the outcome of the election may well be where his support comes from this time.

CHAPTER FIVE

OTHER PARTIES

The Scottish National Party

The Scottish National Party (SNP) was formed in 1934 from the merger of the Scottish Party and the National Party of Scotland. They returned one MP in 1945 but their first real breakthrough came with Winnie Ewing's victory over Labour in the Hamilton by-election in November 1967. She lost the seat to Labour in the subsequent (1979) general election but the party's consolation was to see Donald Stewart, the Provost of Stornaway, gain the seat of Western Isles from Labour. The SNP began to build up support on a platform of 'It's Scotland's Oil' and it was the two 1974 elections which marked their post-War electoral peak. They took seven seats in the February election, and 11 seats in October.

Such was the nationalist success that a reluctant Labour Government was driven to bring in legislation to devolve power to a Scottish Assembly. But by the time of the referendum in March 1979, opinion was only narrowly in favour of such devolution (the 'yes' vote was short of the required 40 per cent of the total Scottish electorate). In the election shortly afterwards, the SNP vote fell and they lost all but two seats (losing no deposits in October 1974, they lost 29 in 1979). By 1983, their support fell further, and they lost their deposit in 53 out of the 72 Scottish seats. In 1987 their share of the vote in Scotland rose to 14 per cent. The result of the Glasgow, Govan by-election in November 1988 transformed their fortunes. With a swing of 33 per cent they overturned a Labour majority of nearly 20,000 and Jim Sillars was elected. The System Three/*Glasgow Herald* poll sampled after the by-election showed a jump of 10 per cent in SNP support across Scotland (with Labour's support falling 6 per cent and that for the Conservatives by 2 per cent); and in their early January 1989 poll the SNP's share rose to 32 per cent – the highest in this Parliament. However, their renewed attacks upon Labour over the Poll Tax did not deliver the coup de grace. Labour fought back by attacking the SNP campaign for non-payment of the tax. By the European elections in June 1989 it was Labour which won the last two Conservative Euro seats in Scotland, when one of them (*North East*) could just as easily have fallen to the SNP. The SNP share of the vote in Scotland rose by 11.6 per cent over the 1987 general election but Labour held its share of the 1987 vote as well as the Westminster by-election seat of Glasgow Central fought on the same day as the Euro elections. The party's renaissance cannot be denied. In the 1988 Scottish District elections their share of the vote put them ahead of the Conservatives for the first time. This second place position was repeated in the 1990 Scottish Regional elections when they ate into the Labour vote. Looking at the total votes cast in the five Scottish parliamentary by-elections since 1987, the SNP took 27.9 per cent compared with Labour's 34.7 per cent (the Lib Dems took 17.9 per cent and the Conservatives 16.2 per cent).

Scotland saw considerable tactical voting in the 1987 election, with voters deciding seat by seat which party was best placed to 'dish the Tories'. If Labour enters the next election campaign with a real prospect of winning nationally then they could well see-off a serious SNP challenge. But if the Scots sense another repeat of the last three general elections – when their support for Labour was drowned by Conservative victory in England – then Labour could well find itself with a battle royal in one of its principal heartlands.

The Scottish National Party Vote 1970-87

Election	MPs elected	Scottish vote%
1970	1	11.4
1974 (Feb)	7	21.9
1974 (Oct)	11	30.4
1979	2	17.3
1983	2	11.8
1987	3	14.0

Plaid Cymru

Formed in 1925, Plaid Cymru enjoyed little political success until a by-election victory in Carmarthen in July 1966, when Gwynfor Evans took the seat from Labour. He lost it in the 1970 general election but for the first time the party contested every seat in Wales. But they never matched the SNP breakthrough in the two 1974 elections – in October 1974 the SNP secured 30.4 per cent of the Scottish vote: at the same election Plaid secured 10.8 per cent of the vote in Wales – slightly lower than their 1970 vote. Where Plaid grew strong was in the Welsh-speaking north and west of Wales, where they maintained their hold on two seats in 1983 despite the continued decline in their overall share of the vote. The party has (with a few exceptions) found it more difficult to make headway in the industrial, non-Welsh-speaking parts.

The referendum on devolution for Wales in March 1979 resulted in a resounding 80 per cent 'No' vote. By 1987 Plaid gained only 7.8 per cent of the Welsh vote. Since 1987 Plaid has not escaped its role as the poor relation of nationalism in Britain. In the four parliamentary by-elections in Wales since the last election it has registered a significant protest vote in the two which were safe Labour seats (Pontypridd and Neath) but it was Labour which won the two other seats from the Conservatives (Vale of Glamorgan and Monmouth) and the impact of Plaid was negligible. Looking at the total votes cast in those by-elections, Labour took 47.9 per cent, the Conservatives 24.6 per cent, Plaid 11.9 per cent and the Lib Dems 10 per cent. In the 1989 European Parliament elections, whilst Plaid's share of the Welsh vote increased by 5.6 per cent compared with 1987, they were pushed into fourth place by the Greens in three out of the four Welsh Euro seats. It seems that Plaid will do well to retain its current three Westminster seats.

The Plaid Cymru Vote 1970-87

Election	MPs elected	Welsh vote %
1970	0	11.8
1974 (Feb)	2	10.7
1974 (Oct)	3	10.8
1979	2	8.1
1983	2	7.8
1987	3	7.3

The Green Party

Founded in 1975 as the Ecology Party, 1979 was their first serious attempt to fight a general election. They fielded 53 candidates and performed well among the minor parties, receiving a total of 39,918 votes. At the 1983 election their number of candidates rose to 108 and their vote to 53,848. In September 1985 they were relaunched as the Green Party and by the 1987 election they fielded a record 133 candidates registering 89,753 votes (0.3 per cent of the total). But the spectacular rise and fall of the party occurred after the 1987 election. Only one month before the European Parliament elections the opinion polls registered 2 per cent support for the Greens. Yet, on 15 June 1989 they received 2.3 million votes – 14.9 per cent of all those cast in Britain. Two years after a general election, when their best constituency performance was 3.6 per cent of the vote in Weston-super-Mare, they came second in six out of 78 Euro seats and third in a further 62, without losing a single deposit. Subsequent opinion surveys showed that the Greens were most popular among women, those aged 18-34, and the middle class. Yet their support declined after the Euro elections. They might have chosen to capitalise upon their vote then and become a major force for environmental change outside the party political system. However, perhaps not surprisingly, they chose instead to compete within that system. This was their undoing. Britain's electoral system is no friend to minor parties and by December 1990 the average monthly poll ratings for the Greens was 2 per cent and this level persisted throughout 1991. Their main impact at the next election will probably be in the University towns, where their support is above average. The unresolved question is whether their vote will disproportionately damage any one of the other parties in some of the key marginals where the outcome of the next election will be decided.

Northern Ireland

The old Conservative and Unionist hegemony was broken during the 1970-74 Heath Government. The Sunningdale Agreement (December 1973) with its power-sharing arrangements between Protestants and Catholics and proposed Council of Ireland bitterly divided the Unionist Party. Both sides saw the February 1974 general election as a referendum on these issues. The dissenting Unionists swept the board in that election and, ever since, none has taken the Conservative whip at Westminster.

Northern Ireland is unique in the United Kingdom in that its non-Westminster elections are fought on the basis of proportional representation. The electorate has become more sophisticated and often varies its party support between local, European and Westminster elections.

In 1989, for the first time since 1974, the Conservative party began to organise and canvass support in the province. Part of the grass roots pressure to organise resulted from the near-26,000 first preference votes which an unofficial Conservative candidate received in the European Parliament elections in Northern Ireland. An official Conservative candidate lost his deposit with 3 per cent of the vote in the Upper Bann by-election in May 1990. Nevertheless in this general election they are putting up candidates for all 17 constituencies.

The British government, as the Nineties arrived, had still not succeeded in establishing devolved government with cross-community support in Northern Ireland. The Anglo-Irish Agreement of 1985 between Britain and the Republic of Ireland was met with great opposition from the Unionist parties. They argued that they had not been consulted in the run-up to the signing of the Agreement, and, once it was signed, all Unionist Westminster MPs resigned their seats and fought subsequent by-elections as a protest against it.

Active support for the campaign, 'Ulster Says No' began to wane after considerable initial civil disorder. Although many were opposed, the Agreement was vague enough to frustrate attempts to resist it – in practice life changed little in the province which may have disillusioned Catholics but allowed Protestants to relax. The two main Unionist parties – the Official Unionists and the Democratic Unionists – forged an electoral pact (whereby neither party challenged the other in seats they held in the 1983 general election) in order to present a common front against the Agreement. The pact lasted four years until November 1989 when Ian Paisley of the DUP declared he had decided to break it in constituencies where this would not 'give the enemies of Ulster the chance to be elected'.

OFFICIAL UNIONIST PARTY

The Ulster Unionists are descended directly from the old Unionist organisation and James Molyneaux became its leader in 1979. Under his leadership the party has had to fend off the challenge from the DUP as well as the ever closer cooperation between London and Dublin. Since 1974, Official Unionism has moved away from Westminster and became more than ever centred in the province. Molyneaux has been generally successful in staunching the loss of grass-roots support to the DUP and often succeeded in reversing the trend back in his party's favour. Official Unionists opposed the Agreement largely through elections and demonstrations in line with their political aim, reflecting the influence of Enoch Powell, of integration with Britain.

The best represented Northern Ireland party at Westminster with nine MPs, the OUP will be seeking to win back Down South from the SDLP which they lost at the last election.

DEMOCRATIC UNIONIST PARTY

Ian Paisley has led the party since it was founded in 1971 and it is represented by three MPs at Westminster. Its conservative Unionism, coupled with economic and social populism, has proved a potent formula. Based on religious fundamentalism, the DUP commands support from the more extremist and working-class voters in the Protestant community. Since the 1980s, Paisley has supported devolution as the only chance Protestants would have of holding power again in the province. The DUP initially wanted to make Northern Ireland ungovernable in protest at the Anglo-Irish-Agreement but while their rhetoric remains unchanged any notions of success on that score have been abandoned.

At this election they will be seeking to win constituencies from the OUP in safe Unionist seats following the demise of their electoral pact.

SOCIAL DEMOCRATIC LABOUR PARTY

Created out of the civil rights campaign of the late 1960s and formed in 1970, the SDLP is the principal Catholic party in Northern Ireland. Gerry Fitt, their first leader, stood down in 1979, concerned with the party's move towards nationalism. His successor, John Hume, is widely regarded as one of the main architects of the Anglo Irish Agreement. Under his leadership the SDLP turned away from hardline socialist principles and incorporated constitutional nationalism (represented in the party by Seamus Mallon, his deputy leader). Hume made much of the potential for reconciliation in the Agreement to placate the Unionists and gained one marginal seat from them in the 1986 by-elections, and another in the 1987 general election. However, talks with Sinn Fein in 1988, which attempted to persuade Gerry Adams that violence was no longer necessary, were unsuccessful.

The SDLP has three MPs at Westminster and will be seeking to increase their number at this election. Their share of the vote is slowly rising. They will be aiming to win Belfast West from Gerry Adams in this election.

PROVISIONAL SINN FEIN

The political wing of the Provisional Irish Republican Army is represented by one MP, its leader Gerry Adams. He won Belfast West in 1983, when Gerry Fitt split the SDLP vote by standing as an Independent, and held it in 1987 with a reduced majority. The Anglo-Irish Agreement was aimed at gaining greater support for the constitutional nationalism of the SDLP and to undermine the bullet and ballot policy of Sinn Fein. During the 1980s the Catholic community's split into more moderate and more extremist groupings was translated into voting patterns. The early 1980s saw an increase in the Sinn Fein vote at the expense of the SDLP, reflecting its change in emphasis to a better organised, grass roots party. However the SDLP fought back, exploiting the methods of fund-raising used by Sinn Fein, and the 1987 general election saw the latter's share of the vote drop by 2 per cent compared with 1983, whilst the SDLP share of the vote increased by over 3 per cent. The broadcasting ban of late 1988, while resisted by broadcasters and civil liberty campaigners, did achieve the government's aim and deprived the party of much-needed public promotion and further limited its political appeal. However, the ban will be lifted during the next general election and they must hope this will help them hold onto Belfast West.

CHAPTER SIX

A 'HUNG' PARLIAMENT?

Despite the emphasis on single-party government in the years since the Second World War, it is nevertheless a fact that Britain has spent almost a quarter of this century under coalition or minority governments.

Since 1945, the Conservative and Labour parties have alternated in power, with just two brief periods of minority rule in the 1970s. The rise of the Liberal-SDP Alliance in the mid-1980s threatened but failed to create a three-cornered challenge for power. Nevertheless, the two-party share of the vote has declined markedly in the last two decades, as the accompanying table shows:

GENERAL ELECTIONS IN GREAT BRITAIN

	Con	Lab	Lib	Two party share of vote
	%	%	%	%
1945	39.4	49.0	9.3	88.4
1950	43.0	46.8	9.3	89.8
1951	47.8	49.4	2.6	97.2
1955	49.3	47.4	2.7	96.7
1959	48.8	44.6	6.0	93.4
1964	42.9	44.8	11.4	87.7
1966	41.4	48.8	8.6	90.2
1970	46.2	43.9	7.6	90.1
1974 (Feb)	38.8	38.0	19.8	76.8
1974 (Oct)	36.7	40.2	18.8	76.9
1979	44.9	37.8	14.1	82.7
			Alliance	
1983	43.5	28.3	26.0	71.8
1987	43.3	31.5	23.1	74.8

Three decisive Conservative victories since 1979, with overall majorities between 43 and 144, have appeared to modify the trend that emerged in the 1970s. But the Liberal Democrats and other parties (including the 17 Northern Ireland MPs) only have to secure 30 seats between them, for it to be unlikely there would be a clear overall majority unless the two major parties are separated by at least three per cent of the vote. A 4 per cent lead would probably generate a majority in single figures (see David Butler: *Governing Without a Majority*, second edition, Macmillan 1986, p.27).

In fact, five out of the 21 general elections this century failed to produce a clear majority and one (October 1974) produced a margin so small that the government was pushed into a minority within two years.

'Hung' Parliaments, however, do not necessarily lead to coalition governments, which this century have been the products of wartime (1916 and 1940) and the special circumstances of Ramsey MacDonald's National Government in 1931. In fact, the precedents show the usual outcome of a 'hung' parliament has been not a coalition but a minority government (1910, 1923, 1929 and February 1974).

The Constitutional Arguments
THE ROLE OF THE QUEEN

The role of the monarch in Britain's unwritten constitution has been progressively eroded over the last four centuries, as political power has passed to ministers responsible to Parliament. The most significant prerogative powers that remain occur when no single political party has control of the House of Commons. Constitutional experts argue fiercely to what extent the Sovereign is free to exercise them but they are twofold: **1** the selection of a Prime Minister to form a government when no party has a clear majority; **2** the power to decide whether to grant a dissolution of Parliament.

THE OUTGOING PRIME MINISTER

It is modern political practice for a defeated Prime Minister to resign from office when the election result becomes known. But it is also the case that the Prime Minister in office may decide to wait, to allow time for negotiations with other parties or to see whether he or she can obtain a majority in the new Commons.

In February 1974, the Conservatives ended up as the second largest party with four seats fewer than Labour but Edward Heath stayed on for four days while he negotiated with the Liberals. This caused some political and constitutional controversy. There is no example this century of a Prime Minister staying on to meet Parliament as the leader of the second largest party (although there is no clear convention against it).

But if the party of the incumbent Prime Minister returns with the largest number of seats, he would be within his rights to stay on to see if he could secure a majority in the Commons. He could explore the possibility of surviving as a minority government with the tacit consent of one or more parties. A further option would be to ask the Queen to dissolve Parliament for a second time.

A lot depends in practice on the precise electoral arithmetic and, in particular, on how far short any party is from the 326 seats needed to command the Commons. Much also depends on the timing of events: there would certainly be political uproar if the outgoing Prime Minister hung on to office in the certain knowledge of defeat when Parliament met.

CHOOSING AN ALTERNATIVE PRIME MINISTER

If the outgoing Prime Minister has resigned, it is thought the Sovereign would then send for the party leader with the largest (or next largest) number of seats, assuming he would have the best chance of forming a government. He would have the same options, with the crucial test being whether he could survive the vote on the Queen's Speech – the programme of government legislation.

Some constitutional experts argue this is not the Sovereign's only choice: that if Labour, for instance, as the largest party had no chance of forming a stable government, the Queen would have the right to appoint a party leader who could – if such a choice existed. But the Sovereign has to remain politically impartial and her advisers would be unlikely to let her move into such uncharted waters, unless circumstances made it unavoidable.

Further, it is argued the Prime Minister does not have to be appointed immediately, but instead, the appointment could be conditional on the ability to form a stable government. In support of this the case of Sir Alec Douglas-Home in 1963 is cited, who, when invited by the Queen to form a government, said he would have to go away and see if it was possible. Those circumstances, however, were rather different from a post-election 'hung' parliament.

THE RIGHT TO A DISSOLUTION

Fact: no request to dissolve Parliament has been refused by the monarch this century.

Fact: most constitutional experts argue that the Queen still has the right to refuse such a request.

This is the most politically sensitive aspect of the royal powers. Constitutionally, the Sovereign possesses the power to dissolve Parliament. At the same time, she must stay above politics in exercising that power. The safest way to do so would be to grant the request for a dissolution when a minority Prime Minister asks for it, however briefly he may have been in office. To refuse it would mean the resignation of the Prime Minister and the possibility that no other Prime Minister could survive in the Commons either.

But some constitutional experts – and some politicians – argue that the Sovereign may refuse a dissolution if: **1** She has substantial grounds for believing an alternative government could be formed; **2** that another general election so soon would be detrimental to the national interest. In this event, the Queen would seek out an alternative government by summoning the leader of the next largest party – and if that fails, the third party. The risk she would run would be the possibility of being forced to grant to one party leader a dissolution which she had refused to another.

There are a number of precedents from around the Commonwealth which emphasise the political risks. The most recent occurred in 1975 when the Governor-General of Australia, Sir John Kerr, dismissed the Labour Prime Minister, Gough Whitlam, for refusing to advise a dissolution as a means of resolving a political deadlock. The Leader of the Opposition, Malcolm Fraser, became caretaker Prime Minister and was granted a dissolution instead. Fraser won the ensuing election but the Queen's representative was seen to have acted in a partisan manner.

So there is little doubt that refusing a dissolution would involve the Crown in heated political controversy. The majority view is that the Queen would grant the first request for a dissolution. This is the conclusion Vernon Bogdanor comes to: 'The Queen's approach, then, will be dictated by caution and she would be unlikely to refuse a dissolution unless the arguments for such a course were quite incontrovertible' (Vernon Bogdanor:*No Overall Majority* published by The Constitutional Reform Centre, London March 1986).

However, if a subsequent general election resulted in yet another 'hung' parliament then the situation might change. The Sovereign might well feel justified in deciding that a third election would be undesirable unless all the possible alternatives of forming a government had been explored. In June 1991, Lord Armstrong, Secretary of the Cabinet between 1979-87, threw some light onto Whitehall thinking about these issues in an interview for BBC Radio 4's 'Analysis' programme. Asked what would happen if there were two hung Parliaments in succession, he said: 'Not only I, but none of us has any experience or precedents to guide us and so I can't say that I know the answer to that question'. However, he went on express his own view that the politicians would be expected: '...to acknowledge that yet another election was out of the question and it was up to them to agree among themselves upon an agreement which would enable the government to be carried on without another election'.

ATTEMPTS TO BROADEN THE GROUND RULES

Prior to the 1987 general election, the Liberal-SDP Alliance tried to open up the constitutional debate, arguing that a new era of multi-party politics meant the old rules were out of date. Unlike Labour and Conservative, they saw positive virtues in coalition. They wanted to introduce new principles: **1** that no party leader in a 'hung' parliament should accept more than a conditional commission from the Queen – to see whether he or she could form a government; **2** that no request for a dissolution should be made until the possibilities of negotiation with other parties had been exhausted.

'The Time has Come', the Alliance policy document, stated that Liberal and Social Democrat MPs would not vote for any Queen's Speech presented by a minority administration unless it had been negotiated with the Alliance and agreed. They were determined that no minority Prime Minister should be allowed to form an administration – and hence be able to claim a dissolution – without first obtaining the support of a majority in the Commons.

In a joint letter to candidates (15 May, 1986) David Steel and David Owen said they were ready to force a second election. If a Conservative or Labour minority government put its programme before Parliament without negotiating with the Alliance, 'we shall be ready for them and they will pay a heavy price because we are confident that our prospects would be even better in such an election'. The two main sticking points on policy were proportional representation and agreement on appropriate measures for economic recovery.

The Conservative and Labour parties, however, said they would have nothing to do with the kind of negotiations advocated by the Alliance, indicating they would prefer to take their chances as minority governments. Indeed, both main parties preferred to maintain the post-war tradition of single-party government, because co-operation with the Alliance heralded a long-term shift to coalition politics, which neither wanted.

Mrs Thatcher (6 January 1987) said, 'What I hate about a hung parliament or these coalitions is that the first thing you have to do is to part from everything which you have got, perhaps the biggest number of seats in an election, and compromise it. There is something that is not quite as honest as I would like about that'.

Neil Kinnock, referring to the Alliance demand for negotiations in exchange for supporting a minority Labour government, said (28 September 1986), 'That would be putting their own vanity considerably above either political integrity or the interests of the country. That might be the price they demand but I'm not in the buying business'.

The Unionist parties also indicated they were not interested in any deals. Many politicians argue that in the highly pressurised circumstances of a hung parliament, the declared standpoints of the parties would in practice be modified swiftly. In the event, the arguments were in vain; the result was once again decisive.

Since 1987 it has been accepted that the arguments about what could or should happen in the event of a 'hung' parliament proved counter-productive for the Alliance. By focussing public attention on the issue of negotiations with other parties, the Alliance reduced their chances of emphasizing their own policies and their own appeal. Instead, the two-headed Alliance leadership increasingly found themselves confronted with questions they did not want to answer, about which of the two main parties they preferred to do a deal with and on what terms. It did not help that David Steel appeared to be pulling more towards Labour and David Owen towards the Conservatives.

This time, whilst the Liberal Democrats have tried to avoid the trap, they have had to respond to inevitable questions. For most of this Parliament Paddy Ashdown said as little as possible on the subject, using a well-tried formula about 'not being afraid' of a 'hung' parliament, but preferring to talk (however improbably) about the merits of a Liberal Democrat government. Following his party's spectacular by-election victories in Eastbourne and Ribble Valley, their poll ratings improved as those for the Conservatives and Labour narrowed to neck and neck. Following Ribble Valley, possibly seeking to reassure his party's new support from among previous Conservative voters, Paddy Ashdown spoke about the possibility of a 'hung' parliament deal with John Major's Conservative party. This caused a flurry of comment – not least from Labour who claimed that he had nailed his colours firmly to the Tory mast.

By April the Lib Dems had hardened their negotiating position. Speaking on BBC Radio, Paddy Ashdown declared: 'I say to Mr Major and Mr Kinnock, if that situation [a hung parliament] comes about, don't even pick up the 'phone unless you are prepared to talk about a fair voting system'. Just prior to the September 1991 Lib Dem Party Conference, he admitted, in conversation with several journalists, that he and senior colleagues had been practising 'war games' on the subject of 'hung' parliaments. The party's campaign director, Des

Wilson, warned delegates of the 'supreme folly' of repeating the mistakes of 1987 by campaigning this time for a 'hung' parliament and speculating about the terms they might set for supporting a minority government. However, these events simply underlined the problems faced by the party. They claim that Labour is incapable of winning the next election and they are therefore better placed to defeat the Conservatives. Yet, since the last election, they have never approached the higher levels of poll support they regularly received during the 1983-7 period. Their best realistic hope is to hold the balance between the two main parties.

But neither of those two main parties will see any advantage in responding to Lib Dem conditions when to do so would publicly acknowledge that they might not win the outright victory they both publicly proclaim is in their grasp. However, if opinion polls during the election campaign point to a close result, the rights and wrongs of a 'hung' parliament will undoubtedly surface again.

The Precedents

Five general elections this century have produced an inconclusive result, leading to minority governments. In each case, a single party took office but relied on the support of at least one other party to stay in power. In addition, one general election (October 1974) generated an overall majority of only three seats which led two years later to a period of minority government.

There have been only three periods of genuine coalition government this century, two of them in wartime. The only peacetime coalition took place in the exceptional circumstances of 1932, circumstances which make it difficult for the Labour party to contemplate such a move again.

1910
The Liberal government of Herbert Asquith lost its huge overall majority in the election of January 1910, which had been fought on the issue of Lloyd George's People's Budget and the House of Lords attempt to block it. Asquith was forced to rely on the support of Irish Nationalist and Labour MPs. A second election in December that year, intended to give the government a mandate to reduce the powers of the Lords, produced almost exactly the same result. But Asquith had a stable majority, mainly because of the government's legislation on Irish Home Rule meant continuing support from the Irish MPs.

1915

Conservatives under Bonar Law joined the Asquith government to form a wartime coalition, of which Lloyd George became Prime Minister the following year. Labour were also represented in the inner War Cabinet. In 1918, the so-called 'coupon election' was fought by the Conservatives together with 150 coalition Liberals in an election pact. The coalition was now predominantly Conservative but Lloyd George remained Prime Minister until 1922.

1923

Conservative Prime Minister, Stanley Baldwin, lost his overall majority but as leader of the largest party stayed in office for six weeks until his programme was defeated in the Commons. Ramsey MacDonald, as the leader of the second largest party, then formed the first Labour minority government. With more than 60 seats fewer than the Conservatives, MacDonald relied on tacit Liberal support. Within nine months, MacDonald asked King George V for a dissolution. It was granted after the King had satisfied himself that no alternative government could be formed.

1929

The Conservatives lost the election and this time Baldwin waited only four days before resigning. Labour was the largest party and again formed a minority government. To conciliate the Liberals, a Committee was set up to investigate electoral reform. But as the economic crisis worsened, the Labour Cabinet split over cuts in welfare payments. King George V was unwilling to accept MacDonald's offer of resignation, asking him instead to form an all-party coalition. It is questionable whether such use of the Sovereign's prerogative would be acceptable today. Only four Labour Cabinet ministers and eight MPs followed MacDonald into the National Government and what was intended as a temporary coalition lasted (in name at least) until 1940. MacDonald remained Prime Minister until 1935 but after the landslide election of 1931 it was overwhelmingly a Conservative government.

1940

The Labour party joined the wartime coalition government established under Winston Churchill after the fall of Neville Chamberlain. The coalition lasted for the duration of the war and was a genuine National Government supported by all significant groupings in the Commons.

1974 (February)

The Conservatives, under the outgoing Prime Minister, Edward Heath, emerged from the February election with four seats fewer than Labour (although nearly 230,000 votes more), with Liberals and Unionists holding the balance. Mr Heath did not resign for three days but held much-publicised negotiations with the Liberal leader, Jeremy Thorpe. Constitutional experts remain divided over his right to do this, since his party did not have the largest number of seats. Approaches to the Unionists also failed. Harold Wilson instead formed a minority Labour government, making it clear he would seek a dissolution if defeated in the Commons. In the event, Wilson went to the country the following October by his own choice. He emerged with an overall majority of just three.

1977

From March 1977, the Liberal party agreed to support in office the Labour government of James Callaghan. The Lib-Lab pact was the result of Labour's loss of an overall majority in the Commons and the Liberals, too, were electorally vulnerable in the wake of the Thorpe affair. It was very far from a coalition – no Liberal MP took office in the Government – but was rather an agreement of mutual support around a number of policy objectives. The pact was marked by a good working relationship between David Steel and the Prime Minister, but the Labour left (including Neil Kinnock, who made an unsuccessful attempt to get the parliamentary party to vote against it) never liked it. It was justified as creating a period of relatively stable government, during which some aspects of the economy did improve. But David Steel was criticised for not achieving greater concessions, in particular for allowing the Prime Minister to avoid a firm commitment to introduce proportional representation for the first elections to the European Parliament in 1979 (Labour MPs and Ministers were allowed a free vote). The pact was ended by the Liberals after 18 months and the Callaghan government continued to survive, thanks in part to deals with other minority MPs. Labour was eventually defeated by one vote on a motion of no confidence on 28 March 1979.

THE RULES OF THE GAME

In September 1991, the Hansard Society published 'Agenda for Change', the report of its Commission on Election Campaigns (16 Gower Street, London WC1E 6DP). In support of its claim that a review of Britain's electoral arrangements is long overdue, it reminded us that the ground rules have barely changed this century: 'Today's laws on electoral administration date largely from 1918; the procedure for counting votes from 1872; the rules on campaign expenditure and party advertising from 1883; and conventions concerning timing and calling of elections from an even more distant past....The only major adjustments since the First World War have concerned the broadcast media, and even those rules have remained substantially unaltered since the 1960s.'

Election Timing

When people say that the United Kingdom does not have 'fixed-term' elections, they mean that the governing party is not obliged by law to face the electorate at a fixed date so many years hence. However, a limit is placed upon the length of time any Parliament can last. For most of the previous two centuries the duration of a Parliament was fixed at seven years. However, the Parliament Act of 1911 reduced that term to five years. A Prime Minister can effectively decide to call a general election before the five-year term has ended (Neil Kinnock made public his preference for fixed term elections in September 1991). Mrs Thatcher always called polls at four-year intervals. John Major has until 11 June, 1992, to set a date for going to the country. Usually, sixteen working days are allowed between the calling of an election and polling day. The statutory general election timetable is set out below:

Event	Day
Royal Proclamation and issue of writs	0
Receipt of writs	1
	2
Notice of election	3
Earliest day for nomination	4
	5
Latest day for nomination	6
Run-up to polling day	7 – 16
Polling day	17

N.B. For the purposes of the timetable, Saturday, Sunday, Christmas Eve, Christmas Day, Maundy Thursday, Good Friday, a bank holiday and any day appointed for public thanksgiving or mourning are disregarded.

Once the Prime Minister announces the date of the dissolution, the Clerk of the Crown in Chancery issues Writs of Election and the timetable above commences. At this time the date of meeting for the new Parliament is also announced. Although they cease to be MPs, government ministers continue in office throughout the election campaign but, like all other former MPs, they may not enter or use the facilities of the House of Commons.

By custom (but not law) the election will be held on a Thursday. The last occasion when this was not so was in 1931 when the General Election was held on a Tuesday. Of the 13 General Elections since the War, four were held in October (1951, 1959, 1964 and 1974); three were held in June (1970, 1983 and 1987); two each in February (1950 and 1974) and May (1955 and 1979); and one each in March (1966) and July (1945).

The Voters
THE ELECTORATE
General Elections are a game that everyone can play – well, almost everyone. There are more than 43 million potential voters on the electoral roll. To qualify, you must be aged 18 or over and a British citizen – or a citizen of the Commonwealth or Irish Republic resident in Britain on 10 October. This is the date when all eligible voters are expected to have registered. Excluded from voting are those under 18, people of unsound mind, Peers, aliens, prisoners and those guilty of illegal election practices. It was not always so this century. The 1918 General Election was the first where women could vote – but only those aged 30 or more. It was not until the 1929 General Election that the right to vote was extended to women aged 21 or more (the same basis as for men). The last great reform took place at the 1970 General Election when the minimum age for all voters was reduced from 21 to 18.

OVERSEAS VOTERS
The Representation of the People Act of 1985 introduced the concept of overseas voting by opening the franchise (for parliamentary and European elections) to British citizens who have lived abroad for up to 5 years but intended to return to the United Kingdom. That enfranchised an estimated 500,000 ex-patriates but left a number of official hurdles for them to clear before they could exercise their right to vote. Those hurdles were largely swept away by the 1989 Representation of the People Act, which offered a proxy vote to any British citizen who had left in the last 20 years, to be cast in the constituency in which they were last registered. A proxy vote allows a person who is eligible to vote to receive a ballot paper and vote on behalf of a

registered voter at a polling station or by post. For the first time, people who had become 18 after leaving the U.K. were also given the right to vote. This group can exercise a proxy vote in the constituency where they used to live, or where their parent or guardian was last registered. An estimated 2,000,000 Britons living abroad will now be eligible to vote, although few of them look like taking the opportunity. At the 1987 general election 11,100 overseas electors were registered. The Conservatives claimed that up to 80,000 ex-patriates would be registered in time for this election but official figures for 1991 showed the number had only increased to just under 35,500. The Conservatives say they expect to win around 80 per cent of the ex-patriate vote – and have set up an organisation called 'Conservatives Abroad' to encourage registration. One-third of its 45 branches are in Spain and its islands. They argue that Britain is among the last of the Western democracies to extend the vote to expatriates and that US citizens retain a lifelong right to vote – wherever they live in the world. Labour, who let the 1989 Act through the House virtually unopposed, say the whole exercise has been 'a damp squib'. However, they subsequently seemed to regret their failure to make an issue of this particular extension of the franchise and tried to make up for it when figures were published in April 1990 showing the sums to be spent in 1990/1 to publicise voter registration. These revealed that the Home Office budget for advertising and publicity on overseas electoral registration was £760,000, compared with a total expenditure of £486,000 in the previous year for 'domestic' voter registration campaigns.

THE ARMED FORCES
The majority of servicemen and women are based in Britain, voting in the constituency where they either live in barracks or married quarters. But special arrangements are made to ensure that those serving abroad are not disenfranchised.

When the 1945 election took place, many soldiers, sailors and airmen were still overseas and it took several weeks before their votes were finally collated. This was a massive operation, involving more than 1,200,000 postal votes being issued and just over 1 million returned. Nowadays, the procedure is much quicker. Servicemen and women overseas (along with embassy officials and other Crown servants) are allowed a proxy vote, regardless of how long they have been abroad.

THE ELECTORAL REGISTER
A register is compiled annually for each constituency by the local Electoral

Registration Officer. Employed by the local authority, he or she sends out forms to every household, asking the names of eligible voters who will be resident on the qualifying date – 10 October in Britain, 15 September in Northern Ireland.

A provisional register is published on 28 November and remains open for public inspection until 16 December, during which time errors and omissions can be corrected. Anyone left off can ask for their name to be included on the final register. This is published on 16 February each year, remaining in force until 15 February the following year. The register is, therefore, already four months out of date when it comes into force – and 16 months out of date by the end of its life.

Census figures have suggested that 1.6 million more adults are eligible to vote than the numbers appearing on the register. As some people, for instance students and those with second homes, sometimes appear twice, this suggests a total of around two million people are wrongly omitted from the register. To help correct this, supplementary registers are published every month, enabling Electoral Registration Officers to add names accidentally left off. An extra factor affecting the accuracy of the register this time could be the effect of the Poll Tax. Although the community charge register is separate from the electoral roll, some estimate that non-registration in an effort to avoid the tax could result in a one per cent reduction in the number of entries. The Home Office say that the downward trend in registration in recent years pre-dates the introduction of the tax. However, the Office of Population Censuses and Statistics (OPCS) threw a statistical bomb into all this conjecture with their publication 'Population Trends 64' in June 1991. They found that the 1991 level of electoral registration was the lowest since at least 1976 (the earliest year for which they had comparable data). Whilst citing a number of possible reasons, they added: 'It is not possible from the evidence available to separate the impact of these influences, or the effect upon them of the community charge. The combined net effect has been to reduce the numbers on the electoral register by around 2.5 per cent – just over one million – in Great Britain, compared with numbers which would have been expected if the proportion of the population had remained at the level obtaining in 1984.' They also recorded an 11 per cent fall in the number of 'attainers' (under-18s registering in advance of their 18th birthday) when population trends would have suggested only 6 per cent.

Voting
About 46,000 polling stations across the United Kingdom – often in local schools and community centres – open at 7 am on election day and it is here

that the vast majority of electors will cast their votes. The presiding officers ask voters for the electoral registration number printed on the poll card sent to every individual before election day (or their name and address if they do not have it). The voter's name is then crossed off a copy of the register to ensure that no-one votes more than once – a criminal offence known as personation. A ballot paper is perforated by a punch machine (to protect against individuals using illegal counterfeits or stolen ballot papers) and then handed to the voter. It lists the names of all the candidates standing in the constituency in alphabetical order, with their party affiliation or other description (the listing of party affiliation has only been allowed since the 1970 general election).

On entering or leaving the polling station, voters are often approached by party supporters, or tellers, seeking a name or voting number. While no-one is under an obligation to give them, these details enable the parties to cross an individual's name off the electoral register as having voted. If a person has previously promised their support to party canvassers and has not had their name crossed off, they may find canvassers back on their doorstep late on polling day, urging them to vote and, if necessary, offering them a lift to the polling station.

Just under a million voters – between 2 and 3 per cent of the electorate – do so by post or, increasingly, by proxy. In the 1987 general election 947,984 postal votes were issued, 818,349 were returned and 793,062 were finally included in the count. Very little is known about how the postal vote divides between the parties: at each count, postal votes are mixed up with all the other ballot papers before the count of votes per candidate begins. Conventional wisdom has it that the Conservatives gain by far the largest share because of their better organisation, underpinned by a large number of full-time agents. Because the eligibility for postal votes widened considerably, the ITN/Harris exit poll in June 1987 made a special effort to assess how it was divided. Harris selected ten seats out of their total sample of 100 and sent out ballot forms to 1,334 postal voters. Some 737 (or 55.3 per cent) were returned and, despite differences in individual seats, in total they broadly mirrored the aggregate share of the vote in the sample of ten seats. This slight evidence suggests that the Conservatives did not have a significant organisational edge.

When the Polls Close
THE COUNT
Polling stations close at 10pm and the ballot boxes are taken off to the local leisure centre, town hall or similar centre to be counted. The overwhelming

majority of constituencies now count their votes on the night, with only a few waiting until the next morning.

Teams of counters – mostly local government staff and specially-recruited 'experts' such as bank tellers – then conduct the two stages of any count. Firstly, they count the number of votes in each ballot box in order to verify that the number tallies with the record of the numbers of ballot papers issued. Once this process is successfully completed they begin the second stage, which is to separate out the votes for each of the candidates. This, the main business of the count, is conducted under the watchful eyes of the candidates and their representatives as the votes are collected together into piles of 50.

DECLARATIONS

When all the votes have been counted and discussed with the party agents, the returning officer – the sheriff in a county constituency, the mayor or chair of the council in urban seats – will declare the result. It could be argued that British elections have lost some of the pageantry of past counts. Certainly Returning Officers today would be hard-pressed to match the declaration of result recorded by the late, incomparable, Fred Craig (quoted in 'British Electoral Facts 1832-87, published by Dartmouth):

'There was so much local interest in the result of the Ashton-under-Lyne by-election (29 October 1928) that the Mayor arranged for coloured rockets indicating the party of the successful candidate to be fired from the roof of the Town Hall. The by-election resulted in a Labour victory and yellow rockets (the local Labour colour) were fired which could be seen throughout the town by many people awaiting the result.'

These days things are more mundane. Something of a race to declare the first result has developed between a handful of constituencies. Torbay, Guildford and Reigate are usually among the first (the two Sunderland seats may be in contention this time); and watch out for Basildon as one of the early seats to provide a pointer as to how the nation is voting. But the timing of declarations in marginal seats is always subject to recounts. However, many of these seats will be considerably affected if the election is held on 7 May. Those seats with local elections on the same day will face serious delays as they separate ballot papers for both sets of results. The only other time this has happened was at the 1979 general election.

RECOUNTS

If the result is close – or if a candidate falls just below the 5 per cent figure needed to save his or her deposit – a recount can be requested. The decision on whether or not to order a recount rests with the returning officer.

If a recount is ordered, it usually involves counting the piles of votes amassed by each candidate. But often candidates or their agents may request that individual piles be checked to ensure that votes have not accidentally been allocated to the wrong candidate. In the case of very close results, a complete recount can take place.

There is no limit on the number of recounts which can be ordered, but if the figures come out the same two or three times on the trot, the Returning Officer will usually decide that requests for further recounts are unreasonable. Since 1945 the prize for the closest-ever result is shared by Peterborough in the 1966 General Election, when the Conservatives won by just three votes and Carmarthen in February 1974 when Labour also won by three votes. The narrowest majorities in 1987 were 56 – for the Liberal Alliance in Brecon and Radnor and for Labour in Mansfield.

TIED CONTESTS

In the unlikely event that recounts fail to separate the candidates and there is a tie, the Returning Officer is required to settle the issue by lot. The candidate whose name comes out of the hat first is deemed to have received an extra vote and, with a sigh of relief, can prepare himself – or herself – for Westminster.

The Candidates

WHO CAN STAND?

Anyone who is a United Kingdom, Commonwealth or Irish citizen may stand as a candidate, provided he or she is at least 21 years old and is not disqualified. Those disqualified include undischarged bankrupts, those gaoled for more than a year, clergy, Peers, judges and many public servants.

ELECTION DEPOSITS

Candidates now have to lodge a deposit of £500 – increased from £150 by the 1985 Representation of the People Act. The deposit of £150 had been introduced in 1918 and the increased figure (originally proposed at £1000) was designed to deter too many 'joke' candidates (voters in the Chesterfield by-election on 1 March 1984 had been confronted with a ballot paper listing 17 names). But the Monster Raving Loony Party of Screaming Lord Sutch and others continue to find money to brighten up the hustings in many parts of the country. For some, the cost is more than repaid by the free publicity they attract. But small parties seeking to maintain a serious national campaign – like the Greens – do find problems. In response to a number of representations the 1985 legislation reduced the share of the vote needed to 'save' the deposit from 12.5 per cent of all the votes cast to 5 per cent.

ELECTION EXPENSES

Another financial restriction on candidates is the limit imposed on election expenses – though here the controls are designed to prevent big parties swamping their smaller rivals with big-spending campaigns.

The maximum expense which can be incurred by a candidate or his agent is £3,648 plus 4.1p for every voter on the electoral roll in a predominantly rural county constituency, or £3,648 plus 3.3p per voter in an urban-based borough constituency, covering a smaller geographical area. The candidate's personal expenses are not taken into account when calculating the maximum. But some costs, such as driving voters to and from polling stations, may not be claimed as expenses. The table below summarises the election expenses incurred at the 1987 general election throughout the United Kingdom:

	£
Personal expenses	266,547
Agents	326,927
Clerks, etc.	107,974
Printing, stationery	6,612,952
Public meetings	88,652
Committee rooms	260,756
Miscellaneous	641,913
Total expenses subject to legal maximum:	**8,039,174**
Number of candidates	2,325

In addition, candidates have a free Post Office delivery of their election address to every home in the constituency and free use of rooms for their election meetings.

There are no restrictions on spending by parties at national level, and in recent elections this has made a big difference to the amount they spend on their campaigns (1983 was the first election where national campaign spending by the Conservatives and Labour was greater than that of their local campaigns). While local expenses rules currently restrict spending to a maximum of around £7,000 in each constituency – making around £4 million altogether, national poster campaigns and newspaper advertising helped push the cost of the Conservative campaign at the 1987 election to almost £20 million. Labour also spent about £4 million on top of their local budgets in that election. At their September 1991 Party Conference, the Lib Dems claimed they were ahead of their target to raise £1.25 million to spend on the general election and hoped to raise £1.5 million if the election was held in 1992. The source of funds for the two main parties has long been a matter of dispute, claim and counter-claim between them. Last September the Conservatives launched a campaign drawing attention to the large sums which trade unions donated to finance the Labour Party. However, *The Sunday Times* that same month revealed that a Greek shipping tycoon, John Latsis, had contributed £2 million to the Conservatives in March 1991. The newspaper's subsequent investigations showed that two Hong Kong businessmen had contributed £1 million and £100,00 respectively. It was also disclosed that Asil Nadir (Polly Peck) had contributed £1.5 million to Conservative funds.

Broadcasters
Unlike newspapers, which have *no* restrictions on their coverage of election campaigns, broadcasters have strict guidelines to ensure political balance. This means that any programme about a particular constituency must include reference to all or none of the candidates in that constituency. Thus candidates can take part only if all their rivals agree to do so. This had led to plans for locally-televised debates being scrapped when one or other of the candidates has refused to take part. However, news coverage of constituency campaigns is not so restricted.

Arrangements for Party Election Broadcasts are supposed to be agreed between the parties and the broadcasting authorities, although there was no such agreement in 1983 or 1987. The amount of time each party is allowed depends in part on the number of candidates it has in the election and its strength in the previous Parliament. In the 1987 election campaign, the Conservatives, Labour and the SDP/Liberal Alliance each had five national television broadcasts. The Green Party had one. The Scottish National Party, Plaid Cymru and the Northern Ireland parties were allocated broadcasts on Scottish, Welsh and Ulster television respectively. All the main parties were also allocated radio broadcasts. Editorial control of Party Election Broadcasts rests with the parties themselves.

They are not allowed to buy advertising time on television or radio, unlike candidates in the United States.

The broadcasting restrictions imposed on parties practising or supporting terrorism or violence in October 1988 will be lifted during the election campaign. This will mean that Sinn Fein candidates, among others, will be able to conduct televised interviews and press conferences over this period. The Home Office accept that it would be difficult for broadcasters to carry out their duty to maintain impartiality in their coverage if the exception were not made.

Boundary Changes
ROLE OF THE BOUNDARY COMMISSIONS
In 1944, four permanent Boundary Commissions were established – one each for England, Northern Ireland, Scotland and Wales – with responsibility for periodically reviewing parliamentary constituency boundaries (they are also responsible for reviewing the boundaries of Euro-Parliamentary constituencies in their areas). To begin with, each Commission was required to report not less than three, or more than seven, years from the date of their previous report. In 1958, these rules were changed to the present requirement of between ten and fifteen years. Each Commission submits its recommendations to the appropriate Secretary of State. He has to present the report to Parliament for approval. If approved, the changes come into effect at the next general election.

Since 1945 there have been four reviews of *all* constituency boundaries involving major changes. The general elections first fought on those revised boundaries were: 1950, 1955, 1974 (February) and 1983.

The purpose of these reviews is to try and ensure that constituencies have broadly equal electorates, but politics is seldom that simple. The Commissions work to different quotas of electors – for example, compared with England, both Scotland and Wales are over-represented in terms of parliamentary seats. But there are also inequalities within England where, currently, London is over-represented. In part these imbalances are due to geography, drifts of population and respecting local community ties, but also because Parliament sets totals for the number of seats in Northern Ireland, Scotland and Wales which seldom change, regardless of population shifts. In London's case, the discrepancies are largely due to the English Commission's decision not to create constituencies which crossed London Borough boundaries.

CHANGES PAST

The boundary changes which took place in 1983 reflected the population shift from north to south, from city to suburbs and from town to country. Overall, the changes favoured the Conservatives and damaged Labour (one estimate suggested a net gain of 30 seats for the Conservatives over Labour).

CHANGES PRESENT

There will be one more MP returning to Westminster after the next general election – 651 instead of the present 650. The English Boundary Commission has taken the highly unusual step of creating a new seat outside of their overall periodic reviews. Milton Keynes – already the constituency with the largest electorate in the country (107,000 and still growing) – is to be split in two. In a review published in 1990, the Commission recommended that the boundaries of Milton Keynes and the neighbouring Buckingham constituency (also too large with 73,000 voters) should be redrawn, creating a new Buckingham seat along with North-East Milton Keynes and Milton Keynes South-West.

Apart from this particular development, the other changes since the last election have been very small. These often affect only a few hundred voters at a time and mainly result from redrawing the Parliamentary boundaries to coincide with those of local government districts. In a report taking effect just after the 1987 election, the English Commission changed the boundaries of 55 constituencies, with the biggest changes taking place in Lancashire. The net effects will be a loss of 1,700 electors from Fylde and a gain of 1,600 for Preston, a loss of 1,000 from Burnley and an addition of 1,100 to Ribble Valley. But none of these changes may be as significant as the switch of 279 voters from marginal Ipswich to neighbouring Suffolk Coastal – a change proposed by the Commission before the last election, but delayed and therefore taking effect for the first time. In 1987, the Conservatives captured Ipswich by just 874 votes, overturning a Labour majority of 1,077.

There are a series of small-scale changes to 21 constituencies in Wales, with a further Commission report proposing 'tidying-up' amendments to six others. The main controversy in the Principality has been over proposed changes in the names of constituencies. There are no changes in Northern Ireland and only minor changes to 40 Scottish seats. The most unusual change north of the border is the redrawing of the boundary between North Tayside and Stirling from the south bank of Loch Tay to the middle of the loch. No constituents are affected, but Stirling gains a few fish.

CHAPTER EIGHT

REGIONAL SURVEY

By Robert Waller
The Harris Research Centre

Greater London

Indicator	1979	latest	change
Population (thousands)	6,888	6,794	-1.4%
Area (sq km)		1,579	n.a.
Unemployment: number	110,700	378,000	241.5%
rate	2.7%	9.0%	n.a.
Employment (thousands)	n.a.	3,782	n.a.
GDP per head	£8,333	£10,405	24.9%
Manufacturing GDP (£m, 1990)	11,181	9,239	-17.4%
Average earnings (per week, 1991)	£278.20	£408.70	46.9%
Car ownership	53.6%	60.5%	n.a.
Offences recorded by police	564,187	916,648	62.5%
Average house prices	£25,793	£84,863	229.0%
Housebuilding	15,744	9,988	-36.6%
Housing tenure: owner occupied	48.5%	61.5%	n.a.
council/new town	31.6%	24.7%	n.a.
Birth rate	13.2	15.6	17.8%
Death rate	11.7	10.1	-13.8%
Infant mortality rate	12.7	7.9	-37.8%

General Election Voting

	Conservative	Labour	Liberal Democrat
	%	%	%
1974 (Feb)	37.6	40.5	20.8
1974 (Oct)	37.4	43.9	17.0
1979	46.0	39.6	11.9
1983	43.9	29.8	24.7
1987	46.5	31.5	21.3

One need make no apology for starting with the capital. It is always foolish to pick out any single region or social group as holding the key to the outcome of a General Election, but there should be no doubt that more of Labour's vital target seats are in Greater London than anywhere else. Labour need almost exactly 100 gains in order to form a government with an overall majority in the Commons. There are 21 Conservative-held seats with a majority over Labour of less than 16 per cent in London. It is reasonable to add to these the three seats won last time by the SDP-Liberal Alliance. No region, never mind any other city, has so many marginals.

It is, therefore, a great worry for Labour that they have in recent years so often performed worse in London than in any other part of Britain: so much opportunity, so little achievement. In the 1987 General Election,Labour lost only six seats nationally, but three of them were in London – Battersea, Walthamstow, and Fulham (reversing a 1986 by-election triumph). Labour did not make a single gain. Instead there was a small net swing *to* the Conservatives from Labour. Labour have now not gained any seat in Greater London at a General Election since 1974. The Conservatives hold 57 of the capital's 84 seats, Labour only 23 (the remainder are made up of two SDP, one Liberal Democrat and the current Speaker, Mr Bernard Weatherill of Croydon N.E.).

Nor do recent local council results suggest that Labour is likely to achieve the gains in London that they need it to contribute if they are to regain power. In May 1990 the Conservatives did well enough in London's borough elections for challenges to Mrs Thatcher's leadership to recede, if only for the time being. The only council that Labour gained in those important contests, dominated by the issue of the Poll Tax, was Merton. They signally failed to win other targets, such as the prestigious Tory 'model boroughs' of Westminster and Wandsworth – indeed they lost most of their existing council seats in the latter.

Worse still, Labour lost overall control in Brent, where the council had been likened to Pol Pot's dictatorship by none other than Ken Livingstone, and they lost Ealing to the Tories. They saw the Liberal Democrats strengthen their grip on Tower Hamlets, in the heart of the East End. The 'London Factor' still seemed to be at work.

Why has Labour performed so badly in London in the past 15 years or so? The reputation of the London Labour Party, especially as seen in the policies and behaviour of Labour-controlled boroughs, may be a major part of the answer.
Many Londoners, including traditional Labour supporters, have formed the impression that the party has been dominated by extreme left wingers, wasteful and inefficient in administering local authorities, charging high rates and community charge levels for inadequate services, and showing undue favour to minority groups of all kinds.

The contrast with councils like Wandsworth, with its Poll Tax of under £200 per

Conservative
Battersea (61)
Beckenham (80)
Bexleyheath (51)
Brent North (5)
Brentford &
 Isleworth (39)
Carshalton &
 Wallington (73)
Chelsea (62)
Chingford (11)
Chipping Barnet (7)
Chislehurst (53)
City of London &
 Westminster
 South (46)
Croydon Central (82)
Croydon NE (81)
Croydon NW (75)
Croydon South (74)
Dulwich (78)
Ealing, Acton (40)
Ealing, North (35)
Edmonton (10)
Eltham (54)
Enfield North (9)
Enfield, Southgate (8)
Erith & Crayford (22)
Feltham & Heston (38)
Finchley (14)
Fulham (63)

Hampstead
 & Highgate (32)
Harrow East (4)
Harrow West (3)
Hayes & Harlington (36)
Hendon North (6)
Hendon South (13)
Hornchurch (21)
Hornsey &
 Wood Green (15)
Ilford North (18)
Ilford South (25)
Kensington (42)
Kingston-upon-
 Thames (67)
Lewisham East (56)
Lewisham West (79)
Mitcham & Morden (71)
Old Bexley &
 Sidcup (52)
Orpington (84)
Putney (64)
Ravenbourne (83)
Richmond &
 Barnes (65)
Romford (19)
Ruislip, Northwood (2)
Streatham (16)
Surbiton (68)
Sutton & Cheam (72)
Twickenham (66)

Upminster (20)
Uxbridge (1)
Walthamstow (17)
Wanstead &
 Woodford (12)
Westminster North (43)
Wimbledon (69)

Labour
Barking (24)
Bethnal Green &
 Stepney (47)
Bow & Poplar (48)
Brent East (33)
Brent South (34)
Dagenham (23)
Ealing, Southall (37)
Hackney North &
 Stoke Newington (30)
Hackney South &
 Shoreditch (29)
Hammersmith (41)
Holborn &
 St Pancras (44)
Islington North (31)
Islington South &
 Finsbury (45)
Lewisham,
 Deptford (57)
Leyton (28)
Newham NE (26)

Newham NW (27)
Newham South (49)
Norwood (77)
Peckham (59)
Tooting (70)
Tottenham (16)
Vauxhall (60)

Lib Dem
Southwark &
 Bermondsey (58)

Independent
Greenwich (55)
Woolwich (50)

head, was not lost on the electorate in May 1990 – or, in 1987 when the Wandsworth constituency of Battersea fell to the Tories. There is a clear link between municipal and parliamentary politics.

It is also true that there have been demographic changes which have hurt Labour in many parts of the capital – gentrification as the middle classes seek property near to the centre of the city. However, the Conservatives have benefited more from a long term swing away from Labour among white working class voters – Barking and Dagenham have not been noticeably gentrified, but the Labour majorities in those two seats have slipped from nearly 20,000 in the 1960s to barely 3,000 in 1987. Nearly all Labour's remaining safe seats have high proportions of ethnic minorities, ranging from about 20 per cent to nearly 50 per cent in the cases of Brent South and Southall. Next time they need to expand their appeal and recapture their former supporters.

If so, Labour can hope to start ticking off their long lists of target. It starts with Dulwich, where Gerald Bowden's Conservative majority is a mere 180. Many are close, but often there seem to be reasons why they might be harder to win than the figures imply. Battersea, the next most marginal (majority 857 or 1.8 per cent) elected nearly a full slate of Tory Councillors in May 1990, and would require an almost complete change of heart between local and General Elections. More likely Labour gains are two seats on London's northern heights, where the sitting MPs are retiring, Hornsey/Wood Green and Hampstead/Highgate, where Labour field a glamorous candidate, the actress Glenda Jackson. Walthamstow may prove easier to regain than Battersea. Streatham includes a substantial part of the centre of Brixton, and is situated in the Borough of Lambeth, which now appears to be forgetting the days in the early 1980s of a radical left wing council under 'Red Ted' Knight. Westminster North (majority 3,310, 7.9 per cent) is another seat situated in an electorally popular Tory council, and many thousands of voters have disappeared from the register in recent years.

A pair of Lewisham seats, West and East (where Colin Moynihan, the former Sports Minister, is MP) would have to fall if Labour is to win the election as a whole. So would Feltham/Heston in Hounslow, a moderate Labour controlled Borough. Croydon North West is the only Labour target in the borough – Labour will be assisted by its 20 per cent non-white population. As the list goes on, the task gets still steeper: it would be a genuine surprise if the Conservatives were to lose the controversial right-winger Terry Dicks in Hayes/Harlington, or former Minister Peter Bottomley in Eltham, or to lose

Fulham again, or Ilford South, or Kensington which they held in a by-election in 1988, or Erith and Crayford whose politics have been permanently affected by the defection of its last Labour member to the SDP. Mitcham and Morden is at least in Merton, the Borough which saw the only Labour local election triumph in May 1990.

Labour's best chances of gains in London are probably the two seats won last time by members of David Owen's SDP, now defunct as a national party: John Cartwright in Woolwich and Rosie Barnes in Greenwich, where she now faces Nick Raynsford, once briefly MP for Fulham. It is hard to see any hope for these two, whatever arrangement they might come to with the Liberal Democrats. The Liberal Democrats' own Simon Hughes (Southwark and Bermondsey) seems better established, but Labour will always feel they should be able to regard such working class inner city territory as their own. Meanwhile, the Liberal Democrats will be hoping that they can at last convert their almost complete domination of Richmond upon Thames Borough Council into a Commons seat for their new candidate at Richmond/Barnes, Jennifer Tonge. It is unlikely they will be able to make gains as a result of their local strength in the other boroughs they control, Sutton and Tower Hamlets.

It is clear, then, that the Conservatives can nurture high hopes of retaining a comfortable majority of the seats in Greater London, which will go a considerable way towards guaranteeing them a fourth consecutive term of office. Nor, if the polls come to favour them, should they write off the prospects of further gains in the capital, which has proved such good ground for them.

On the basis of the latest local election results, Tooting, Labour's last seat in the Borough of Wandsworth, cannot be regarded as entirely safe. Nor can Ken Livingstone's Brent East. Labour has not produced a good performance in London for a very long time. They still have a mountain to climb here.

The South East

Indicator	1979	latest	change
Population (thousands)	10,064	10,664	6.0%
Area (sq. km.)		25,643	n.a.
Unemployment: number	111,300	356,700	220.5%
rate	2.5%	7.0%	n.a.
Employment (thousands)	n.a.	4,794	n.a.
GDP per head, 1990	£6,979	£9,256	32.6%
Manufacturing GDP (£ million,1990)	19,185	19,403	1.1%

Average earnings (per week, 1991)	244.70	£333,40	36.2%
Car ownership	66.2%	76.1%	n.a.
Offences recorded by police	394,552	826,728	109.5%
Average house prices	£24,675	£77,356	213.5%
Housebuilding	47,129	30,249	-35.8%
Housing tenure: owner occupied	63.2%	74.7%	n.a.
council/new town	24.2%	14.5%	n.a.
Birth rate	12.8	13.5	5.3%
Death rate	11.2	10.5	-6.0%
Infant mortality rate	11.3	6.6	-41.6%

General Election Voting

	Conservative	Labour	Liberal Democrat
	%	%	%
1974 (Feb)	45.0	27.6	27.1
1974 (Oct)	45.1	30.8	23.8
1979	54.8	26.8	17.5
1983	54.5	15.8	29.0
1987	55.6	16.8	27.2

The most populous of the Standard Regions of the UK – and the one with the most parliamentary constituencies – is the South East of England. The dozen or so counties which make up the South East have 108 seats between them. Yet as far as recent General Elections have been concerned, the contests have been less, not more, interesting than in most regions. The reason is simple: they are so one-sided. In 1987 the Conservatives won 107 of the 108 seats. There is no doubt that they have a good chance to put the 'ton' up again next time. This remains a good bet despite their traumatic loss in October 1990 of Ian Gow's old seat, Eastbourne, which fell in a by-election to an East Sussex local councillor, David Bellotti.

The other non-Tory in the region is Andrew Smith of Oxford East, a Labour gain in 1987. This served only to make up for Labour's loss of Thurrock in the same year. There was only one net charge, as the Conservatives gained the Isle of Wight on the retirement of its popular and long-serving Liberal MP, Stephen Ross. Overall the South East was Labour's most disappointing region except for London.

There *are* winnable target seats for Labour in the South East, though not as many as in Greater London. They must hope to regain Thurrock from the far

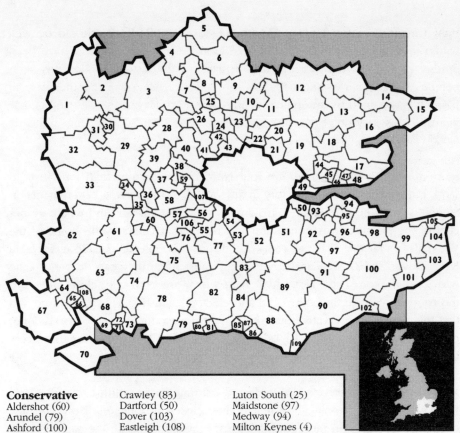

Conservative

Aldershot (60)
Arundel (79)
Ashford (100)
Aylesbury (28)
Banbury (2)
Basildon (45)
Basingstoke (61)
Beaconsfield (38)
Bedfordshire Mid (6)
Bedfordshire North (5)
Bedfordshire SW (7)
Berkshire East (58)
Bexhill & Battle (90)
Billericay (44)
Braintree (13)
Brentwood &
   Ongar (19)
Brighton,
   Kemptown (86)
Brighton Pavilion (87)
Broxbourne (22)
Buckingham (3)
Canterbury (99)
Castle Point (46)
Chelmsford (18)
Chertsey & Walton (56)
Chesham &
   Amersham (40)
Chichester (78)
Colchester North (14)
Colchester South
   & Maldon (16)

Crawley (83)
Dartford (50)
Dover (103)
Eastleigh (108)
Epping Forest (21)
Epsom & Ewell (54)
Esher (55)
Fareham (68)
Faversham (98)
Folkestone &
   Hythe (101)
Gillingham (95)
Gosport (69)
Gravesham (93)
Guildford (76)
Hampshire East (74)
Hampshire NW (62)
Harlow (20)
Harwich (15)
Hastings & Rye (102)
Havant (73)
Henley (29)
Herts & Stortford (11)
Herts North (9)
Herts SW (41)
Herts West (26)
Hertsmere (43)
Horsham (82)
Hove (85)
Isle of Wight (70)
Kent Mid (96)
Lewes (88)
Luton North (8)

Luton South (25)
Maidstone (97)
Medway (94)
Milton Keynes (4)
Mole Valley (77)
New Forest (67)
Newbury (33)
Oxford West &
   Abingdon (31)
Portsmouth North (72)
Portsmouth South (71)
Reading East (35)
Reading West (34)
Reigate (53)
Rochford (17)
Romsey &
   Waterside (64)
Saffron Waldon (12)
Sevenoaks (51)
Shoreham (80)
Slough (59)
Southampton,
   Itchen (66)
Southampton, Test (65)
Southend East (48)
Southend West (47)
Spelthorne (107)
St Albans (24)
Stevenage (10)
Surrey East (52)
Surrey NW (57)
Surrey SW (75)
Sussex Mid (74)

Thanet North (105)
Thanet South (104)
Thurrock (49)
Tonbridge &
   Malling (92)
Tunbridge Wells (91)
Wantage (32)
Watford (42)
Wealdon (89)
Welwyn Hatfield (23)
Winchester (63)
Windsor &
   Maidenhead (37)
Witney (1)
Woking (106)
Wokingham (36)
Worthing (81)
Wycombe (39)

Labour
Oxford East (30)

Lib Dem
Eastbourne (109)

right winger, Timothy Janman. Another Essex seat, Basildon, should be well within their grasp. New Towns like Basildon do however seem to have been drifting away from the Labour Party in each of the last three Elections – do people change their voting habits as they migrate? Harlow is another case in point: it was gained by an original young Tory, Jerry Hayes, in 1979, and he has increased his majority each time since: now it is over 10 per cent, or nearly 6,000 votes.

In Hertfordshire, where there are four New Towns, Labour held four seats in 1974, but were not close to victory in any in 1987. They have a better chance in Slough, where the Conservative majority is only 7.3 per cent and where 20 per cent of the population is non-white, and perhaps in Luton South, home of the Vauxhall car factory (9.6 per cent). There are a couple of outside chances in Kent: Dover and Gravesham. Finally, they must hope they can do well in the two Southampton seats, Test and Itchen, which are both very close indeed to the national average, in both social and electoral statistics. That this is true and that the current Conservative majority in Test, for example, is 6,954 or 12.3 per cent, shows the magnitude of Labour's task – or at least, how far they were behind in 1987.

Most of the 107 Conservative MPs elected last time in the South East of England had Liberal-SDP Alliance candidates as their closest challengers. However, few of them were close on the Tories' heels. At Portsmouth South the gap was only 205 votes, but this was an unusual case – the Conservative David Martin recovered the seat which had been lost in a mid-term by-election to Mike Hancock of the SDP. Even if that party were still a force, it would be more likely that Portsmouth South would soon return to its previous safe Conservative status.

There are no other seats vulnerable to the Liberal democrats with a majority of less than 9 per cent (Oxford West/Abingdon, held by the Home Office Minister John Patten). They will of course hope that David Bellotti can pull off the mighty task of holding Eastbourne in a General Election, after a relatively short opportunity to build up an 'incumbency factor' in his favour. The omens in such cases are very mixed.

The South East will remain overwhelmingly Conservative. It is the heart of prosperous, middle class England, and it is solidly true blue too. No wonder then that seven Cabinet Ministers hold seats in the region: Douglas Hurd and Michael Heseltine in Oxfordshire, Kenneth Baker in Surrey, Peter Lilley in

Hertfordshire, Michael Howard in Kent and Anthony Newton and John Wakeham in Essex.

The South West

Indicator	1979	latest	change
Population (thousands)	4,335	4,667	7.6%
Area (sq km)		23,849	n.a.
Unemployment: number	74,700	182,400	144.2%
rate	4.0%	8.2%	n.a.
Employment (thousands)	1,744	2,063	18.3%
GDP per head, 1990	£5,920	£7,779	31.4%
Manufacturing GDP (£ million, 1990)	6,634	7,375	11.2%
Average earnings (per week,1991)	£222.50	£297.10	33.5%
Car ownership	65.1%	75.9%	n.a.
Offences recorded by police	155,207	402,995	159.7%
Average house prices	£20,494	£62,826	206.6%
Housebuilding	22,317	14,523	-34.9%
Housing tenure: owner occupied	63.2%	73.7%	n.a.
council/new town	22.1%	14.6%	n.a.
Birth rate	11.6	12.6	8.2%
Death rate	12.8	11.9	-7.3%
Infant mortality rate	12.5	6.8	-45.6%

General Election Voting

	Conservative	Labour	Liberal Democrat
	%	%	%
1974 (Feb)	43.3	26.2	29.4
1974 (Oct)	43.4	28.9	27.3
1979	51.6	24.6	22.5
1983	51.4	14.7	33.2
1987	50.6	15.9	33.0

The counties of England's western peninsula – Cornwall, Devon, Dorset and Somerset – have long been associated with Liberalism: this goes back to the Nonconformist religious and political traditions of the nineteenth century. The further one proceeds towards Cornwall, the less 'English' is the ambience, and the less firm the Tory grip. However, for all the Liberal connections – the late David Penhaligon in Cornwall, the former leader Jeremy Thorpe in North Devon and now Paddy Ashdown in Yeovil, Somerset – in fact the vast majority of MPs here are Conservative.

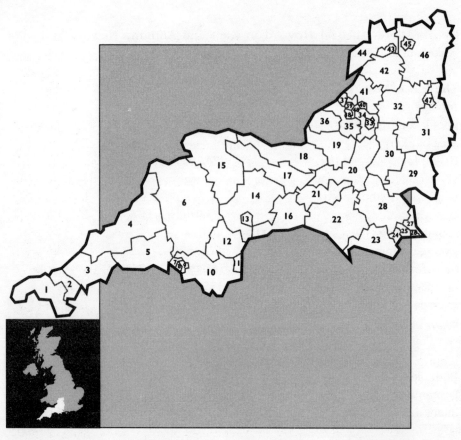

Conservative
Bath (33)
Bournemouth East (26)
Bournemouth West (25)
Bridgewater (18)
Bristol East (48)
Bristol NW (37)
Bristol West (39)
Cheltenham (45)
Christchurch (27)
Cirencester &
  Tewkesbury (46)
Cornwall North (4)
Cornwall SE (5)
Devizes (31)
Devon North (15)
Devon West &
  Torridge (6)
Dorset North (28)

Dorset South (23)
Dorset West (22)
Exeter (13)
Falmouth &
  Cambourne (2)
Gloucester (43)
Gloucestershire
  West (44)
Honiton (16)
Kingswood (40)
Northavon (41)
Plymouth, Drake (8)
Plymouth, Sutton (9)
Poole (24)
Salisbury (29)
Somerton & Frome (20)
South Hams (10)
St Ives (1)
Stroud (42)

Swindon (47)
Taunton (17)
Teignbridge (12)
Tiverton (14)
Torbay (11)
Wansdyke (34)
Wells (19)
Westbury (30)
Weston-super-Mare (36)
Wiltshire North (32)
Woodspring (35)

Labour
Bristol South (38)

Lib Dem
Truro (3)
Yeovil (21)

Independent
Plymouth, Devonport
(7)

The Liberal Democrats have just two seats: Matthew Taylor, still the youngest MP, who has held Truro since the by-election caused by David Penhaligon's tragic death a few months before the 1987 General Election; and the party leader Paddy Ashdown.

There is also the SDP leader David Owen in Plymouth Devonport, but he is leaving the Commons and his future seems unclear. We know now that the SDP will not be making any gains in the South West (or any other region), but the Liberal Democrats, their former partners in the Alliance, must still hope to catch a sufficient anti-Tory vote to win a few more divisions: North Devon, North Cornwall and West Devon each have a majority of around 10 per cent. The Conservative vote declined west of Bristol in 1987, and this independently minded region may well give them a few more problems in the forthcoming General Election. Nor should we forget that the Conservative Party Chairman, Chris Patten, tipped by some as a future leader of the Conservative party, had a majority of only 1,412 in 1987 – though that was over the SDP's Malcolm Dean, a *Guardian* journalist.

Labour has hopes too, in the more urban parts of the region, principally the county of Avon. They hold only one seat at present, Bristol South, and that only just. Other marginals in the Bristol area which they must win if they are going to win the election are Bristol East (where Tony Benn was defeated by Jonathan Sayeed in 1983) and Kingswood. Bristol North West (12.0 per cent) is a third target. Labour's other chances are at Plymouth Devonport, a 'natural' seat for them but for the mercurial career of David Owen; and Swindon, that booming town along the M4 'corridor', which has been sliding away towards the Tories since 1979.

One other seat should be mentioned. 'Celebrities' from other fields rarely make the transition to politics in Britain, but we can find an exception in Falmouth and Camborne. The local Conservatives were delighted when Sebastian Coe offered himself as a candidate, and he powered his way to a comfortable selection. He might have to run hard to be actually elected, though, as the Alliance halved the Tory majority in 1987, putting Coe firmly in his rivals' sights in the finishing straight.

East Anglia

Indicator	1979	latest	change
Population (thousands)	1,864	2,059	10.5%
Area (sq km)		12,573	n.a.
Unemployment: number	25,800	66,200	156.6%
rate	3.1%	6.5%	n.a.
Employment (thousands)	781	952	21.9%
GDP per head, 1990z	£6,125	£8,408	37.3%
Manufacturing GDP (£ million, 1990)	3,241	3,831	18.2%
Average earnings (per week,1991)	£230.00	£300.20	30.5%
Car ownership	67.9%	73.4%	n.a.
Offences recorded by police	67,452	154,924	129.7%
Average house prices	£18,461	£59,442	222.0%
Housebuilding	11,604	8,809	-24.1%
Housing tenure: owner occupied	58.3%	70.2%	n.a.
council/new town	26.4%	17.1%	n.a.
Birth rate	12.8	12.9	-1.0%
Death rate	11.1	10.8	-3.1%
Infant mortality rate	12.6	6.9	-45.2%

General Election Voting

	Conservative	Labour	Lib-Dem
	%	%	%
1974 (Feb)	42.8	32.0	24.9
1974 (Oct)	43.8	35.5	20.6
1979	50.8	32.6	16.0
1983	51.0	20.5	28.2
1987	52.1	21.7	25.7

The smallest of the standard regions, with only 20 MPs, is East Anglia. This does not mean that it is politically without interest. Three seats changed hands in 1987 in a variety of directions. Labour gained one from the Conservatives (Norwich South) but lost one of them in another large town (Ipswich).

The Liberals' only seat in East Anglia disappeared as Clement Freud was defeated by the Tory Malcolm Moss as Cambridgeshire North East. There was no change in the other contests but there was a fascinating three-way battle at Cambridge where both Labour and Shirley Williams of the SDP failed in their bids to oust Robert Rhodes James, the sitting Conservative MP.

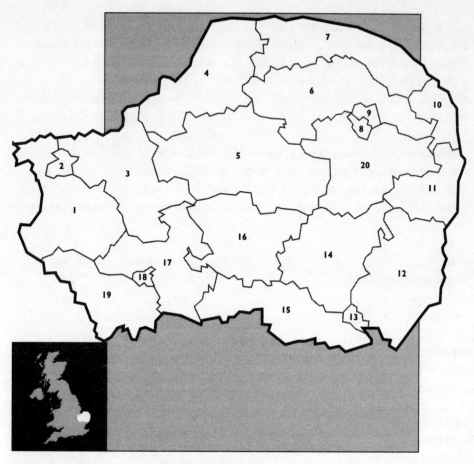

Conservative
Bury St Edmunds (16)
Cambridge (18)
Cambridgeshire NE (3)
Cambridgeshire SE (17)
Cambridgeshire SW (19)
Great Yarmouth (10)
Huntington (1)
Ipswich (13)
Norfolk North (7)
Norfolk NW (4)

Norfolk South (20)
Norfolk SW (5)
Norfolk Mid (6)
Norwich North (9)
Peterborough (2)
Suffolk Central (14)
Suffolk Coastal (12)
Suffolk South (15)
Waveney (11)

Labour
Norwich South (8)

Mrs Williams – and her former party – have now left the political scene, and Labour probably have the best chance of taking Cambridge now. Labour's other targets in this prosperous and rapidly growing region are the ultra-marginal Ipswich, and, if they do well and are in the hunt for an overall majority, Norwich North and Peterborough. The Liberal Democrats cannot realistically hope to regain Clement Freud's old seat, and are well behind in all the others.

Although only a small region consisting of three counties, East Anglia, houses the constituencies of three Cabinet Ministers: John MacGregor of Norfolk South, John Selwyn Gummer of Suffolk Coastal and, with the largest majority of any Conservative (27,044), the Prime Minister himself, John Major, at Huntingdon.

Wales

Indicator	1979	latest	change
Population (thousands)	2,810	2,881	2.5%
Area (sq km)		20,768	n.a.
Unemployment: number	68,800	120,700	75.4%
rate	5.5%	9.3%	n.a.
Employment (thousands)	1,157	1,170	1.1%
GDP per head,1990	£5,533	£6,960	25.8%
Manufacturing GDP (£ million,1990)	4,252	5,472	28.7%
Average earnings (per week,1990)	£236.60	£280.10	18.4%
Car ownership	61.5%	66.9%	n.a.
Offences recorded by police	127,467	262,710	106.1%
Average house prices	£17,061	£45,952	169.3%
Housebuilding	11,426	9,566	-16.3%
Housing tenure: owner occupied	59.3%	72.0%	n.a.
council/new town	29.0%	19.2%	n.a.
Birth rate	12.9	13.5	4.7%
Death rate	12.8	11.8	-7.8%
Infant mortality rate	12.4	6.9	-44.4%

General Election Voting

	Conservative	Labour	Liberal Democrat	Plaid
	%	%	%	%
1974 (Feb)	25.9	46.8	16.0	10.7
1974 (Oct)	23.9	49.5	15.5	10.8
1979	32.2	48.6	10.6	8.1
1983	31.1	37.5	23.2	7.8
1987	29.5	45.1	17.9	7.3

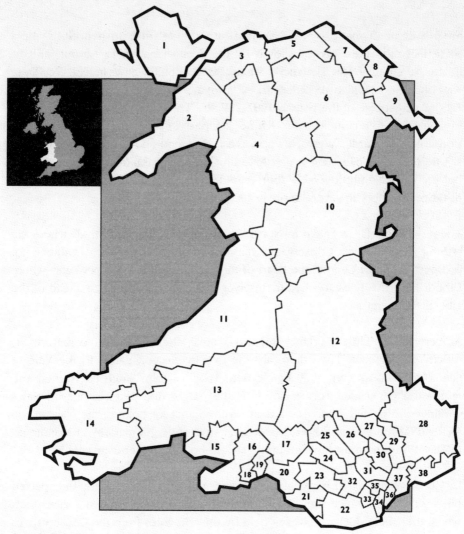

Conservative
Cardiff North (35)
Cardiff Central (34)
Clwyd NW (5)
Conwy (3)
Delyn (7)
Pembroke (14)

Labour
Aberavon (20)
Alyn & Deeside (8)
Blaenau, Gwent (27)
Bridgend (21)
Caerphilly (31)
Cardiff South &
  Penarth (36)
Cardiff West (33)

Carmarthen (13)
Clwyd SW (6)
Cynon Valley (25)
Gower (16)
Islwyn (30)
Llanelli (15)
Merthyr Tydfil &
  Rhymney (26)
Monmouth (28)
Neath (17)
Newport East (38)
Newport West (37)
Ogmore (23)
Pontypridd (32)
Rhondda (24)
Swansea East (19)
Swansea West (18)

Torfaen (29)
Vale of Glamorgan (22)
Wrexham (9)

Lib Dem
Brecon & Radnor (12)
Ceredigion &
  Pembroke North (11)
Montgomery (10)

Plaid Cymru
Caernarfon (2)
Meirionnydd
  Nant Conwy (4)
Ynys Môn (1)

Much has been made of the 'North-South divide' in British politics, most particularly the great favour shown by the Scottish nation to Labour, and its hearty rejection of Mrs Thatcher's otherwise triumphant government. Yet there was one region which recorded an even greater increase than Scotland in the Labour percentage of the vote in 1987 – Wales. There the Labour share went up by over 7.5 per cent and Mr Kinnock's party made four gains from the Conservatives: Cardiff West, Newport West, Bridgend and Clwyd South West. It is true that 1983 has been a disappointing year for Labour in the principality, but the dramatic improvement four years later has left the party within striking distance of victory in several more seats.

The most likely fall is Delyn in North Wales (around Flint and Mold) where the retiring Keith Raffan's Conservative majority is only 2.3 per cent. Another hot prospect is Cardiff Central, the heart of the capital (majority 4.8 per cent) where Labour have finally established themselves in a clear second place ahead of the Liberal Democrats.

At Pembroke, 'Little England Beyond Wales', the Conservative majority is exactly 10 per cent. Then there are the two by-election gains. In the Vale of Glamorgan, in an April 1989 by-election, Labour's John Smith overturned and reversed a 6,000 plus Tory majority as the party's fine performance in Wales continued. Mr Smith probably has an even chance of holding the Vale in the General Election. Huw Edwards overcame an even larger majority at Monmouth in May 1991, and must have an uphill task to hold off Roger Evans again.

Labour have one other reasonable prospect, although it is a slightly unexpected one, and one in which they are at present in third place: Brecon and Radnor, which the Liberal Richard Livesey held by only 56 votes from the Conservatives in 1987. But the Labour candidate was only 2,329 votes (5.6 per cent) behind, and a fascinating three-way battle can be expected.
The Liberal Democrats can be more confident of holding their other two seats in Wales, Ceredigion/Pembroke North and Montgomery, both of which have a far longer tradition of Liberalism than Brecon and Radnor. They have only one outside chance of a gain, at Conwy, where the Tory Lead over the Rev. Roger Roberts last time was only 3,024.

There is, of course, a fourth party in Welsh politics. Plaid Cymru's support is largely confined to Welsh-speaking areas, but this does enable them to concentrate their vote sufficiently to win three seats in Gwynedd, the county in the north-western corner of the country. In 1987, benefiting partially from the enforced retirement of the Conservative MP (who had attempted to buy too many British Telecom shares), Ieuan Wyn Jones became the MP for Ynys Mon (Anglesey). Thus he joined his two well-established colleagues who have taken it in turns to be party leader, Dafydd Wigley (Caenarfon) and Dafydd Elis Thomas (Meirionnydd nant Conwy). All three are probably safe now and there are no realistic prospects for further nationalist gains.

The Conservatives have slipped from 14 seats to 8 in Wales in 1987, and as seen above, could lose another three to Labour and just possibly one to the Liberal Democrats, as well as failing to regain the Vale of Glamorgan and Monmouth. This leaves only two near certainties, but one of those also has an unhappy recent history. Cardiff North poses few problems, but the other 'safe' seat has seen its MP retired by the local party against his will: Clwyd North West's Sir Anthony Meyer, who dared to stand against Mrs Thatcher for the party leadership in 1989.

As in the case of Scotland, the Conservative government rules Wales while holding only a small minority of the seats there, and this situation could pertain again after the next election: Tory predominance in England can easily outvote the other constituents of the United Kingdom. Mr Kinnock can at least take pleasure from the knowledge that the land of his birth will again elect an absolute majority of members of his own party, just as it did in 1987 and even in the grim year of 1983. The last three leaders of the Labour Party have all represented Welsh constituencies, as did the founding father, Keir Hardie. It remains one of the party's ancestral homelands.

West Midlands

Indicator	1979	latest	change
Population (thousands)	5,179	5,219	0.8%
Area (sq km)		13,013	n.a.
Unemployment: number	100,400	244,300	143.3%
rate	4.0%	9.4%	n.a.
Employment (thousands)	2,382	2,339	-1.8%
GDP per head,1990	£6,253	£7,612	21.7%
Manufacturing GDP (£ million, 1990)	13,270	12,364	-6.8%
Average earnings (per week, 1991)	£237.30	£291.10	22.7%
Car ownership	61.3%	65.0%	n.a.
Offences recorded by police	243,697	486,377	99.6%
Average house prices	£18,493	£58,721	217.5%
Housebuilding	21,617	14,711	-31.9%

Housing tenure: owner occupied	56.7%	67.8%	n.a.
council/new town	32.9%	23.5%	n.a.
Birth rate	13.2	14.4	9.4%
Death rate	11.2	10.9	-2.6%
Infant mortality rate	13.8	9.9	-28.3%

General Election Voting

	Conservative	*Labour*	*Lib-Dem*
	%	%	%
1974 (Feb)	40.8	43.1	21.5
1974 (Oct)	37.5	43.9	17.8
1979	47.1	40.1	11.5
1983	45.0	31.2	23.4
1987	45.5	33.3	20.8

The Midlands, especially the West Midlands with its giant conurbation of one and a half million voters, is often described as the crucial hinge or cockpit of British electoral politics. It is sometimes rather crudely seen as holding the balance between a largely Labour North and a largely Conservative South.In fact the whole of the Midlands has barely as many critical marginal constituencies as London or the North West, and individually the West and East Midlands cannot be regarded as such vital battlegrounds. The 'marginal Midlands' is something of a myth. It is not the sole key to the outcome of the battle.

That is not to say that it can be ignored. There are indeed plenty of important and close contests every General Election. In 1987 Labour made no net progress here, gaining the Wrekin (Telford New Town) from the Tories but losing Wolverhampton North East to them. They must do better next time if they are to knock out the national Conservative majority of around 100.

Much will depend on the state of the economy. The West Midlands has been one of the cradles of initial manufacturing industry, particularly metalwork – ranging from the iron and steel artifacts of all sizes associated with the Black County in the nineteenth century to the automobiles of the twentieth. It remains to be seen whether the region's prosperity can withstand the nationwide decline of manufacturing and the switch to service industries and finance. The West Midlands suffered heavily from the unemployment of the early 1980s, but recovered well in the second half of the decade. Perhaps this accounts for the continuing favour shown to Mrs Thatcher's government in 1987. Besides, the

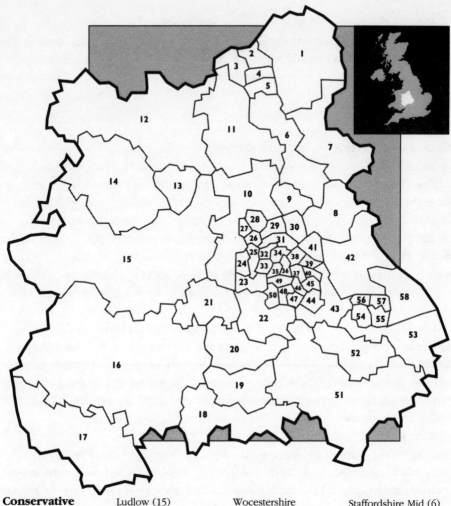

Conservative
Aldridge,
  Brownhills (30)
Birmingham,
  Hall Green (47)
Birmingham,
  Edgbaston (49)
Birmingham,
  Northfield (50)
Birmingham,
  Selly Oak (48)
Birmingham,
  Yardley (45)
Bromsgrove (22)
Burton (7)
Cannock &
  Burntwood (9)
Coventry SW (54)
Dudley West (24)
Halesowen &
  Stourbridge (23)
Hereford (17)
Leominster (16)

Ludlow (15)
Meriden (43)
Nuneaton (58)
Rugby &
  Kenilworth (53)
Shrewsbury &
  Atcham (14)
Shropshire North (12)
Solihull (44)
Stafford (11)
Staffordshire
  Moorlands (1)
Staffordshire South (10)
Staffordshire SE (8)
Stratford-on-Avon (51)
Sutton Coldfield (41)
Warwick &
  Leamington (52)
Warwickshire North (42)
Wolverhampton NE (28)
Wolverhampton SW (27)
Worcester (19)
Worcestershire Mid (20)

Wocestershire
  South (18)
Wyre Forest (21)

Labour
Birmingham,
  Erdington (39)
Birmingham,
  Hodge Hill (40)
Birmingham,
  Ladywood (36)
Birmingham,
  Perry Barr (38)
Birmingham,
  Small Heath (37)
Birmingham,
  Sparkbrook (46)
Coventry NE (57)
Coventry NW (56)
Coventry SE (55)
Dudley East (25)
Newcastle-under-
  Lyme (3)

Staffordshire Mid (6)
Stoke-on-Trent
  Central (4)
Stoke-on-Trent North (2)
Stoke-on-Trent South (5)
Walsall North (29)
Walsall South (31)
Warley East (35)
Warley West (33)
West Bromwich
  East (34)
West Bromwich
  West (32)
Wolverhampton SE (26)
The Wrekin (13)

recapture of Wolverhampton North East, a swing of 3 per cent from Conservative to Labour would win Birmingham Selly Oak, Cannock/Burntwood, Warwickshire North and Birmingham Northfield. A further 3 per cent would see the fall of only three more seats: Birmingham Yardley, Coventry South West and Nuneaton.

These are all predominantly 'white' constituencies: in the cosmopolitan West Midlands, most of the seats with a large ethnic population are already safely Labour. The threat of Muslim defections and candidates of the Islamic Party is more likely to cause mere embarrassment, say to Roy Hattersley, Labour's Deputy Leader, in Birmingham Sparkbrook or over the selection of a new candidate to replace Denis Howell at Birmingham Small Heath. Labour really should not be worrying about losing any seats in the West Midlands – if they were in a position to do so the result of the General Election would be a foregone conclusion anyway:-another landslide win for the Conservatives.

The West Midlands is not good ground for the Liberal Democrats. They have only held one seat here at any time since the Second World War, and that was Birmingham Ladywood which was won from Labour in a by-election in 1969 and lost the next year. There is one perennial hope, though, in the most rural part of the region: Hereford, where they restricted the Tory majority to 1,413 in 1987 and where they control the city council with a large majority.

One more seat should be mentioned. Labour's best by-election result for very many years came in March 1990 when Sylvia Heal increased their vote at Mid Staffordshire by over 24 per cent, turning a Conservative majority of over 14,000 into a Labour win by over 9,000. It is true that this was at the time of maximum government unpopularity over the Poll Tax, but the formidable Mrs Heal may just be able to hold it in the General Election – when it would count as one of Labour's precious gains in their bid to form their first government for well over a decade.

East Midlands

Indicator	1979	latest	change
Population (thousands)	3,818	4,019	5.2%
Area (sq km)		15,630	n.a.
Unemployment: number	58,600	157,200	168.3%
rate	3.3%	8.1%	n.a.
Employment (thousands)	1,671	1,778	6.4%
GDP per head, 1990	£6,250	£8,054	28.9%

Manufacturing GDP (£ million,1990)	8,261	9,371	13.4%
Average earnings (per week, 1991)	£234.40	£292.60	24.8%
Car ownership	59.9%	70.9%	n.a.
Offences recorded by police	182,155	410,605	125.4%
Average house prices	£15,836	£55,835	252.6%
Housebuilding	18,285	12,980	-29.0%
Housing tenure: owner occupied	59.0%	70.6%	n.a.
council/new town	28.7%	19.6%	n.a.
Birth rate	12.9	13.6	5.5%
Death rate	11.4	10.7	-6.1%
Infant mortality rate	12.4	7.8	-37.1%

General Election Voting

	Conservative	Labour	Liberal Democrat
	%	%	%
1974 (Feb)	37.2	36.8	20.2
1974 (Oct)	38.5	41.8	18.3
1979	46.8	38.6	13.7
1983	47.2	28.0	24.1
1987	48.6	30.0	21.0

Unlike the West Midlands, the East Midlands has no vast conurbations or Metropolitan Boroughs. It does have several very substantial proud and independent towns, though, with a wide variety of industry: Leicester, Nottingham, Derby and Northampton are just the largest of these. There are a number of crucial marginal seats in these towns, and elsewhere in the region, that make the East Midlands disproportionately a focus of attention at General Election time.

In 1987 Labour gained two seats in Leicester and one in Nottingham. Now they have their eyes set on the other two Nottingham seats (East and South), and Derby North, to complete their hold over the representation of the three largest towns in the region. Their other targets are a mixed bunch.

Corby is a New Town whose *raison d'être* was the steel industry which attracted thousands of Scottish migrants between the wars but which suffered severe closures in the early 1980s. Leicestershire North West is based on an ex-coalfield; Sherwood on the other hand is the heart of the Nottinghamshire mining area which was opened up between the wars, still remains viable, and has largely supported the breakaway UDM against Arthur Scargill's National

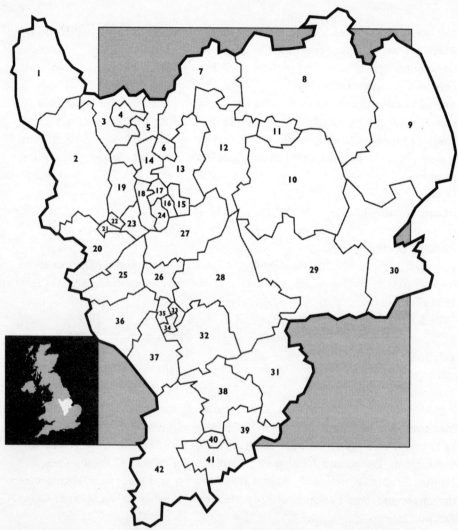

Conservative
Amber Valley (19)
Blaby (37)
Bosworth (36)
Broxtowe (18)
Corby (31)
Daventry (42)
Derby North (22)
Derbyshire South (20)
Derbyshire West (2)
Erewash (23)
Gainsborough &
  Horncastle (8)
Gedling (15)
Grantham (10)

Harborough (32)
High Peak (1)
Holland with
  Boston (30)
Kettering (38)
Leicestershire NW (25)
Lincoln (11)
Lindsey East (9)
Loughborough (26)
Newark (12)
Northhampton
  North (40)
Northhampton
  South (41)
Nottingham East (16)

Nottingham South (4)
Rushcliffe (27)
Rutland & Melton (28)
Sherwood (13)
Stamford &
  Spalding (29)
Wellingborough (39)

Labour
Ashfield (14)
Bassetlaw (7)
Bolsover (5)
Chesterfield (4)
Derby South (21)
Derbyshire NE (3)

Leicester East (33)
Leicester South (34)
Leicester West (35)
Mansfield (6)
Nottingham North (17)

Union of Mineworkers. It remains to be seen whether this factor will assist the Conservatives as it did last time (when the Tories came within 56 votes of capturing Mansfield, the metropolis of the Nottinghamshire coalfield).

Lincoln is one of the most socially and electorally typical towns in the whole of England. Other seats may be just out of Labour's grasp, with majorities of a little over 15 per cent: Northampton North, and four in Derbyshire: High Peak, Erewash, Amber Valley, and last but not least, Edwina Currie's Derbyshire South.

The East Midlands may well be the Liberal Democrats' weakest region. The closest they have come to securing representation here since 1945 came in the West Derbyshire by-election of 1986, when they failed by merely a round 100 votes. But the Conservative victor, Patrick McLoughlin (unusually for his party, an ex-miner) restored his lead to over 10,000 in the subsequent General Election. The battle for the East Midlands remains predominantly a 'major party' affair.

The North West

Indicator	1979	latest	change
Population (thousands)	6,498	6,389	-1.7%
Area (sq km)		7,331	n.a.
Unemployment: number	157,700	306,900	94.6%
rate	5.1%	10.1%	n.a.
Employment (thousands)	2,890	2,709	-6.3%
GDP per head, 1990	£6,259	£7,422	18.6%
Manufacturing GDP (£ million, 1990)	15,039	13,816	-8.1%
Average earnings (per week, 1991)	£239.60	£300.30	25.3%
Car ownership	54.6%	61.9%	n.a.
Offences recorded by police	365,683	701,703	91.9%
Average house prices	£16,902	£52,185	208.8%
Housebuilding	23,496	15,350	-34.7%
Housing tenure: owner occupied	59.2%	68.3%	n.a.
council/new town	29.7%	22.1%	n.a.
Birth rate	13.1	14.4	9.7%
Death rate	12.9	11.9	-7.7%
Infant mortality rate	13.5	8.2	-39.3%

General Election Voting

	Conservative	Labour	Liberal Democrat
	%	%	%
1974 (Feb)	36.2	39.9	21.0
1974 (Oct)	36.9	44.8	17.9
1979	43.8	42.6	13.0
1983	40.0	36.0	23.4
1987	38.0	41.2	20.6

The North West of England vies with Greater London for the 'honour' of being the region with the largest number of marginal seats. It is a populous and, in the main, urbanised area containing the two former metropolitan counties of Greater Manchester and Merseyside as well as the industrial towns and valleys of Lancashire, which became a world centre for textile production in the Industrial Revolution but which have been forced to adapt to a different and wider economic base. there are many marginal 'ex-textile' seats on both sides of the Pennines, where high owner-occupation and a lack of a strong trade union tradition have stimulated a considerable degree of working-class Conservatism. The small terraced houses typical of the region, though, have been subjected to high community charges, and some opinion polls have suggested that the Conservatives might face a degree of hostility in the North West.

They can do without that, as they have many vulnerable seats. These are not in Manchester or Liverpool themselves, where all Tory representation has already been eliminated. But each swing to Labour of 1 per cent would knock over vulnerable targets: up to 1 per cent Wallasey in Merseyside and Bolton North East; up to 2 per cent West Lancashire; up to 3 per cent Hyndburn (formerly Accrington), Pendle and Bury South; up to 4 per cent Stockport and Warrington South; up to 5 per cent Bolton West, Rossendale/Darwen and the City of Chester. And there are 18 in all, within Labour's top 100 hopes of a gain.

Labour also believe they can pick up some seats from another source. With Sir Cyril Smith's retirement at Rochdale, it is highly likely that the seat will revert to Labour: his tenure was almost entirely based on personal, not party, appeal. David Alton (Mossley Hill) must also be vulnerable to Labour's strength in Liverpool. Indeed, all three Liberal democrat seats are shaky, for Ronald Fearn has a hefty task in holding on to traditionally true-blue Southport, after just one term in Parliament. But the Liberal Democrats have hopes of counter-attack too: they have one of their best hopes of a gain anywhere at Hazel Grove, once held for the Liberals by Dr Michael Winstanley and now represented by Sir

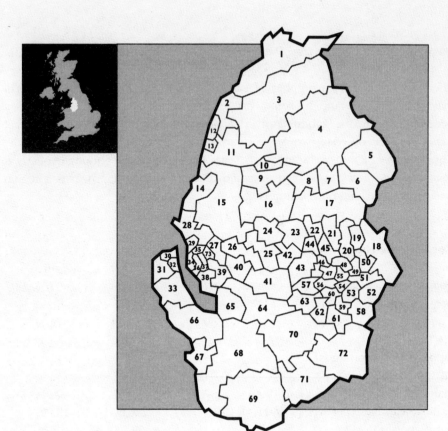

Conservative
Altrimcham & Sale (63)
Blackpool North (12)
Blackpool South (13)
Bolton NE (22)
Bolton West (23)
Bury North (21)
Bury South (45)
Cheadle (61)
Chester, City of (67)
Chorley (16)
Congleton (71)
Crosby (28)
Davyhulme (57)
Eddisbury (68)
Ellsmere Port &
  Neston (66)
Fylde (11)
Hazel Grove (58)
Hyndburn (7)
Lancashire West (15)
Lancaster (3)
Littleborough &
  Saddleworth (18)
Macclesfield (72)

Morecambe &
  Lunesdale (1)
Pendle (5)
Rossendale &
  Darwen (17)
South Ribble (9)
Stockport (59)
Tatton (70)
Wallasey (30)
Warrington South (64)
Wirral South (33)
Wirral West (31)
Wyre (2)

Labour
Ashton-under-Lyne (51)
Birkenhead (32)
Blackburn (8)
Bolton SE (44)
Bootle (29)
Burnley (6)
Crewe & Nantwich (69)
Denton & Reddish (53)
Eccles (46)
Halton (65)

Heywood &
  Middleton (20)
Knowsley North (27)
Knowsley South (39)
Leigh (42)
Liverpool,
  Broadgreen (37)
Liverpool, Garston (38)
Liverpool, Riverside (34)
Liverpool, Walton (35)
Liverpool,
  West Derby (73)
Makerfield (25)
Manchester,
  Blackley (48)
Manchester Central (55)
Manchester, Gorton (54)
Manchester,
  Withington (60)
Manchester,
  Wythenshawe (62)
Oldham Central &
  Royton (50)
Oldham West (49)
Preston (10)

Salford East (47)
St Helens North (26)
St Helens South (40)
Stalbridge & Hyde (52)
Stretford (56)
Warrington North (41)
Wigan (24)
Worsley (43)

Lib Dem
Liverpool,
  Mossley Hill (36)
Ribble Valley (4)
Rochdale (19)
Southport (14)

Tom Arnold, the Conservative Party Vice-Chairman for candidates and research.

There are, of course, a number of Labour seats in the North West with small majorities, but it would be somewhat misleading to call them marginals, as a general swing to the Labour Party is anticipated. If they were to lose any of these, the Election result would be clear: a massive three-figure majority for the Conservatives. Even excluding such seats from the picture, though, nearly a third of the North West's 73 seats could possibly change hands. It is a region well worth watching on Election Night.

Yorkshire & Humberside

Indicator	1979	latest	change
Population (thousands)	4,921	4,952	0.6%
Area (sq km)		15,420	n.a.
Unemployment: number	93,300	221,100	137.0%
rate	4.1%	9.2%	n.a.
Employment (thousands)	2,145	2,175	1.4%
GDP per head, 1990	£6,042	£7,562	25.2%
Manufacturing GDP (£ million, 1990)	9,878	9,882	0.0%
Average earnings (per week, 1991)	239.30	286.60	19.8%
Car ownership	49.1%	59.2%	n.a.
Offences recorded by police	255,097	568,552	122.9%
Average house prices	£15,003	£52,728	251.4%
Housebuilding	17,869	11,844	-33.5%
Housing tenure: owner occupied	55.9%	66.3%	n.a.
council/new town	32.2%	24.1%	n.a.
Birth rate	12.7	13.9	9.6%
Death rate	12.3	11.5	-6.8%
Infant mortality rate	13.9	8.9	-36.0%

General Election Voting

	Conservative	Labour	Liberal Democrat
	%	%	%
1974 (Feb)	33.8	41.4	23.2
1974 (Oct)	32.7	47.1	19.4
1979	39.4	44.5	15.1
1983	38.7	35.3	25.5
1987	37.4	40.6	21.7

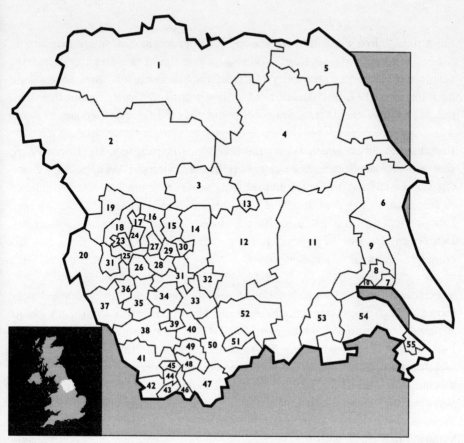

Conservative
Batley & Spen (26)
Beverley (9)
Boothferry (11)
Bridlington (6)
Brigg &
  Cleethorpes (54)
Calder Valley (20)
Colne Valley (37)
Elmet (14)
Harrogate (3)
Keighley (19)
Leeds NE (15)
Leeds NW (16)
Pudsey (17)
Richmond (Yorks) (1)
Ryedale (4)

Scarborough (5)
Selby (12)
Sheffield, Hallam (42)
Shipley (18)
Skipton & Ripon (2)
York (13)

Labour
Barnsley Central (39)
Barnsley East (40)
Barnsley West &
  Penistone (38)
Bradford North (24)
Bradford South (25)
Bradford West (23)
Dewsbury (35)
Don Valley (50)

Doncaster Central (51)
Doncaster North (52)
Glanford &
  Scunthorpe (53)
Great Grimsby (55)
Halifax (21)
Hemsworth (33)
Huddersfield (36)
Hull East (7)
Hull North (8)
Hull West (10)
Leeds Central (29)
Leeds East (30)
Leeds South &
  Morley (28)
Leeds West (27)
Normanton (31)

Pontefract &
  Castleford (32)
Rother Valley (47)
Rotherham (48)
Sheffield, Attercliffe (46)
Sheffield, Brightside (45)
Sheffield, Central (44)
Sheffield, Heeley (43)
Sheffield,
  Hillsborough (41)
Wakefield (34)
Wentworth (49)

Labour made five gains in Yorkshire and Humberside in 1987, more than in any other region but Scotland. These were Halifax, Bradford North, Glanford/Scunthorpe, Dewsbury (all from the Conservatives) and Leeds West from the Liberal Michael Meadowcroft. They will need to make more than that, though, to form even a minority government after the General Election.

Unfortunately, there are not a goodly number of possibilities. The Conservative seat with the smallest majority anywhere in the country is York, held by Conal Gregory in 1987 by 147 votes; but the only other constituencies with Tory leads of less than 10 per cent are Batley and Spen, Elmet, and Colne Valley (where Labour were in third place in 1987, but just behind the Liberal Democrats). Labour are just over 10 per cent behind at Calder Valley and Keighley, but this completes the total of possible gains.

The Liberal Democrats presumably hope they might triumph at Colne Valley too, although their strength there really lay in the personality of Richard Wainwright MP, up to his retirement in 1987. They have a number of long shots too – Pudsey and Leeds North West, for example – but this is a disappointing area for them: they have in the past flattered only to deceive by spectacular by-election victories (Ripon 1973, Ryedale 1986) which have been reversed at subsequent General Election. Michael Meadowcroft, the former MP for Leeds West, is not a Liberal Democrat but a leader of a small group which – never having much truck with the Alliance or the SDP – still use the historic name 'The Liberal Party'.

Yorkshire is a vast and varied county and this is reflected in this region, which spreads over the broad acres from the Labour strongholds of the 'Socialist Republic of South Yorkshire' through the great ex-textile (chiefly woollen) centres of Leeds and Bradford to the Pennines, and also to the vast open countryside of the North Yorkshire Dales and Moors. The politics are similarly kaleidoscopic, and always capable of springing the odd surprise next time.

The Northern Region

Indicator	1979	latest	change
Population (thousands)	3,130	3,075	-1.8%
Area (sq km)		15,401	n.a.
Unemployment: number	93,200	149,800	60.7%
rate	6.4%	10.7%	n.a.
Employment (thousands)	1,325	1,245	-6.0%
GDP per head, 1990	£5,923	£7,233	22.1%

Manufacturing GDP (£ million, 1990)	6,214	6,171	-0.7%
Average earnings (per week, 1991)	£240.40	£289.30	20.3%
Car ownership	48.2%	60.7%	n.a.
Offences recorded by police	181,240	404,353	123.1%
Average house prices	£15,443	£44,177	186.1%
Housebuilding	12,518	7,360	-41.2%
Housing tenure: owner occupied	47.1%	60.3%	n.a.
council/new town	39.7%	29.0%	n.a.
Birth rate	13.3	13.2	-0.8%
Death rate	12.6	12.2	-2.8%
Infant mortality rate	13.3	7.9	-40.6%

General Election Voting

	Conservative	Labour	Liberal Democrat
	%	%	%
1974 (Feb)	29.0	45.8	17.3
1974 (Oct)	30.5	51.3	16.8
1979	35.9	50.2	12.4
1983	34.6	40.2	25.0
1987	32.3	46.4	21.0

The five northern counties of England – Cumbria, Northumberland, Tyne and Wear, Durham and Cleveland – constitute Labour's strongest area in the most populous of the four nations which make up the United Kingdom. Of the 36 seats here, Labour won 27 in 1987 – precisely three-quarters. The Conservatives won eight, as they did before the 1987 election, and the Liberal Democrats just one – that of Alan Beith, who has now won Berwick upon Tweed six times.

Why is the far North so strongly Labour? The answer lies primarily in economics, and economic history. No area was as badly affected by the unemployment of the inter-war years, and it is not by coincidence that the jobless march on London in the 1930s started on Tyneside, at Jarrow. The great staple industries of the North East – and of Cumbria – were coal, steel and shipbuilding, all in massive decline for most of this century. Shipyards, mines and steelworks such as Consett have all been subject to the grim cycle of decline and closure. Small wonder that a socialist tradition still flourishes here.

Labour's strength is likely to increase further next time. They won the November 1991 by-election at Langbaurgh on a small swing with an Asian candidate, Ashok Kumar. Most of the seven remaining Tory seats are very

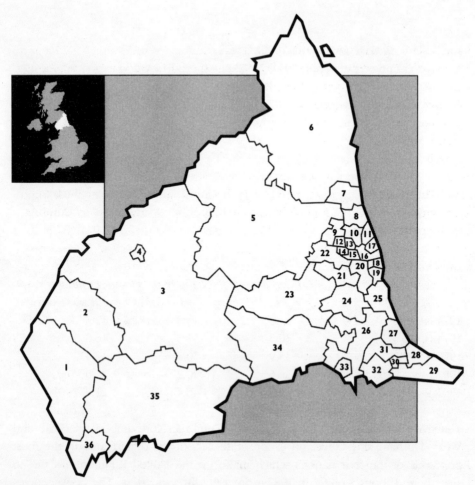

Conservative
Barrow & Furness (36)
Darlington (33)
Hexham (5)
Penrith &
   The Border (3)
Stockton South (32)
Tynemouth (11)
Westmorland &
Lonsdale (35)

Labour
Bishop Auckland (34)
Blaydon (22)
Blyth Valley (8)
Carlisle (4)
Copeland (1)

Durham, City of (24)
Durham North (21)
Durham NW (23)
Easington (25)
Gateshead East (15)
Hartlepool (27)
Houghton &
   Washington (20)
Jarrow (16)
Langbaurgh (29)
Middlesborough (30)
Newcastle-upon-Tyne
   Central (12)
Newcastle-upon-Tyne
   East (13)
Newcastle-upon-Tyne
   North (9)

Redcar (28)
Sedgefield (26)
South Shields (17)
Stockton North (31)
Sunderland North (18)
Sunderland South (19)
Tyne Bridge (14)
Wallsend (10)
Wansbeck (7)
Workington (2)

Lib Dem
Berwick-upon-
   Tweed (6)

vulnerable – Tynemouth and Darlington have majorities of less than 3,000; and Barrow and Furness less than 4,000; to them should be added Stockton South, the closest three-way fight in the country in 1987, with a bare 2,233 votes or 3.7 per cent separating the Conservatives, SDP and Labour; Labour are probably favourites to leap from third place to first, given the effective demise of the Social Democrats.

Were Labour to slip up in a major way, there are seats they might conceivably lose. The Shadow Cabinet member Jack Cunningham has usually looked somewhat insecure in Copeland (the area around Whitehaven in Cumbria, which includes Sellafield), and has been elected by less than 2,000 votes on the last two occasions. In Blyth Valley the far left Labour candidate Ronnie Campbell only held on by 853 votes against a strong SDP challenge based in the private 'new town' of Cramlington. However, a further Labour decline from their dire performances of 1983 and 1987 seems very unlikely, and the North is more likely to contribute handsomely to a Labour recovery of some magnitude.

Scotland

Indicator	1979	latest	change
Population (thousands)	5,204	5,102	-2.0%
Area (sq km)		77,080	n.a.
Unemployment: number	139,900	226,400	61.8%
rate	5.7%	9.1%	n.a.
Employment (thousands)	2,262	2,243	0.8%
GDP per head, 1990	£6,157	£7,592	23.3%
Manufacturing GDP (£ million, 1990)	9,173	8,345	-9.0%
Average earnings (per week, 1991)	£242.90	£299.50	23.3%
Car ownership	51.5%	56.8%	n.a.
Offences recorded by police	346,700	559,700	61.4%
Average house prices	£19,371	£47,887	147.2%
Housebuilding	23,116	20,762	-10.2%
Housing tenure: owner occupied	35.3%	51.6%	n.a.
council/new town	54.1%	39.4%	n.a.
Birth rate	13.2	13.0	-1.5%
Death rate	12.7	12.1	-4.7%
Infant mortality rate	12.8	7.7	-39.8%

General Election Voting

	Conservative	Labour	Liberal Democrat	SNP
	%	%	%	%
1974 (Feb)	32.9	36.6	8.0	21.9
1974 (Oct)	24.7	36.3	8.3	30.4
1979	31.4	41.6	9.0	17.3
1983	28.4	35.1	24.5	11.8
1987	24.0	42.4	19.3	14.0

Scotland, as is well known, is the best example of the division of response to Mrs Thatcher's government. While cruising in 1987 to her second consecutive landslide victory with an overall majority of over 100, Scotland proved an unmitigated disaster for the Conservative party. They lost over half of their 21 seats, being reduced to a mere 10 out of 72. Between a quarter and a fifth of all Labour's MPs now sit for constituencies north of the border; less than 3 per cent of Conservatives do. The Scottish Conservative Party has subsequently been publicly and noisily split, with rapid exchanges of Chairman, all creating a highly difficult position for successive Scottish Secretaries, Malcolm Rifkind and Ian Lang. In November 1991 the Liberal Democrats' Nicol Stephen easily seized Kincardine & Deeside after the death of its Tory MP, Alick Buchanan-Smith.

Several parties benefited from the Conservative collapse in 1987. The Scottish National Party made three gains in the rural north east of the country (while losing their previous two seats to Labour). The Liberal Democrats gained Argyll and Bute on the west coast and Fife North East on the east. Labour, of course, did best of all, seizing half a dozen Conservative seats and making a net gain of nine to reach a grand total of 50.

Much has been written on why the Conservatives now do so badly in Scotland – it has not always been so; in 1955 they won half the seats. Mrs Thatcher personally and her government in general appeared to be seen as thoroughly English, uncaring about Scotland and willing to adopt harmful policies without giving the Scots an adequate say in their own affairs. Moreover, the Scots seem to be willing to espouse more left wing principles and views than their English counterparts; this applies even to middle-class areas. The majority middle-class, owner-occupier constituency of Strathkelvin and Bearsden in the Glasgow suburbs fell to Labour's Sam Galbraith (admittedly a brain surgeon) in 1987; a seat with such an economic and social makeup would never have 'defected' south of the border. It is clear that the Tories have lasting problems in Scotland. However, it is not so clear that their decline will continue at the forthcoming

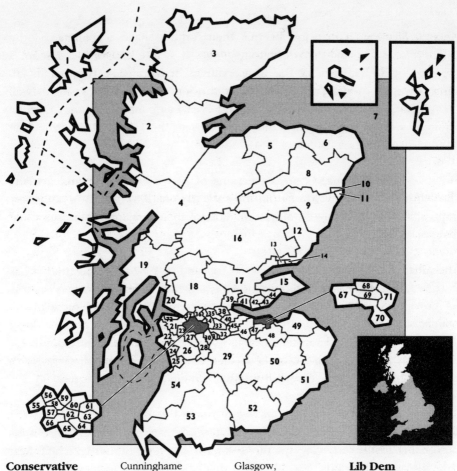

Conservative
Aberdeen South (11)
Ayr (25)
Dumfries (52)
Eastwood (27)
Edinburgh,
  Pentlands (47)
Edinburgh West (67)
Galloway &
  Upper Nithsdale (53)
Perth & Kinross (17)
Stirling (18)
Tayside North (16)

Labour
Aberdeen North (10)
Angus East (12)
Carrick, Cumnock
  & Doon Valley (54)
Clackmannan (39)
Clydebank &
  Milngavie (37)
Clydesdale (29)
Cumbernauld &
  Kilsyth (35)
Cunninghame
  North (22)

Cunninghame
  South (24)
Dumbarton (20)
Dundee East (14)
Dundee West (13)
Dunfermline East (42)
Dunfermline West (41)
East Kilbride (28)
East Lothian (49)
Edinburgh
  Central (69)
Edinburgh East (71)
Edinburgh, Leith (68)
Edinburgh South (70)
Falkirk East (40)
Falkirk West (38)
Fife Central (44)
Glasgow, Cathcart (65)
Glasgow Central (62)
Glasgow,
  Garscadden (56)
Glasgow, Hillhead (58)
Glasgow, Maryhill (59)
Glasgow, Pollok (66)
Glasgow, Provan (61)
Glasgow,
  Rutherglen (64)

Glasgow,
  Shettleston (63)
Glasgow,
  Springburn (60)
Greenock &
  Port Glasgow (72)
Hamilton (30)
Kilmarnock &
  Loudoun (26)
Kirkaldy (43)
Linlithgow (45)
Livingston (46)
Midlothian (48)
Monklands East (33)
Monklands West (34)
Motherwell North (32)
Motherwell South (31)
Paisley North (55)
Paisley South (23)
Renfrew West &
  Inverclyde (21)
Strathkelvin &
  Bearsden (36)
Western Isles (1)

Lib Dem
Argyll & Bute (19)
Fife NE (15)
Gordon (8)
Inverness, Nairn &
  Lochaber (4)
Kincardine &
  Deeside (9)
Orkney & Shetland (7)
Roxborough &
  Berwickshire (51)
Tweeddale, Ettrick &
  Lauderdale (50)
Caithness &
  Sutherland (3)
Ross, Cromarty &
  Skye (2)

SNP
Banff & Buchan (6)
Glasgow, Govan (57)
Moray (5)

General Election. It may just be that their fortunes have plummeted to the extent where they may have 'bottomed out'. It is true that one can script a scenario by which most of the Conservatives' remaining seats will fall: Ian Lang's own Galloway/Upper Nithsdale, Perth/Kinross and North Tayside may all be vulnerable to the SNP; Ayr, Stirling and even Edinburgh Pentlands (Malcolm Rifkind's seat) to Labour; and Edinburgh West to the Liberal Democrats. That would leave only two, Dumfries and Eastwood.

However, the Regional Council elections of May 1990 in Scotland actually showed a slight improvement from the dark days of 1987, and it is not totally impossible that they might hold all or most of their remaining nine seats and even pick up one or two.

The Alliance won nine of its 22 seats in Scotland in 1987, but since then it has fractured, the SDP has folded, and the Liberal Democrats dropped very sharply in the opinion polls in Scotland. Unless the ten MPs can hold on with the benefit of a personal vote and/or the Scottish tendency to vote tactically to keep the Tories out (well demonstrated in 1987) some look less than irremovable – particularly the less well-established, such as Menzies Campbell (Fife North East) and Mrs Ray Michie (Argyll/Bute), who entered the Commons in 1987.

Labour did lose one seat, Glasgow Govan, to the SNP's dynamic (and ex-Labour) Jim Sillars in a 1988 by-election. It will be very interesting to see if his personal charisma can overcome the teak-hard long-term Labour vote here near the old Clyde Shipyards; but the SNP cannot be expected to make any other inroads at Labour's expense in Scotland's central industrial belt.

Even if further humiliation does not await the Scottish Conservatives, everyone knows that a solid and increasingly able and influential 'delegation' of Labour MPs will be sent to Westminster again next time, among them John Smith, Gordon Brown and Donald Dewar, all likely Cabinet Ministers. It would be ironic if this considerable numerical and intellectual contribution were ever to be reduced by the logic that states that any increased degree of devolution to Scotland would have to be matched by a reduction of the number of Westminster Scottish MPs – for Scotland is heavily over-represented at the moment, its seats on average 15,000 electors smaller than England's.

Until they get their own Assembly, many Scots may continue to feel stymied – and it is still the Labour Party which will benefit from that frustration.

Northern Ireland

Indicator	1979	latest	change
Population (thousands)	1,530	1,589	3.9%
Area (sq km)		13,483	n.a.
Unemployment: number	52,900	102,900	94.5%
rate	7.9%	14.2%	n.a.
Employment (thousands)	598	622	4.0%
GDP per head, 1990	£5,130	£6,181	20.5%
Manufacturing GDP (£ million, 1990)	1,791	1,728	-3.5%
Average earnings (per week, 1991)	£225.20	£269.70	19.8%
Car ownership	51.0%	66.5%	n.a.
Offences recorded by police	54,262	57,198	5.4%
Average house prices	£21,824	£33,273	52.5%
Housebuilding	6,467	7,464	15.4%
Housing tenure: owner occupied	51.9%	65.8%	n.a.
council/new town	39.0%	28.7%	n.a.
Birth rate	18.4	16.7	-9.2%
Death rate	11.0	9.7	-11.7%
Infant mortality rate	14.8	7.5	-49.3%

General Election Voting

	Ulster Unionist *	DUP	SDLP Fein	Sinn	Alliance	Others
	%	%	%	%	%	%
1974 (Feb)	42.9	8.2	22.4	n.a.	3.2	23.3
1974 (Oct)	49.6	8.5	22.0	n.a.	6.3	13.6
1979	42.3	10.2	18.2	n.a.	11.9	17.4
1983	37.0	20.0	17.9	13.4	8.0	3.7
1987	40.3	11.7	21.1	11.4	10.0	5.5

* *In both 1974 elections includes Vanguard Unionist Progressive Party; in 1979 includes United Ulster Unionist Party; in 1983 and 1987, includes Ulster Popular Unionist Party.*
Yet again, a firm forecast can be made about the destiny of all 17 of Northern Ireland's seats in the forthcoming United Kingdom general election: none each for the Conservatives, Labour and Liberal Democrats – once more 'Others', that label which covers a multitude of stances, will score 17.

This is no brave prediction. Politics in Northern Ireland are based on truly different cleavages and motivations from the other side of the Irish Sea – essentially the division between republicans and those who wish to retain the

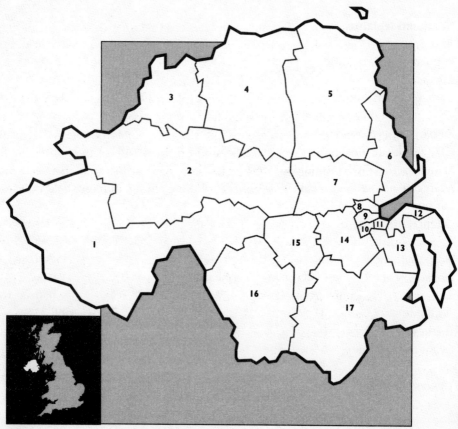

DUP
Antrim North (5)
Belfast East (11)
Ulster Mid (2)

PSF
Belfast West (9)

SDLP
Down South (17)
Foyle (3)
Newry & Armagh (16)

UUP
Antrim East (6)
Antrim South (7)
Belfast North (8)
Belfast South (10)
Down North (12)
Fermanagh &
    South Tyrone (1)
Lagan Valley (14)
Londonderry East (4)
Strangford (13)
Upper Bann (15)

union with Westminster (although very much on their own terms). In turn that divide correlates all too clearly with that between Roman Catholic and Protestant communities.

Northern Ireland's continuing appalling problems of poverty, unemployment and bad housing still press on both sides of the sectarian barrier, yet do not bring the people together on grounds of class or common interest. The battles this time, as so often before, will depend on the ability of the nationalist and unionist camps to bring out their votes, and also on the splits between more moderate and more extreme exponents of those strong and long-held policies.

Traditionally, and most particularly since their combined opposition to the 1986 Anglo-Irish Hillsborough agreement led them all to resign their seats, the unionists have been better at forming non-opposition pacts and then making them stick. As a result, the nationalist parties have rarely been able to win all the seats where they command a majority of the electorate, although in 1986 and 1987 respectively they did manage to add Newry and Armagh and South Down (taken from Enoch Powell) to West Belfast and Foyle, the seats of Gerry Adams and John Hume. They are also close to a majority at Fermanagh and South Tyrone and Mid Ulster, those war-torn rural areas in the centre of the province, but fail because the division between Provisional Sinn Fein and the SDLP lets in the single unionist candidate in each case.

Since this is likely to continue to be so, at least in marginal seats, we can expect little change next time in those seats. There are one or two where the outcome is unclear, though. In West Belfast, Gerry Adams, who has not taken his seat in the Commons since he was first elected in 1983, won by only 2,000 plus votes from the SDLP last time, and it will be interesting to judge the mood of Northern Ireland's largest concentration of nationalist voters. Also, one of the more curious contests of 1987 occurred in the rather middle class seat of North Down, where an independent unionist MP, James Kilfedder, was pressed very close (within 4,000 votes) by Robert McCartney, standing as a Real Unionist.

This contest may now be repeated, but with at least an element of extra spice. Since 1987, the Conservatives at least have decided to contest some seats in Northern Ireland, which gives the electorate an opportunity to vote for or against a party with a chance of government at Westminster. The North Down branch of the party was one of the very first to be formed, and indeed the Conservatives already have councillors in North Down District. However, no one seriously thinks the Conservatives will win North Down or any other seat, and they underwent a very depressing start to their campaigning in the Upper

Bann by-election of early 1990, where they lost their deposit.

Northern Ireland will continue to 'do different', and to return a disparate bloc of MPs, who may just acquire a little more influence at Westminster, should the next General Election result in a hung parliament where all 'Others' will perforce be courted by would-be claimants to government: one more intriguing prospect that a close election would open up.

Notes and definitions

Population Resident population at mid-year, 1979 and 1990

Area In hectares

Unemployment Unemployed claimants as a percentage of the workforce, seasonally adjusted on current concepts, May 1979 and November 1991

Employment Civilian workforce in employment, June 1979 and June 1991

GDP per head GDP at factor cost at 1990 prices, 1979 and 1990. The figures are converted from cash using the national GDP deflator at factor cost in the absence of regional price data; this does not necessarily measure regional differences in price changes

Manufacturing GDP GDP at factor cost in manufacturing industries in £ million at 1990 prices, 1979 and 1990. See above for notes on price basis

Earnings Average gross weekly earnings at April 1991 prices (using Retail Price Index) of full-time male employees on adult rates whose earnings were not affected by absence, April 1979 and April 1991 (except Northern Ireland where latest figures are for April 1990). The 1979 figures are adjusted from data covering males aged 21 and over.

Car ownership Percentage of households with use of car or van, 1978/79 (combined) and 1989/90 (combined)

Crime For England and Wales, notifiable offences recorded by the police, 1979 and year ending September 1991. The figures for London cover the City of London and Metropolitan Police Force areas which extend slightly beyond the Greater London area. The figures for the rest of the South East similarly cover a slightly smaller area than the region. For Scotland, crimes recorded by the police in 1979 and year ending June 1991 (provisional). The coverage of these figures is not the same as for the rest of the UK. For Northern Ireland, notifiable offences known to the police, 1979 and 1990

House prices Average prices at mortgage completion stage, 1979 and 1991 second quarter. Based on 5 per cent sample of building society mortgages only; not adjusted for changes in dwelling unit

Housing tenure Percentage of dwelling stock (a) owner-occupied and (b) rented from local authorities or new towns, December 1979 and June 1991 (provisional). Privately rented, housing association and other dwellings are not covered

Birth rate Live births per thousand population, 1979 and 1990. Not adjusted for differences between regions in age and sex structure

Death rate Deaths per thousand population, 1979 and 1990. Not adjusted for differences between regions in age and sex structure

Infant mortality rate Deaths in first year per thousand live births, 1979 and 1990

CANDIDATES

CONSERVATIVE MPS RETIRING AT THE 1992 GENERAL ELECTION

By December 1991, a total of 56 Conservative MPs were retiring at this election and one has been deselected, roughly 15 per cent of the Parliamentary party. Thirty-two are leaving seats with over 20 per cent majorities but nine are leaving seats with a Conservative majority of less than 10 per cent.

Name	Constituency	Year	Maj %
Julian Amery	Brighton Pavilion	1969-	21.1
{*Derek Spencer*}	{*Leicester S*}		
William Benyon	Milton Keynes	1970-	18.5
[*Peter Butler*]	[*NE*]		
[*Barry Legg*]	[*SW*]		
Sir Peter Blaker	Blackpool South	1964-	15.9
[*Nicholas Hawkins*]			
Robert Boscawen	Somerton & Frome	1970-	17.4
[*Mark Robinson*]	{*Newport W*}		
Sir Bernard Braine	Castle Point	1950-	38.8
[*Dr Robert Spink*]			
John Browne	Winchester	1979-	12.1
[*Gerald Malone*]	{*Aberdeen S*}		
Sir Antony Buck	Colchester N	1961-	21.8
[*Bernard Jenkin*]			
Sir Williams Clark	Croydon S	1959-	39.8
[*Richard Ottaway*]	{*Nottingham N*}		
Sir Paul Dean	Woodspring	1964-	29.6
[*Dr Liam Fox*]			
Sir John Farr	Harborough	1959-	31.7
[*Edward Garnier*]			
Sir Geoffrey Finsberg	Hampstead & Highgate	1970-	4.9
[*Oliver Letwin*]			
Sir Ian Gilmour	Chesham & Amersham	1962-	35.1
[*Cheryl Gillan*]			
Sir Alan Glyn	Windsor & Maidenhead	1959-	29.8
[*Lord Michael Trend*]			
Sir Philip Goodhart	Beckenham	1957-	30.4
[*Piers Merchant*]	{*Newcastle Central*}		
Sir Eldon Griffiths	Bury St Edmunds	1964-	30.6
[*Richard Spring*]			

Name	Constituency	Year	Maj %
Christopher Hawkins [*Charles Hendry*]	High Peak	1983-	16.9
Sir Barney Hayhoe [*Nirj Deva*]	Brentford-Isleworth	1970-	14.5
Sir Geoffrey Howe [*Peter Ainsworth*]	East Surrey	1970-	39.5
Sir Charles Irving [*John D.B.Taylor*]	Cheltenham	1974-	7.9
Michael Latham [*Alan Duncan*]	Rutland & Melton	1974-	38.5
Nigel Lawson [*Andrew Robotham*]	Blaby	1974-	35.5
Sir Ian Lloyd [*David Willetts*]	Havant	1964-	29.0
Sir Richard Luce [*Michael Stephen*]	Shoreham	1971-	30.9
Sir Robert McCrindle [*Eric Pickles*]	Brentwood & Ongar	1970-	35.5
Sir Michael McNair-Wilson [*Judith Chaplin*]	Newbury	1968-	28.4
Sir Neil Macfarlane [*Lady Olga Maitland*]	Sutton & Cheam	1974-	32.2
Robin Maxwell-Hyslop [*Angela Browning*]	Tiverton	1960-	16.9
Sir Anthony Meyer* [*Roderick Richards*]	Clwyd NW	1970-	23.7
Sir Hal Miller [*Roy Thomason*]	Bromsgrove	1974-	31.4
Norman Miscampbell [*Harold Elletson*]	Blackpool N	1962-	17.0
John Moore [*Sir Paul Beresford*]	Croydon C	1974-	32.2
Sir Charles Morrison [*Lord Michael Ancram*]	Devizes {Edinburgh S}	1964-	26.9
Sir Peter Morrison [*Gyles Brandreth*]	City of Chester	1974-	9.3
David Mudd [*Sebastian Coe*]	Falmouth & Camborne	1970-	9.3

Name	Constituency	Year	Maj %
Cecil Parkinson	Hertsmere	1970-	32.8
[*James Clappison*]			
Sir David Price	Eastleigh	1955-	19.3
[*Stephen Milligan*]			
Keith Raffan	Delyn	1983-	2.3
[*Michael Whitby*]			
Timothy Raison	Aylesbury	1970-	28.9
[*David Liddington*]			
Robert Rhodes James	Cambridge	1976-	9.4
[*Mark Bishop*]			
Nicholas Ridley	Cirencester & Tewkesbury	1959-	19.4
[*Geoffrey Clifton-Brown*]			
Sir Julian Ridsdale	Harwich	1954-	21.4
[*Iain Sproat*]			
Sir Hugh Rossi	Hornsey & Wood Green	1966-	3.0
[*Andrew Boff*]			
Peter Rost	Erewash	1970-	16.5
[*Angela Knight*]			
Sir Michael Shaw	Scarborough	1966-	25.0
[*John Sykes*]			
Ivor Stanbrook	Orpington	1970-	27.1
[*John Horam*]			
Ian Stewart	Hertfordshire North	1974-	17.9
[*Oliver Heald*]			
Sir John Stokes	Halesowen & Stourbridge	1970-	22.3
[*Warren Hawksley*]	{*Wrekin*}		
Norman Tebbit	Chingford	1970-	41.2
[*Iain Duncan-Smith*]			
Margaret Thatcher	Finchley	1959-	22.2
[*Hartley Booth*]			
John Wakeham	Colchester S & Maldon	1974-	24.3
[*John Whittingdale*]			
Peter Walker	Worcester	1961-	19.8
[*Peter Luff*]			
Sir Dennis Walters	Westbury	1964-	15.2
[*David Faber*]			
Kenneth Warren	Hastings & Rye	1970-	14.1
[*Jacqui Lait*]			

Name	Constituency	Year	Maj %
Bernard Weatherill	Croydon NE	1964-	28.5
[David Congdon]			
Mike Woodcock	Ellesmere Port & Neston	1983-	3.2
[Andrew Pearce]			
George Younger	Ayr	1964-	0.3
[Phil Gallie]			

[ ] *denotes replacement candidate*

{ } *indicates service in other constituency*

* *deselected MP*

LABOUR MPS RETIRING AT THE 1992 GENERAL ELECTION

A total of 23 Labour MPs, about 10 per cent of the Parliamentary party, will not be contesting the next general election. Two of these have been deselected. Sixteen are leaving seats with a Labour majority of over 20 per cent, and only three are leaving a Labour majority of less than 10 per cent. In addition, Terry Fields, Liverpool, Broadgreen and Dave Nellist, Coventry South East, have been expelled from the Labour Party and may stand as Independents at the next election.

Name	Constituency	Year	Maj %
Peter Archer	Warley W	1966-	13.4
[John Spellar]	{Birmingham Northfield}		
Jack Ashley	Stoke on Trent S	1966-	9.7
[George Stevenson MEP]			
Sydney Bidwell*	Ealing, Southall	1966-	15.2
[Piara Khabra]			
Ron Brown*	Edinburgh Leith	1979-	26.4
[Malcolm Chisholm]			
Bob Clay	Sunderland North	1983-	27.5
[Billy Hetherington]			
Stanley Crowther	Rotherham	1976-	37.6
[James Boyce]			
Dick Douglas (now SNP)	Dunfermline W	1970-	24.0
[Rachel Squires]			
Sir Patrick Duffy	Sheffield Attercliffe	1970-	35.1
[Clive Betts]			
Alexander Eadie	Midlothian	1966-	26.3
[Erik Clarke]			

Name	Constituency	Year	Maj %
Harry Ewing [Michael Connarty]	Falkirk E	1971-	35.5
Martin Flannery [Helen Jackson]	Sheffield Hillsborough	1974-	5.5
Michael Foot [Llewellyn Smith MEP]	Blaenau Gwent	1945-	64.4
Ted Garrett [Steve Byers]	Wallsend	1964-	33.6
Frank Haynes [Geoff Hoon MEP]	Ashfield	1979-	8.1
Denis Healey [George Mudie]	Leeds East	1952-	22.1
Denis Howell [Roger Godsiff]	Birmingham Small Heath	1955-	45.2
John Hughes* [Bob Ainsworth]	Coventry NE	1987-	25.0
David Lambie [Brian Donohoe]	Cunninghame S	1970-	44.5
James Lamond [Bryan Davies]	Oldham C & Royton {Enfield North}	1970-	13.8
Ted Leadbitter [Peter Mandelson]	Hartlepool	1964-	14.6
Allen McKay [Mick Clapham]	Barnsley W& Penistone	1978-	30.8
Merlyn Rees [John Gunnell]	Leeds S & Morley	1963-	15.5
Michael Welsh [Kevin Hughes]	Doncaster North	1979-	37.4

LIBERAL DEMOCRAT MPs RETIRING AT THE 1992 GENERAL ELECTION

Sir Cyril Smith [Elizabeth Lynne]	Rochdale	1972-	5.4

SDP MPs RETIRING AT THE 1992 GENERAL ELECTION

David Owen [Harold Luscombe]	Plymouth Devonport	1966-	13.0

NATIONALIST MPs RETIRING AT THE 1992 GENERAL ELECTION

Name	Constituency	Year	Maj%
Dafydd Elis Thomas (PC)	Merionnydd	1974-	11.7
[*Elwyn Llwyd*]			

[ ] *denotes replacement candidate*
{ } *indicates service in other constituency*
* *deselected MP*

WOMEN CANDIDATES IN THE 1992 GENERAL ELECTION

	Woman MPs in the last Parliament	Women Candidated in 1992
Conservative	16	60
Labour	24	133
Liberal Democrat	1	124
Nationalist	1	1?
IND	1	1
Total	**42**	**318**

	Women as % of Parliamentary Party		Women as % of party candidates	
Conservative	4.3	(3.6)	9.2	(7.0)
Labour	10.4	(5.8)	22.0	(16.0)
Liberal Democrat	4.5	(4.2)	19.6	(15.6)

( )*Figures for 1987*

Although underrepresentation of women in Parliament is still a potent issue, especially the absence of a single woman in John Major's Cabinet, there are more women candidates in this election than ever before.

Twenty-two Conservative women candidates are defending seats with a Conservative majority, and a further six are facing majorities of less than 10 per cent. However a third of candidates face majorities against them of over 20 per cent. Twenty-eight of the Labour women are defending seats with a Labour majority, and a further 12 are contesting seats with a majority of less than 10 per cent but 60 per cent of their candidates face majorities of over 20 per cent. The Liberal Democrats have two women defending seats with a majority and five seeking to overturn a majority of less than 10 per cent. 78 per cent of their candidates face majorities of over 20 per cent.

This means a total of 52 women are standing in seats where their party has a majority, potentially just over 8.2 per cent of the House, an increase from 5.5 per cent in 1987. A further 23 are facing majorities of under 10 per cent, a further 3.6 per cent of the House. But 42 per cent of the total are facing majorities of at least 30 per cent; in 1987 it was a third. The 300 Group, which campaigns for greater representation of women in Parliament, points out that their target of 300 women MPs by the year 2000 will not be achieved without a radical change in attitude towards methods of selection.

CONSERVATIVE WOMEN CANDIDATES*

Name	Constituency	Con Maj%
Marion Roe MP	Broxbourne	43.3
Gillian Shepherd MP	Norfolk South West	36.2
Cheryl Gillan	Chesham & Amersham	35.1
Lady Olga Maitland	Sutton & Cheam	32.1
Teresa Gorman MP	Billericay	29.3
Judith Chaplin	Newbury	28.4
Virginia Bottomley MP	Surrey South West	25.1
Dame Jill Knight MP	Birmingham Edgbaston	22.9
Dame Peggy Fenner MP	Medway	21.2
Ann Widdecombe MP	Maidstone	18.6
Angela Browning	Tiverton	16.9
Angela Knight	Erewash	16.5
Edwina Currie MP	Derbyshire South	15.9
Ann Winterton MP	Congleton	14.5
Dame Elaine Kellett -Bowman MP	Lancaster	14.3
Jacqui Lait	Hastings & Rye	14.1
Angela Rumbold MP	Mitcham & Morden	12.9
Emma Nicholson MP	Devon West and Torridge	11.1
Dame Janet Fookes MP	Plymouth, Drake	8.0
Elizabeth Peacock MP	Batley and Spen	2.3
Lynda Chalker MP	Wallasey	0.5
Maureen Hicks MP	Wolverhampton North East	0.4
Elizabeth Holt	The Wrekin	-2.3
Mary Scanlon	Fife North East	-3.6
Jeannie France-Hayhurst	Montgomery	-8.1
Roma Hossack	Moray & West Banff	-8.2
Annabel Goldie	Renfrew West & Inverclyde	-9.0

Name	Constituency	Con Maj%
Jacqueline Foster	Newham South	-9.3
Fiona Burkeman	Yeovil	-10.2
Caroline Spelman	Bassetlaw	-10.6
Elizabeth Gibson	Birmingham Hodge Hill	-11.8
Shirley Finlay-Maxwell	Roxburgh & Berwickshire	-12.0
Christine Smith	Leyton	-12.1
Sarah Whitehouse	Warley West	13.4
Patricia Morris	Oldham Central & Royton	-13.8
Agnes Hill	Coventry North West	-14.3
Jane Kenyon	Huddersfield	-14.5
Brenda Binge	Burnley	-14.6
Angela Emmett	Newport East	-16.9
Martine Hyams	Coventry South East	-17.5
Teresa O'Neil	Lewisham Deptford	-17.9

* *Women candidates either defending majorities or facing majorities of up to 20 per cent.*

LABOUR WOMEN CANDIDATES*

Name	Constituency	Lab Maj %
Ann Clwyd MP	Cynon Valley	56.7
Maria Fyfe MP	Glasgow Maryhill	54.8
Joyce Quin MP	Gateshead East	35.3
Kate Hoey MP	Vauxhall	33.9
Harriet Harman MP	Peckham	28.8
Clare Short MP	Birmingham Ladywood	26.3
Rachel Squire	Dunfermline West	23.9
Audrey Wise MP	Preston	23.9
Hilary Armstrong MP	Durham North West	22.5
Diane Abbott MP	Hackney Nth & Stoke Newington	19.8
Joan Lestor MP	Eccles	19.4
Joan Ruddock MP	Lewisham Deptford	17.9
Sylvia Heal MP	Staffordshire Mid	16.8
Dr Marjorie Mowlem MP	Redcar	16.0
Joan Walley MP	Stoke-on-Trent North	15.7
Irene Adams MP	Paisley North	14.6
Judith Chegwidden	Putney	14.4
Mildred Gordon MP	Bow and Poplar	13.6
Betty Boothroyd MP	West Bromwich West	13.3
Jo Richardson MP	Barking	9.9

Name	Constituency	Lab Maj%
Llin Golding MP	Newcastle Under Lyme	9.6
Helen Jackson	Sheffield Hillsborough	5.5
Margaret Beckett MP	Derby South	3.2
Dawn Primarolo MP	Bristol South	2.8
Alice Mahon MP	Halifax	2.1
Gwyneth Dunwoody MP	Crewe and Nantwich	1.9
Ann Taylor MP	Dewsbury	0.8
Tessa Jowell	Dulwich	-0.5
Kate Phillips	Stirling	-2.1
Eunice Durkin	Batley & Spen	-2.3
Barbara Roche	Hornsey and Wood Green	-3.0
Ann Holmes	Kensington	-3.4
Lynne Jones	Birmingham Selly Oak	-4.9
Glenda Jackson	Hampstead & Highgate	-4.9
Hazel Blears	Bury South	-5.2
Estelle Morris	Birmingham Yardley	-6.0
Ann Coffey	Stockport	-6.1
Jenny Edwards	Westminster North	-7.9
Jean Corston	Bristol East	-8.2
Janet Anderson	Rossendale & Darwen	-8.3
Bridget Prentice	Lewisham East	-10.9
Anne Campbell	Cambridge	-11.7
Siobhain McDonagh	Mitcham & Morden	12.9
Ruth Henig	Lancaster	-14.2
Ann Keen	Brentford & Isleworth	-14.5
Irene Kitson	Edinburgh West	-15.2
Julie Owens	Peterborough	-15.8
Betty Williams	Conwy	-16.4
Jane Slowey	Birmingham Hall Green	-16.7
Judith Church	Stevenage	-16.7
Patricia Muddyman	Burton	-17.1
Janet Thomas	Northampton North	17.9
Diana Organ	Gloucestershire West	-18.5
Julie Morgan	Cardiff North	-18.6

* Women candidates either defending majorities or facing majorities of up to 20 per cent.

LIBERAL DEMOCRAT WOMEN CANDIDATES*

Name	Constituency	Lib Maj %
Elizabeth Lynne	Rochdale	5.9
Ray Michie MP	Argyll & Bute	3.8
Kay Kirkham	Stockton South	-1.3
Dr Jenny Tonge	Richmond & Barnes	-3.9
Jenny Randerson	Cardiff Central	-7.7
Valerie Cox	Plymouth Drake	-8.0
Mrs Terrye Jones	Falmouth & Camborne	-9.3
Barbara Pearce	Leeds North West	-10.1
Flo Clucas	Crosby	-10.2
Moira Craig	Eastwood	-12.2
Rosie Cooper	Liverpool Broad Green	-12.6
Frances David	Monmouth	-14.5
Elizabeth Shields	Ryedale	-14.8
Vivienne Rayner	Westbury	-15.2
Nina Stimson	Southend West	-16.3
Barbara Waterfield	Strathkelvin & Bearsden	-16.7
Irene Keith	Aberdeen South	-16.8
Christine Napier	Wiltshire North	-17.1
Jackie Ballard	Taunton	-17.6
Monica Howes	St Albans	-18.0
Linda Cufley	Folkestone & Hythe	-18.1
Hilary Campbell	Edinburgh Leith	-18.6
Paula Yates	Maidstone	-18.7
Eve Warlow	Cardiff North	-18.8
Patsy Calton	Cheadle	-19.2
Anne Corris	Stockport	-19.3
Pat Frankish	Great Grimsby	-19.4
Maisie Jamieson	Erith & Crayford	-19.9

* *Women candidates either defending majorities or facing majorities of up to 20 per cent.*

NATIONALIST WOMEN CANDIDATES*

Name	Constituency	Lib Maj %
Margaret Ewing MP	Moray	8.2
Roseanna Cunningham	Perth & Kinross	-12.0
Frances McFarlane	Western Isles	-14.2

* *Women candidates either defending majorities or facing majorities of up to 20 per cent.*
[19.4 per cent of SNP candidates are women]
[17.6 per cent of Plaid Cymru's candidates are women]

IND WOMEN CANDIDATES

Name	Constituency	Lib Maj %
Rosie Barnes MP	Greenwich	5.7

Ethnic candidates in the 1992 General Election

The 1987 General Election saw four ethnic Members of Parliament elected for the first time in over half a century. All four MPs came from the Labour Party with the addition of Ashok Kumar as a result of the recent Langbaurgh by-election. This election will probably result in an increase in ethnic MPs. The Conservative Party has eight ethnic candidates standing, three more than the last election; the Labour Party has seven, seven less than last time; and the Liberal Democrats five, two less than in 1987.

Two of the Conservative candidates, Nirj Deva and John Taylor, are standing with majorities behind them and a further two are facing majorities of less than 10 per cent. Five of the Labour candidates are sitting MPs and Mr Khabra defends a strong Labour seat. But the remaining candidates are fighting large majorities. No Liberal candidate is standing in a seat with a majority of less than 25 per cent.

This means that of the 22 ethnic candidates put up by the major parties, a total of eight, over one-third, are standing with majorities behind them. A further two are fighting majorities of less than 10 per cent. However, 12 black candidates, one-half of those standing, are facing a majority against them of at least 24 per cent.

CONSERVATIVE ETHNIC CANDIDATES

Name	Constituency	Con Maj %
Nirj Deva	Brentford and Isleworth	14.5
John Taylor	Cheltenham	7.9

Name	Constituency	Con Maj%
Andrew Popat	Bradford South	-0.6
Andrew Charalambous	Tottenham	-8.3
Lurline Champagnie	Islington North	-24.7
Mohammed Riaz	Bradford North	-34.9
Mohammed Khamisa	Birmingham Sparkbrook	-35.1
Abdul Qayyum Chaudhary	Birmingham Small Heath	-45.2

LABOUR ETHNIC CANDIDATES

Name	Constituency	Lab Maj %
Diane Abbott MP	Hackney Nth & Stoke Newington	19.8
Paul Boateng MP	Brent South	19.5
Piara Khabra	Ealing Southall	15.2
Bernie Grant MP	Tottenham	8.3
Ashok Kumar MP	Langbaurgh	3.8
Keith Vaz MP	Leicester East	3.6
Claude Ajith Moraes	Harrow West	-28.1
Doreen Cameron	Ashford	-29.2
Kingsley Abrams	Wimbledon	-29.3

LIBERAL DEMOCRAT ETHNIC CANDIDATES

Name	Constituency	Lib Maj %
Verona Marfo	Hackney North & Stoke Newington	-29.5
Zerbanoo Gifford	Hertsmere	-32.8
Marcello Verma	Cynon Valley	-32.9
Pash Nandhra	Ealing Southall	-37.4
Akbar Ali	Liverpool Riverside	-61.9

CHAPTER TEN

THE LAST TIME AROUND

The 1987 General Election campaign

The general election campaign of 1987 was called just after 2pm on Monday May 11. Mrs Thatcher ended weeks of speculation by saying 'it was best to end the uncertainty so that we can all plan for the future.' The Conservatives had been leading the opinion polls for months and favourable results in the May local elections made it inevitable. Much of the legislative programme had to be abandoned, except the 2p cut to a 27 per cent standard rate of income tax, to complete Commons business in time. Mr Denis Healey, Labour's Foreign Affairs Spokesman, made the first gaffe of the campaign by announcing that the Soviet authorities 'were praying for a Labour victory.' Opinion polls remained remarkably static helped no doubt by the majority of electors claiming to have made their mind up before the campaign started.

Both the Alliance and Conservative strategies were drawn up on the assumption that the Alliance would be challenging Labour for second place. However a well-orchestrated Labour campaign concentrating on the 'caring' issues restored Labour's position as the main Opposition party. Both Conservatives and Alliance had too rigid and too dependent original game plans which forced them onto the defensive early in the campaign from which position the Alliance never really recovered. The Conservative's slow start gathered momentum with the most expensive advertising blitz ever in the last week of the campaign. Labour were seen to have run a good, professional campaign with effective advertising and none of the sense of impending defeat of the 1983 campaign. Without their unilateralist defence policy they might have run the Conservatives closer. Neil Kinnock's personal standing increased dramatically. The Alliance's expected surge never materialised as Labour's campaign forced them significantly further back into third place compared with the 1983 election.

MONDAY 11 MAY: Mrs Thatcher announced the date of the General Election. A Harris poll for London Weekend Television the previous day put the Conservatives on 44 per cent, Labour on 33 per cent and the SDP/Liberal Alliance on 21 per cent.

TUESDAY MAY 12: Labour's Shadow Cabinet and National Executive met and approved a manifesto stripped of many traditional left wing commitments with little acrimony, demonstrating Neil Kinnock's dominance of the party. Labour's unilateral defence policy was seen to be the most difficult part to 'sell' to the electorate.

WEDNESDAY MAY 13: The Alliance leaders seized the initiative, catching headlines and touring the regions. Labour highlighted the issue of hospital waiting lists.

THURSDAY MAY 14: Conservatives received additional boost from the unemployment figures showing a fall for the tenth month in succession. Labour accused the government of 'fiddling' the figures. Mrs Thatcher refused to take part in a TV debate with Mr Kinnock.

FRIDAY MAY 15: Mrs Thatcher and Mr Kinnock both opened their campaigns outside Westminster. She addressed a Conservative rally in Scotland pledging an intensified drive for popular capitalism and warning Labour had an 'iceberg manifesto' with nine-tenths of socialism concealed. He mocked her yearning for immortality: 'she must not be allowed to go on and on....with a one-person government.'

MONDAY 18 MAY: Parliament was dissolved. The Alliance manifesto was launched by Dr Owen and Mr Steel concentrating their assault on the Conservatives, dismissing Labour as 'unelectable and irrelevant'.

TUESDAY 19 MAY: Conservative and Labour manifestos were launched. The Conservatives' manifesto was a radical programme promising further privatisation and opt-out schemes for hospitals and schools. Labour's promised a £12 billion package to tackle unemployment, poverty and crime.

WEDNESDAY 20 MAY: Dr Owen was infuriated by Conservative claims that the Alliance shared Labour's defence policy. The defence row went on for days with the Opposition parties objecting to the use of the Union Jack in a Conservative election broadcast implying only the Tory party was patriotic. Labour lifted unemployment briefly to the top of the agenda by wrongfooting Norman Tebbit on remarks he made before the election on the 3 million unemployed.

THURSDAY 21 MAY: Mrs Thatcher launched the full election campaign, making defence the centre of her attack on Labour. Defence became an increasingly important issue during the campaign. Labour succeeded in lifting interest in the NHS and education.

FRIDAY 22 MAY: The radical Conservative programme became something of an embarrassment as details of the education plan had not been fully thought out. Similar confusion occurred a few days later with housing plans.

MONDAY 25 MAY: Mr Kinnock's tour of the regions backed up by well-organised shadow ministers' speeches on specific issues showed the Labour machine in fighting trim. He came across as confident and concerned about the plight of the less well-off. Labour did blunder with confusion about its local government finance policy.

TUESDAY 26 MAY: The Alliance seemed rooted at around 20-21 per cent as the two leaders ceased dual appearances on TV. Mr Kinnock sold the image of a semi-socialist Labour party while the Conservatives continued to play the defence card attacking Mr Kinnock for speaking of Russian occupation.

WEDNESDAY 27 MAY: Nominations closed. Neil Kinnock was accused of dodging the national press by failing to appear for more than a handful of the morning press conferences in London, a duty Mrs Thatcher attacked with relish.

THURSDAY 28 MAY: A Gallup poll in the *Daily Telegraph* put the state of the parties at: Conservatives 44.5 per cent, Labour 36 per cent and the Alliance 18 per cent. Mr Kinnock held a 'make or break' Press Conference on defence and withstood heavy questioning without deepening Labour's problems.

FRIDAY 29 MAY (the last weekend in May): Polls put Conservative support above 40 per cent. Mrs Thatcher emphasised the 'winter of discontent' which ended the last Labour Government and declared: 'we are building one nation' in response to accusations of creating a divided Britain. She was forced to declare no VAT on food or electricity, gas and fuels after heavy opposition questioning. Gerald Kaufman said Mrs Thatcher's values could be said to be: 'want it, own it, get it, grab it'. The Alliance mood was more subdued realising that public talk of a two-horse race made it more vulnerable to a two-party squeeze in the final stages rather than the surge predicted by Dr Owen. He also predicted they would hold the balance in a hung parliament.

MONDAY 1 JUNE: Campaign hotted up when Mr Kinnock launched a personal attack on Margaret Thatcher's style of leadership labelling her an 'ambitious would-be empress' surrounded by a 'palace guard' and with 'spineless' Cabinet ministers. Mrs Thatcher said she was merely paying the price for the resolution of her administration. She said this was an attempt to deflect attention from the 'real issues' by focusing on her personality.

TUESDAY 2 JUNE: The Conservatives still maintain a substantial lead despite conflicting polling from the marginals. Mrs Thatcher stepped up her attack on Labour, predicting the TUC would run a Labour government and that they would repeal trade union legislation. As Britain's foreign reserves reached a new record, she said Tories had transformed a 'lame duck economy into a bulldog economy.' Labour sought to make the key issues the north-south divide and unemployment. Nigel Lawson predicted Labour's economic plans would push inflation up to 14 per cent. Mr Kinnock accused Mrs Thatcher of creating a 'Divided Kingdom'. Dr Owen launched a strong attack on Labour's 'lethal left' saying the left-wing were hidden thorns behind Labour's rose.

WEDNESDAY 3 JUNE: City prices dipped nervously as a BBC Newsnight poll put Labour ahead on average in 27 marginal seats. Speculation at prospect of hung parliament led Mr Steel and Dr Owen to differ publicly: Mr Steel would prefer to negotiate with Labour while Dr Owen refused to rule out a deal with

Mrs Thatcher. Mr Kinnock again ruled out any question of a deal with the Alliance. Roy Hattersley created fresh uncertainty over Labour's plans for Britain's Polaris submarine fleet. Mrs Thatcher, pressed on Conservative plans for the Poll Tax, slammed Labour for proposing capital value rating for local government finance, shrugging off suggestions the Conservatives had run a lacklustre campaign.

THURSDAY 4 JUNE: 'The day the Tory campaign wobbled' as a Gallup poll puts the Conservatives at 40.5 per cent, Labour 36.5 per cent and Alliance 21.5 per cent, opening up the possibility of a hung parliament. Mr Kinnock highlighted the case of a 10-year-old boy waiting 15 months for a heart operation to emphasise Labour's commitment to the NHS forcing Mrs Thatcher to admit she had a private operation at the time of her choosing and to praise the virtues of private health insurance. She in turn launched her most outspoken attack yet on socialism, accusing Left-wing union leaders of promoting class conflict. Dr Owen said Mrs Thatcher's insensitive remarks on the NHS were 'outrageous'. With a week to go the Conservatives, worried by Labour's confidence, took advice from alternative ad-men.

FRIDAY 5 JUNE: A Marplan poll in the *Guardian* puts the Tories back at 44 per cent with Labour at 34 per cent and the Alliance at 20 per cent. Conservatives stepped up attack on Labour's defence policy saying Labour would leave no bargaining counters in arms negotiations and would destabilise NATO, setting out to highlight Mr Kinnock's lack of experience on the defence issue. Mrs Thatcher warned income tax would have to double to support Labour's spending plans. Labour was accused of 'cynical exploitation' of the 10-year-old boy waiting for heart surgery and the Conservatives claimed his condition 'not acute'. Mr Kinnock made an emotional speech claiming the high moral ground. The Alliance leadership seemed to have conceded defeat by predicting a Conservative victory.

SATURDAY 6 JUNE: Mr Lawson contrasts the Conservative commitment to progressive tax reductions with Labour's proposed tax increases and accused the Labour party of 'plain deceit' by failing to list its tax commitments in its manifesto. Mr Kinnock said 'absolutely definitely' no-one earning less that £500 a week would be worse off and dismissed Mr Lawson's claims as 'pure fabrication'. Mr Hattersley appealed to SDP voters to come home to the Labour party in a powerful speech. Dr Owen was disappointed at the Alliance's failure to win votes in the North of England.

SUNDAY 7 JUNE: Mrs Thatcher addressed a campaign rally with showbiz stars at Wembley and predicted thousands of traditional Labour supporters would desert the party. She called the Conservatives the party of peace. Mr Kinnock held his own rally in Islington where he attacked Mrs Thatcher: 'the needy have been denied and deprived'. He also pledged to reintroduce a 25p lower band of tax. Bryan Gould launched a drive to recapture former supporters who had drifted away to the Alliance. Dr Owen said the other two parties were trying to scare people from voting for the Alliance while Mr Steel said there was every prospect Alliance would hold the balance of power.

MONDAY 8 JUNE: Mrs Thatcher was in Venice for a 24-hour economic summit. Furious wrangles over Labour's plans for tax and benefit changes dominated with Mr Lawson accusing Mr Hattersley of 'lying through his teeth'. Labour's previously self-confident election campaign began to wilt under severe pressure from the Conservatives and from seemingly opposing impressions from Hattersley, Kinnock and Gould. Labour refused to give details of the tax bands and allowances they would introduce. Mr Kinnock accused the Prime Minister of lying over VAT increases.

TUESDAY 9 JUNE: A Marplan poll in the *Guardian* puts the Conservatives on 43 per cent, Labour on 35 per cent and the Alliance on 21 per cent. Mrs Thatcher, returning from Venice with an effective repudiation by world leaders of the non-nuclear defence policy of the Labour party, made an impassioned appeal to traditional Labour voters to desert 'the reckless party'. Voters had to choose between economic success and rising taxes and inflation. Both Opposition parties dismissed her Venice trip as a photo-opportunity. Mr Kinnock derided the Conservative's claims to be the party of the family and said Labour were the true 'one nation' party. Labour continued to hold the moral high ground while the Conservatives concentrated on Labour's tax policies. The Alliance appealed to the 'thoughtful voters' to stop Mrs Thatcher enjoying 'unfettered power'. Mr Steel's remarks hinted at an acceptance Mrs Thatcher would be returned with a reduced majority.

WEDNESDAY 10 JUNE: Mr Kinnock likened Mrs Thatcher to a tyrant as he made appeal to voters to reject the Conservative's mean and malicious policies and elect a Labour government. Claimed today was last day of Thatcherism.

THURSDAY 11 JUNE: Polling day – the Conservatives were returned for an historic third term under Mrs Thatcher with an overall majority in the House of Commons of 102, and a majority over Labour of 146.

Campaign Opinion Polls

Despite the problems generated by 'wobbly Thursday' the national opinion polls were remarkably consistent. This may explain why so many people concentrated upon the separate polls of marginal seats, which appeared to be sending a different message – one of a much closer contest. The table below sets out the individual national polls published during the 1987 election campaign (this list excludes telephone polls):

Poll	Date Pub.	Con %	Lab %	Allnc. %	Con Lead over Lab %
Marplan/*Express*	15.5	41	30	26	11
MORI/*S.Times*	17.5	44	30	25	14
Harris/*Observer*	17.5	42	33	23	9
Harris/TV-AM	18.5	42	32	24	10
Marplan/*Today*	19.5	41	33	24	8
Gallup/*Telegraph*	21.5	42	33	24	9
Marplan/*Guardian*	22.5	41	33	21	8
MORI/*S.Times*	24.5	44	31	24	13
Harris/*Observer*	24.5	41	34	22	7
Gallup/*S.Telegraph*	24.5	42	33	23	9
Marplan/*Today*	27.5	42	35	20	7
Gallup/*Telegraph*	28.5	44.5	36	18	8.5
Marplan/*Guardian*	29.5	44	32	21	12
Harris/*Observer*	31.5	41	37	21	4
MORI/*S.Times*	31.5	44	32	23	12
Marplan/*Guardian*	5.6	44	34	20	10
Gallup/*S.Telegraph*	31.5	41.5	34	22.5	7.5
Marplan/*Today*	2.6	44	33	21	11
Gallup/*Telegraph*	4.6	40.5	36.5	21.5	4
Harris/*Observer*	7.6	44	33	21	11
MORI/*S.Times*	7.6	43	32	24	11
Gallup/*S.Telegraph*	7.6	41.5	34.5	22.5	7
Marplan/*Today*	6.6	43	35	21	8
Marplan/*Guardian*	9.6	45	32	21	13
Gallup/*Telegraph*	10.6	41	34	23.5	7
Marplan/*Today*	10.6	43	35	21	8
MORI/*Times*	11.6	44	32	22	12
Marplan/*Guardian*	11.6	42	35	21	7
Actual Result (G.B.)	**11.6**	**43.3**	**31.5**	**23.1**	**11.8**

THE STATE OF THE NATION

How They Voted Last Time Round

All results taken from the 1987 General Election except those marked with an asterisk where subsequent by-elections occured (see Chapter One for changes).

Crosses indicate that the figures shown have been estimated to account for boundary changes affecting the Constituency.

England

PA No.	Seat name	Region	% Majority	Winner	% of Vote	Second	% of Vote	Third	% of Vote
4	Aldershot	SE	29.7	Con	59.0	All.	29.2	Lab	11.8
5	Aldridge, Brownhills	WM	25.0	Con	53.3	Lab	28.3	All.	18.3
6	Altrincham and Sale	NW	27.4	Con	53.5	All.	26.1	Lab	20.5
8	Amber Valley	EM	17.1	Con	51.4	Lab	34.4	All.	14.2
14	Arundel	SE	33.7	Con	61.3	All.	27.6	Lab	11.0
15	Ashfield	EM	8.0	Lab	41.7	Con	33.6	All.	24.7
16	Ashford	SE	29.2	Con	56.5	All.	27.3	Lab	14.7
17	Ashton-under-Lyne	NW	21.5	Lab	51.8	Con	30.3	All.	17.9
18	Aylesbury	SE	28.9	Con	57.5	All.	28.6	Lab	13.9
20	Banbury	SE	32.8	Con	56.2	All.	23.4	Lab	20.4
22	Barking	GL	9.9	Lab	44.3	Con	34.5	All.	21.2
23	Barnsley Central	YH	48.7	Lab	66.8	Con	18.1	All.	15.1
24	Barnsley East	YH	60.5	Lab	74.5	Con	14.0	All.	11.5
25	Barnsley West and Penistone	YH	30.7	Lab	57.3	Con	26.6	All.	16.0
26	Barrow and Furness	N	7.2	Con	46.5	Lab	39.3	All.	14.3
27	Basildon	SE	5.3	Con	43.5	Lab	38.3	All.	18.2
28	Basingstoke	SE	29.8	Con	56.1	All.	26.3	Lab	17.7
29	Bassetlaw	EM	10.6	Lab	48.1	Con	37.5	All.	14.4
30	Bath	SW	2.7	Con	45.4	All.	42.7	Lab	10.6
31	Batley and Spen	YH	2.3	Con	43.4	Lab	41.1	All.	14.3
32	Battersea	GL	1.8	Con	44.2	Lab	42.4	All.	11.9
33	Beaconsfield	SE	42.3	Con	66.0	All.	23.7	Lab	10.3
34	Beckenham	GL	30.4	Con	56.3	All.	25.9	Lab	17.8
35	Bedfordshire Mid	SE	36.0	Con	59.0	All.	23.0	Lab	18.1
36	Bedfordshire North	SE	29.1	Con	52.6	All.	23.5	Lab	23.2
37	Bedfordshire South West	SE	35.9	Con	58.2	All.	22.3	Lab	18.3
42	Berkshire East	SE	34.9	Con	60.3	All.	25.4	Lab	14.3
43	Berwick-upon-Tweed	N	22.6	All.	52.1	Con	29.5	Lab	17.5
44	Bethnal Green & Stepney	GL	16.5	Lab	48.3	All.	31.8	Con	19.2
45	Beverley	YH	20.9	Con	52.2	All.	31.3	Lab	16.4
46	Bexhill and Battle	SE	40.6	Con	66.4	All.	25.8	Lab	7.7
47	Bexleyheath	GL	25.3	Con	53.8	All.	28.5	Lab	17.8
48	Billericay	SE	29.3	Con	55.0	All.	25.6	Lab	19.5
49	Birkenhead	NW	32.4	Lab	58.7	Con	26.4	All.	14.9
50	Birmingham - Edgbaston	WM	23.0	Con	49.8	Lab	26.8	All.	21.0

PA No.	Seat name	Region	% Majority	Winner	% of Vote	Second	% of Vote	Third	% of Vote
51	Birmingham - Erdington	WM	6.6	Lab	45.9	Con	39.2	All.	14.9
52	Birmingham - Hall Green	WM	16.7	Con	44.9	Lab	28.2	All.	27.0
53	Birmingham - Hodge Hill	WM	11.7	Lab	48.7	Con	37.0	All.	14.4
54	Birmingham - Ladywood	WM	26.3	Lab	57.7	Con	31.4	All.	9.3
55	Birmingham - Northfield	WM	5.9	Con	45.1	Lab	39.2	All.	15.6
56	Birmingham - Perry Barr	WM	13.5	Lab	50.4	Con	36.9	All.	12.7
57	Birmingham - Selly Oak	WM	4.9	Con	44.2	Lab	39.3	All.	15.4
58	Birmingham - Small Heath	WM	45.2	Lab	66.3	Con	21.1	All.	10.5
59	Birmingham - Sparkbrook	WM	35.2	Lab	60.8	Con	25.7	All.	11.3
60	Birmingham - Yardley	WM	6.0	Con	42.6	Lab	36.6	All.	20.8
61	Bishop Auckland	N	13.2	Lab	48.0	Con	34.8	All.	17.2
62	Blaby	EM	35.6	Con	60.5	All.	25.0	Lab	14.5
63	Blackburn	NW	9.8	Lab	49.9	Con	40.1	All.	10.0
64	Blackpool North	NW	17.0	Con	48.0	Lab	31.0	All.	21.0
65	Blackpool South	NW	16.0	Con	48.0	Lab	32.1	All.	19.9
67	Blaydon	N	24.9	Lab	50.3	All.	25.5	Con	24.2
68	Blyth Valley	N	1.9	Lab	42.5	All.	40.6	Con	16.9
69	Bolsover	EM	27.9	Lab	56.2	Con	28.3	All.	15.5
70	Bolton North East	NW	1.7	Con	44.4	Lab	42.7	All.	13.0
71	Bolton South East	NW	23.1	Lab	54.3	Con	31.2	All.	14.5
72	Bolton West	NW	8.2	Con	44.3	Lab	36.1	All.	19.6
73	Boothferry	YH	33.3	Con	55.7	All.	22.4	Lab	21.9
74	Bootle	NW	46.8	Lab	66.9	Con	20.1	All.	13.0
75	Bosworth	EM	27.1	Con	54.4	All.	27.3	Lab	17.2
76	Bournemouth East	SW	27.7	Con	58.3	All.	30.6	Lab	11.1
77	Bournemouth West	SW	23.2	Con	55.2	All.	32.0	Lab	12.9
78	Bow & Poplar	GL	13.6	Lab	46.4	All.	32.7	Con	20.1
79	Bradford North	YH	3.3	Lab	42.8	Con	39.5	All.	17.7
80	Bradford South	YH	0.6	Lab	41.4	Con	40.8	All.	17.8
81	Bradford West	YH	15.2	Lab	51.9	Con	36.7	All.	11.4
82	Braintree	SE	27.7	Con	54.2	All.	26.5	Lab	19.3
84	Brent East	GL	4.2	Lab	42.6	Con	38.4	All.	14.5
85	Brent North	GL	35.1	Con	59.9	Lab	24.8	All.	15.3
86	Brent South	GL	19.5	Lab	51.9	Con	32.4	All.	15.7
87	Brentford and Isleworth	GL	14.5	Con	47.7	Lab	33.2	All.	17.5
88	Brentwood and Ongar	SE	35.5	Con	60.5	All.	25.0	Lab	13.2
90	Bridgwater	SW	21.2	Con	51.5	All.	30.3	Lab	18.2
91	Bridlington	YH	29.4	Con	54.8	All.	25.5	Lab	18.1
92	Brigg and Cleethorpes	YH	20.1	Con	48.7	All.	28.6	Lab	22.7
93	Brighton, Kemptown	SE	20.6	Con	53.5	Lab	32.9	All.	13.6
94	Brighton, Pavilion	SE	21.1	Con	50.8	Lab	29.7	All.	19.5
95	Bristol East	SW	8.2	Con	43.6	Lab	35.4	All.	20.4

PA No.	Seat name	Region	% Majority	Winner	% of Vote	Second	% of Vote	Third	% of Vote
96	Bristol North West	SW	12.0	Con	46.6	Lab	34.6	All.	18.8
97	Bristol South	SW	2.8	Lab	40.9	Con	38.1	All.	19.6
98	Bristol West	SW	14.2	Con	45.5	All.	31.3	Lab	20.9
99	Bromsgrove	WM	31.4	Con	54.7	Lab	23.3	All.	22.0
100	Broxbourne	SE	43.3	Con	63.2	All.	19.9	Lab	16.9
101	Broxtowe	EM	29.3	Con	53.6	Lab	24.3	All.	22.1
102	Buckingham	SE	34.7	Con	61.4	All.	26.7	Lab	11.9
103	Burnley	NW	14.5	Lab	48.4	Con	33.8	All.	17.8
104	Burton	WM	17.1	Con	50.7	Lab	33.6	All.	15.7
105	Bury North	NW	12.4	Con	50.1	Lab	37.8	All.	12.1
106	Bury South	NW	5.2	Con	46.1	Lab	40.9	All.	13.1
107	Bury St. Edmunds	EA	37.8	Con	59.3	All.	21.5	Lab	17.3
111	Calder Valley	YH	10.2	Con	43.5	Lab	33.4	All.	23.1
112	Cambridge	EA	9.4	Con	40.0	All.	30.6	Lab	28.3
113	Cambridgeshire North East	EA	2.5	Con	47.0	All.	44.5	Lab	8.5
114	Cambridgeshire South East	EA	31.3	Con	58.8	All.	27.5	Lab	13.7
115	Cambridgeshire South West	EA	28.8	Con	57.7	All.	29.0	Lab	13.3
116	Cannock and Burntwood	WM	4.9	Con	44.5	Lab	39.5	All.	16.0
117	Canterbury	SE	26.5	Con	53.8	All.	27.3	Lab	16.9
122	Carlisle	N	2.1	Lab	42.2	Con	40.1	All.	17.7
125	Carshalton & Wallington	GL	27.8	Con	54.0	All.	26.2	Lab	18.2
126	Castle Point	SE	38.9	Con	59.9	All.	21.1	Lab	19.0
128	Cheadle	NW	19.2	Con	55.1	All.	35.9	Lab	9.1
129	Chelmsford	SE	11.4	Con	51.9	All.	40.5	Lab	6.8
130	Chelsea	GL	46.6	Con	64.6	All.	17.9	Lab	15.4
131	Cheltenham	SW	7.8	Con	50.2	All.	42.3	Lab	7.5
132	Chertsey & Walton	SE	32.4	Con	59.5	All.	27.2	Lab	13.3
133	Chesham and Amersham	SE	35.0	Con	62.2	All.	27.1	Lab	9.3
134	Chester, City of	NW	9.2	Con	44.9	Lab	35.6	All.	19.5
135	Chesterfield	EM	15.9	Lab	45.5	All.	29.6	Con	25.0
136	Chichester	SE	33.5	Con	61.8	All.	28.3	Lab	7.9
137	Chingford	GL	41.2	Con	62.3	All.	21.0	Lab	15.3
138	Chipping Barnet	GL	34.9	Con	57.9	All.	23.0	Lab	19.0
139	Chislehurst	GL	34.6	Con	57.6	All.	23.0	Lab	19.4
140	Chorley	NW	13.3	Con	48.0	Lab	34.7	All.	16.1
141	Christchurch	SW	41.4	Con	65.9	All.	24.6	Lab	9.6
142	Cirencester and Tewkesbury	SW	19.3	Con	55.4	All.	36.0	Lab	8.2
143	C. of London & Westminster Sth	GL	36.0	Con	57.8	All.	21.8	Lab	20.4
149	Colchester North	SE	21.8	Con	52.3	All.	30.5	Lab	17.2
150	Colchester South & Maldon	SE	24.4	Con	54.9	All.	30.6	Lab	14.5
151	Colne Valley	YH	3.0	Con	36.4	All.	33.4	Lab	29.1
152	Congleton	NW	14.5	Con	48.3	All.	33.8	Lab	17.9

PA No.	Seat name	Region	% Majority	Winner	% of Vote	Second	% of Vote	Third	% of Vote
154	Copeland	N	4.3	Lab	47.2	Con	43.0	All.	9.1
155	Corby	EM	3.4	Con	44.3	Lab	40.9	All.	14.8
156	Cornwall North	SW	9.8	Con	51.7	All.	41.9	Lab	6.4
157	Cornwall South East	SW	11.8	Con	51.6	All.	39.8	Lab	8.7
158	Coventry North East	WM	24.9	Lab	54.3	Con	29.3	All.	15.8
159	Coventry North West	WM	14.3	Lab	49.0	Con	34.7	All.	16.3
160	Coventry South East	WM	17.6	Lab	47.5	Con	29.9	All.	21.4
161	Coventry South West	WM	6.2	Con	43.3	Lab	37.0	All.	19.7
162	Crawley	SE	20.6	Con	49.6	Lab	29.0	All.	21.5
163	Crewe and Nantwich	NW	1.9	Lab	44.0	Con	42.1	All.	13.9
164	Crosby	NW	10.3	Con	46.2	All.	35.9	Lab	18.0
165	Croydon Central	GL	32.3	Con	56.6	Lab	24.4	All.	19.0
166	Croydon North East	GL	28.5	Con	55.0	Lab	26.5	All.	18.5
167	Croydon North West	GL	10.0	Con	47.0	Lab	37.0	All.	16.0
168	Croydon South	GL	39.7	Con	64.1	All.	24.3	Lab	9.8
173	Dagenham	GL	6.0	Lab	44.4	Con	38.5	All.	17.1
174	Darlington	N	5.0	Con	46.6	Lab	41.6	All.	11.8
175	Dartford	SE	26.0	Con	53.5	Lab	27.5	All.	18.2
176	Daventry	EM	36.4	Con	57.9	All.	21.6	Lab	20.5
177	Davyhulme	NW	16.2	Con	46.6	Lab	30.4	All.	23.0
179	Denton and Reddish	NW	15.7	Lab	49.6	Con	33.9	All.	16.6
180	Derby North	EM	11.6	Con	48.8	Lab	37.3	All.	13.4
181	Derby South	EM	3.2	Lab	43.7	Con	40.5	All.	15.8
182	Derbyshire North-East	EM	6.7	Lab	44.4	Con	37.7	All.	17.9
183	Derbyshire South	EM	15.9	Con	49.1	Lab	33.2	All.	17.7
184	Derbyshire West	EM	17.9	Con	53.1	All.	35.2	Lab	11.7
185	Devizes	SW	26.9	Con	54.8	All.	27.9	Lab	17.3
186	Devon North	SW	8.1	Con	50.9	All.	42.8	Lab	6.3
187	Devon West & Torridge	SW	11.0	Con	50.3	All.	39.2	Lab	8.5
188	Dewsbury	YH	0.8	Lab	42.4	Con	41.6	All.	16.0
189	Doncaster Central	YH	16.0	Lab	51.2	Con	35.2	All.	13.6
190	Doncaster North	YH	37.4	Lab	61.8	Con	24.4	All.	13.9
191	Don Valley	YH	20.9	Lab	53.1	Con	32.3	All.	14.6
192	Dorset North	SW	20.7	Con	57.0	All.	36.4	Lab	6.6
193	Dorset South	SW	27.4	Con	54.8	All.	27.5	Lab	17.3
194	Dorset West	SW	24.6	Con	56.2	All.	31.7	Lab	12.2
195	Dover	SE	11.9	Con	46.0	Lab	34.1	All.	19.9
198	Dudley East	WM	6.4	Lab	45.9	Con	39.5	All.	14.7
199	Dudley West	WM	15.8	Con	49.8	Lab	34.0	All.	16.2
200	Dulwich	GL	0.5	Con	42.4	Lab	42.0	All.	14.5
207	Durham City of	N	11.8	Lab	44.9	All.	33.2	Con	21.9
208	Durham North	N	33.6	Lab	56.2	All.	22.6	Con	21.2
209	Durham North West	N	22.5	Lab	50.9	Con	28.4	All.	20.7
210	Ealing, Acton	GL	25.6	Con	53.4	Lab	27.8	All.	18.8
211	Ealing North	GL	28.2	Con	56.0	Lab	27.8	All.	15.1
212	Ealing Southall	GL	15.3	Lab	50.7	Con	35.5	All.	13.3
213	Easington	N	51.8	Lab	68.1	Con	16.3	All.	15.6
214	Eastbourne*	SE	30.2	Con	59.9	All.	29.7	Lab	8.8
216	Eastleigh	SE	19.2	Con	51.3	All.	32.0	Lab	16.7
219	Eccles	NW	19.4	Lab	50.8	Con	31.4	All.	17.9
220	Eddisbury	NW	27.5	Con	51.1	All.	23.7	Lab	23.5
227	Edmonton	GL	15.2	Con	51.2	Lab	36.0	All.	12.8

PA No.	Seat name	Region	% Majority	Winner	% of Vote	Second	% of Vote	Third	% of Vote
228	Ellesmere Port & Neston	NW	3.2	Con	44.4	Lab	41.2	All.	14.1
229	Elmet	YH	9.8	Con	46.9	Lab	37.1	All.	16.0
230	Eltham	GL	15.5	Con	47.5	Lab	32.0	All.	20.5
231	Enfield North	GL	27.1	Con	55.5	Lab	28.5	All.	14.7
232	Enfield Southgate	GL	37.9	Con	58.8	All.	20.9	Lab	18.9
233	Epping Forest*	SE	41.6	Con	60.9	All.	19.4	Lab	18.4
234	Epsom and Ewell	SE	39.0	Con	62.2	All.	23.2	Lab	14.6
235	Erewash	EM	16.5	Con	48.6	Lab	32.1	All.	19.3
236	Erith and Crayford	GL	15.6	Con	45.2	Lab	29.5	All.	25.3
237	Esher	SE	39.9	Con	65.6	All.	25.7	Lab	8.8
238	Exeter	SW	12.6	Con	44.4	All.	31.8	Lab	22.5
241	Falmouth and Camborne	SW	9.3	Con	43.9	All.	34.6	Lab	20.9
242	Fareham	SE	31.2	Con	61.1	All.	29.9	Lab	9.1
243	Faversham	SE	23.0	Con	51.1	All.	28.1	Lab	20.8
244	Feltham and Heston	GL	9.1	Con	46.5	Lab	37.4	All.	16.1
248	Finchley	GL	22.3	Con	53.9	Lab	31.7	All.	13.9
249	Folkestone and Hythe	SE	18.1	Con	55.4	All.	37.3	Lab	7.4
251	Fulham	GL	15.1	Con	51.8	Lab	36.7	All.	10.4
252	Fylde	NW	36.5	Con	60.7	All.	24.2	Lab	14.3
253	Gainsborough & Horncastle	EM	18.1	Con	53.3	All.	35.2	Lab	11.5
255	Gateshead East	N	35.3	Lab	59.2	Con	23.9	All.	16.9
256	Gedling	EM	30.6	Con	54.5	Lab	23.9	All.	21.6
257	Gillingham	SE	23.2	Con	53.1	All.	29.9	Lab	17.1
258	Glanford & Scunthorpe	YH	0.9	Lab	43.5	Con	42.6	All.	13.7
270	Gloucester	SW	20.1	Con	49.7	Lab	29.6	All.	20.7
271	Gloucestershire West	SW	18.5	Con	46.2	Lab	27.8	All.	26.0
273	Gosport	SE	26.9	Con	58.5	All.	31.6	Lab	9.9
275	Grantham	EM	35.8	Con	57.1	All.	21.3	Lab	20.5
276	Gravesham	SE	15.2	Con	50.1	Lab	34.8	All.	15.1
277	Great Grimsby	YH	17.0	Lab	45.5	Con	28.5	All.	26.1
278	Great Yarmouth	EA	20.6	Con	51.7	Lab	31.1	All.	17.1
280	Greenwich	GL	5.7	All.	40.6	Lab	34.9	Con	23.3
281	Guildford	SE	21.5	Con	55.5	All.	33.9	Lab	10.6
282	Hackney North & Stoke Newngtn	GL	19.8	Lab	48.7	Con	28.9	All.	19.2
283	Hackney South & Shoreditch	GL	19.1	Lab	47.9	Con	28.7	All.	22.4
284	Halesowen & Stourbridge	WM	22.3	Con	50.1	Lab	27.8	All.	22.1
285	Halifax	YH	2.1	Lab	43.4	Con	41.3	All.	15.4
286	Halton	NW	25.2	Lab	55.5	Con	30.2	All.	14.3
288	Hammersmith	GL	6.9	Lab	45.0	Con	38.1	All.	14.9
289	Hampshire East	SE	35.6	Con	64.5	All.	28.9	Lab	6.7
290	Hampshire North West	SE	24.7	Con	57.8	All.	33.1	Lab	9.1
291	Hampstead & Highgate	GL	4.9	Con	42.5	Lab	37.6	All.	19.3
292	Harborough	EM	31.7	Con	59.4	All.	27.7	Lab	12.9
293	Harlow	SE	10.7	Con	47.2	Lab	36.6	All.	16.2
294	Harrogate	YH	21.2	Con	55.6	All.	34.3	Lab	10.1

PA No.	Seat name	Region	% Majority	Winner	% of Vote	Second	% of Vote	Third	% of Vote
295	Harrow East	GL	30.7	Con	54.2	Lab	23.6	All.	22.2
296	Harrow West	GL	28.0	Con	55.2	All.	27.2	Lab	17.5
297	Hartlepool	N	14.5	Lab	48.5	Con	33.9	All.	14.1
298	Harwich	SE	21.3	Con	51.8	All.	30.5	Lab	17.5
299	Hastings & Rye	SE	14.1	Con	50.1	All.	36.0	Lab	13.1
300	Havant	SE	29.0	Con	57.1	All.	28.1	Lab	14.1
301	Hayes and Harlington	GL	13.8	Con	49.2	Lab	35.5	All.	15.3
302	Hazel Grove	NW	3.4	Con	45.5	All.	42.0	Lab	11.8
303	Hemsworth*	YH	49.8	Lab	67.0	Con	17.2	All.	15.8
304	Hendon North	GL	30.2	Con	55.6	Lab	25.5	All.	18.9
305	Hendon South	GL	32.0	Con	55.6	All.	23.6	Lab	20.9
306	Henley	SE	34.8	Con	61.1	All.	26.3	Lab	12.6
307	Hereford	WM	2.7	Con	47.5	All.	44.8	Lab	7.7
308	Hertford & Stortford	SE	29.2	Con	57.5	All.	28.3	Lab	12.8
309	Hertfordshire North	SE	17.9	Con	49.7	All.	31.8	Lab	18.5
310	Hertfordshire South West	SE	26.9	Con	55.8	All.	28.9	Lab	15.3
311	Hertfordshire West	SE	23.4	Con	49.7	All.	26.3	Lab	24.0
312	Hertsmere	SE	32.8	Con	56.6	All.	23.8	Lab	19.6
313	Hexham	N	17.9	Con	49.6	All.	31.7	Lab	18.0
314	Heywood & Middleton	NW	15.6	Lab	49.9	Con	34.3	All.	15.8
315	High Peak	EM	16.9	Con	45.7	Lab	28.8	All.	25.6
316	Holborn & St. Pancras	GL	19.5	Lab	50.6	Con	31.1	All.	17.6
317	Holland with Boston	EM	37.2	Con	57.9	All.	20.7	Lab	20.6
318	Honiton	SW	28.1	Con	59.2	All.	31.1	Lab	8.5
319	Hornchurch	GL	22.8	Con	51.2	Lab	28.4	All.	20.5
320	Hornsey & Wood Green	GL	3.0	Con	43.0	Lab	40.0	All.	15.1
321	Horsham	SE	38.3	Con	63.7	All.	25.4	Lab	8.7
322	Houghton & Washington	N	36.4	Lab	59.1	Con	22.7	All.	18.2
323	Hove	SE	37.0	Con	58.8	All.	21.8	Lab	18.3
324	Huddersfield	YH	14.5	Lab	45.9	Con	31.4	All.	21.5
325	Hull East	YH	30.3	Lab	56.3	Con	26.0	All.	17.7
326	Hull North	YH	23.8	Lab	51.2	Con	27.3	All.	21.5
327	Hull West	YH	21.6	Lab	51.9	Con	30.3	All.	17.7
328	Huntingdon	EA	42.4	Con	63.6	All.	21.2	Lab	13.9
329	Hyndburn	NW	4.6	Con	44.4	Lab	39.8	All.	15.2
330	Ilford North	GL	27.6	Con	54.9	Lab	27.4	All.	17.7
331	Ilford South	GL	10.9	Con	48.4	Lab	37.5	All.	14.1
333	Ipswich	EA	1.7	Con	44.4	Lab	42.7	All.	12.6
334	Isle of Wight	SE	8.2	Con	51.2	All.	43.0	Lab	5.9
335	Islington North	GL	24.6	Lab	50.0	Con	25.3	All.	21.8
336	Islington South & Finsbury	GL	2.0	Lab	40.1	All.	38.1	Con	20.6
338	Jarrow	N	40.2	Lab	63.4	Con	23.2	All.	13.3
339	Keighley	YH	10.7	Con	45.8	Lab	35.0	All.	19.2
340	Kensington*	GL	14.3	Con	47.5	Lab	33.3	All.	17.3
341	Kent Mid	SE	28.4	Con	55.1	All.	26.8	Lab	18.1
342	Kettering	EM	21.8	Con	51.1	All.	29.3	Lab	19.7
345	Kingston Upon Thames	GL	26.0	Con	56.2	All.	30.2	Lab	13.2

PA No.	Seat name	Region	% Majority	Winner	% of Vote	Second	% of Vote	Third	% of Vote
346	Kingswood	SW	7.5	Con	44.9	Lab	37.4	All.	17.7
348	Knowsley North	NW	53.7	Lab	69.9	All.	16.2	Con	12.5
349	Knowsley South*	NW	42.8	Lab	64.5	Con	21.6	All.	13.9
351	Lancashire West	NW	2.2	Con	43.7	Lab	41.5	All.	14.8
352	Lancaster	NW	14.2	Con	46.7	Lab	32.4	All.	19.9
353	Langbaurgh*	N	3.4	Con	41.7	Lab	38.4	All.	19.9
354	Leeds Central	YH	30.1	Lab	55.6	Con	25.5	All.	17.9
355	Leeds East	YH	22.2	Lab	48.7	Con	26.6	All.	24.7
356	Leeds North East	YH	17.3	Con	45.6	All.	28.3	Lab	25.3
357	Leeds North West	YH	10.1	Con	43.5	All.	33.5	Lab	21.7
358	Leeds South & Morley	YH	15.4	Lab	49.6	Con	34.1	All.	16.3
359	Leeds West	YH	9.6	Lab	43.2	All.	33.6	Con	23.2
360	Leicester East	EM	3.7	Lab	46.2	Con	42.5	All.	11.4
361	Leicester South	EM	3.3	Lab	44.2	Con	40.8	All.	13.8
362	Leicester West	EM	2.4	Lab	44.5	Con	42.1	All.	13.5
363	Leicestershire NW	EM	13.4	Con	47.6	Lab	34.3	All.	17.2
364	Leigh	NW	32.4	Lab	58.6	Con	26.3	All.	15.1
365	Leominster	WM	25.9	Con	57.9	All.	31.9	Lab	8.2
366	Lewes	SE	24.2	Con	56.8	All.	32.6	Lab	8.8
367	Lewisham, Deptford	GL	17.9	Lab	49.6	Con	31.7	All.	17.3
368	Lewisham East	GL	10.9	Con	45.1	Lab	34.2	All.	20.7
369	Lewisham West	GL	8.3	Con	46.2	Lab	37.9	All.	15.9
370	Leyton	GL	11.6	Lab	41.2	All.	29.7	Con	29.1
371	Lincoln	EM	12.8	Con	46.5	Lab	33.7	All.	19.4
372	Lindsey East	EM	15.5	Con	52.2	All.	36.7	Lab	11.1
374	Littleborough & Saddleworth	NW	12.1	Con	43.1	All.	30.9	Lab	26.0
375	Liverpool - Broadgreen	NW	12.6	Lab	48.6	All.	36.0	Con	15.5
376	Liverpool - Garston	NW	29.7	Lab	53.6	Con	23.9	All.	22.4
377	Liverpool - Mossley Hill	NW	4.9	All.	43.7	Lab	38.8	Con	17.5
378	Liverpool - Riverside	NW	59.4	Lab	73.2	Con	13.8	All.	11.2
379	Liverpool - Walton*	NW	43.2	Lab	64.4	All.	21.2	Con	14.4
380	Liverpool - West Derby	NW	46.1	Lab	65.3	Con	19.2	All.	15.5
384	Loughborough	EM	30.2	Con	54.7	Lab	24.5	All.	19.7
385	Ludlow	WM	22.9	Con	53.9	All.	31.0	Lab	15.1
386	Luton North	SE	27.0	Con	53.8	Lab	26.8	All.	19.4
387	Luton South	SE	9.6	Con	46.2	Lab	36.7	All.	17.1
388	Macclesfield	NW	32.4	Con	56.4	All.	24.0	Lab	19.6
389	Maidstone	SE	18.7	Con	52.4	All.	33.8	Lab	12.5
390	Makerfield	NW	29.0	Lab	56.3	Con	27.3	All.	16.5
391	Manchester - Blackley	NW	23.6	Lab	52.4	Con	28.8	All.	18.8
392	Manchester - Central	NW	49.4	Lab	68.2	Scon	18.8	All.	13.1
393	Manchester - Gorton	NW	31.1	Lab	54.4	Con	23.3	All.	21.7
394	Manchester - Withington	NW	6.7	Lab	43.0	Con	36.2	All.	19.8
395	Manchester - Wythenshawe	NW	28.2	Lab	56.8	Con	28.6	All.	14.1
396	Mansfield	EM	0.1	Lab	37.5	Con	37.4	All.	22.2
397	Medway	SE	21.2	Con	51.0	Lab	29.8	All.	18.1
399	Meriden	WM	29.0	Con	55.1	Lab	26.1	All.	18.8
401	Middlesbrough	N	34.7	Lab	59.7	Con	25.0	All.	15.3
403	Milton Keynes NE†	SE	14.9	Con	48.5	All.	33.6	Lab	15.9
404	Milton Keynes SW†	SE	18.1	Con	48.0	Lab	29.9	All.	22.1

PA No.	Seat name	Region	% Majority	Winner	% of Vote	Second	% of Vote	Third	% of Vote
405	Mitcham & Morden	GL	13.0	Con	48.2	Lab	35.2	All.	16.6
406	Mole Valley	SE	30.8	Con	60.8	All.	29.9	Lab	9.3
412	Morecambe & Lunesdale	NW	27.8	Con	52.7	All.	24.9	Lab	22.5
416	Newark	EM	25.8	Con	53.5	Lab	27.7	All.	18.8
417	Newbury	SE	28.4	Con	60.1	All.	31.7	Lab	8.1
418	Newcastle under Lyme	WM	9.6	Lab	40.5	All.	30.9	Con	27.9
419	Newcastle upon Tyne Central	N	5.4	Lab	44.2	Con	38.8	All.	15.8
420	Newcastle upon Tyne East	N	29.8	Lab	56.5	Con	26.7	All.	16.0
421	Newcastle upon Tyne North	N	10.0	Lab	42.7	All.	32.7	Con	24.6
422	New Forest	SE	37.8	Con	64.7	All.	26.9	Lab	8.5
423	Newham North-East	GL	21.1	Lab	51.9	Con	30.8	All.	17.4
424	Newham North-West	GL	30.1	Lab	55.4	Con	25.4	All.	17.4
425	Newham South	GL	9.3	Lab	43.5	Con	34.2	All.	22.2
429	Norfolk, Mid	EA	31.2	Con	56.7	All.	25.5	Lab	17.8
430	Norfolk North	EA	28.3	Con	53.3	All.	25.0	Lab	19.9
431	Norfolk North West	EA	18.6	Con	50.6	All.	31.9	Lab	17.5
432	Norfolk South	EA	19.6	Con	53.4	All.	33.9	Lab	12.7
433	Norfolk South West	EA	36.2	Con	57.6	All.	21.4	Lab	21.0
434	Normanton	YH	15.5	Lab	49.5	Con	34.1	All.	16.4
435	Northampton North	EM	17.9	Con	48.0	Lab	30.1	All.	20.7
436	Northampton South	EM	31.1	Con	55.7	Lab	24.6	All.	18.6
437	Northavon	SW	22.7	Con	54.4	All.	31.7	Lab	13.9
438	Norwich North	EA	15.7	Con	45.8	Lab	30.2	All.	24.0
439	Norwich South	EA	0.7	Lab	37.9	Con	37.3	All.	24.9
440	Norwood	GL	12.5	Lab	48.5	Con	36.0	All.	14.7
441	Nottingham East	EM	1.0	Con	42.9	Lab	42.0	All.	14.7
442	Nottingham North	EM	3.3	Lab	44.9	Con	41.6	All.	11.7
443	Nottingham South	EM	4.2	Con	44.7	Lab	40.5	All.	14.8
444	Nuneaton	WM	10.3	Con	44.9	Lab	34.6	All.	19.2
446	Old Bexley & Sidcup	GL	41.5	Con	62.1	All.	20.6'	Lab	17.3
447	Oldham Central & Royton	NW	13.9	Lab	48.1	Con	34.3	All.	17.6
448	Oldham West	NW	14.5	Lab	49.4	Con	34.9	All.	15.8
450	Orpington	GL	27.2	Con	58.2	All.	31.0	Lab	10.7
451	Oxford East	SE	2.6	Lab	43.0	Con	40.4	All.	15.6
452	Oxford West & Abingdon	SE	9.0	Con	46.4	All.	37.4	Lab	14.9
455	Peckham	GL	28.8	Lab	54.5	Con	25.7	All.	17.8
457	Pendle	NW	5.1	Con	40.4	Lab	35.3	All.	24.3
458	Penrith & The Border	N	31.6	Con	60.3	All.	28.7	Lab	11.0
460	Peterborough	EA	15.8	Con	49.4	Lab	33.6	All.	16.1
461	Plymouth, Devonport	SW	13.0	All.	42.3	Con	29.3	Lab	28.5
462	Plymouth, Drake	SW	8.0	Con	41.3	All.	33.3	Lab	24.1
463	Plymouth, Sutton	SW	7.9	Con	45.8	All.	37.8	Lab	16.4
464	Pontefract & Castleford	YH	45.7	Lab	66.9	Con	21.2	All.	11.3
466	Poole	SW	24.9	Con	57.5	All.	32.6	Lab	9.9
467	Portsmouth North	SE	30.6	Con	55.3	All.	24.7	Lab	20.0

PA No.	Seat name	Region	% Majority	Winner	% of Vote	Second	% of Vote	Third	% of Vote
468	Portsmouth South	SE	0.4	Con	43.3	All.	42.9	Lab	13.0
469	Preston	NW	23.9	Lab	52.5	Con	28.5	All.	19.0
470	Pudsey	YH	11.5	Con	45.5	All.	34.0	Lab	20.5
471	Putney	GL	14.4	Con	50.5	Lab	36.1	All.	12.4
472	Ravensbourne	GL	37.7	Con	63.0	All.	25.3	Lab	11.3
473	Reading East	SE	30.6	Con	53.8	All.	23.2	Lab	21.5
474	Reading West	SE	32.9	Con	55.3	All.	22.4	Lab	21.3
475	Redcar	N	16.0	Lab	47.3	Con	31.3	All.	21.4
476	Reigate	SE	34.8	Con	59.3	All.	24.5	Lab	14.3
479	Ribble Valley*	NW	39.4	Con	60.9	All.	21.4	Lab	17.7
480	Richmond & Barnes	GL	3.9	Con	47.7	All.	43.9	Lab	7.1
481	Richmond (Yorks)*	YH	34.3	Con	61.2	All.	27.0	Lab	11.8
482	Rochdale	NW	5.4	All.	43.4	Lab	38.0	Con	18.7
483	Rochford	SE	33.2	Con	60.4	All.	27.3	Lab	12.3
484	Romford	GL	33.2	Con	56.0	Lab	22.8	All.	20.2
485	Romsey & Waterside	SE	24.4	Con	56.4	All.	32.0	Lab	11.5
487	Rossendale & Darwen	NW	8.3	Con	46.6	Lab	38.3	All.	15.1
488	Rotherham	YH	37.6	Lab	59.7	Con	22.1	All.	18.2
489	Rother Valley	YH	31.5	Lab	56.4	Con	24.9	All.	18.4
491	Rugby & Kenilworth	WM	26.6	Con	51.6	Lab	24.9	All.	23.5
492	Ruislip, Northwood	GL	38.8	Con	62.6	All.	23.9	Lab	13.5
493	Rushcliffe	EM	35.8	Con	58.8	All.	23.0	Lab	16.5
494	Rutland & Melton	EM	38.5	Con	62.0	All.	23.5	Lab	14.5
495	Ryedale	YH	14.8	Con	53.3	All.	38.6	Lab	8.1
496	Saffron Walden	SE	28.7	Con	57.7	All.	29.0	Lab	11.5
497	St. Albans	SE	18.0	Con	52.5	All.	34.5	Lab	11.5
498	St. Helens North	NW	26.4	Lab	53.7	Con	27.3	All.	19.1
499	St. Helens South	NW	27.9	Lab	54.6	Con	26.7	All.	18.7
500	St. Ives	SW	14.5	Con	48.4	All.	33.8	Lab	17.8
501	Salford East	NW	31.4	Lab	58.8	Con	27.4	All.	13.3
502	Salisbury	SW	19.9	Con	54.9	All.	35.0	Lab	9.5
503	Scarborough	YH	24.9	Con	50.7	All.	25.7	Lab	23.6
504	Sedgefield	N	28.2	Lab	56.0	Con	27.9	All.	16.1
505	Selby	YH	24.9	Con	51.6	Lab	26.8	All.	21.7
506	Sevenoaks	SE	31.0	Con	58.9	All.	27.9	Lab	13.2
507	Sheffield Attercliffe	YH	35.2	Lab	57.8	Con	22.7	All.	19.5
508	Sheffield Brightside	YH	54.2	Lab	69.9	Con	15.7	All.	14.4
509	Sheffield Central	YH	50.6	Lab	67.7	Con	17.1	All.	13.9
510	Sheffield Hallam	YH	13.8	Con	46.3	All.	32.5	Lab	20.4
511	Sheffield Heeley	YH	27.1	Lab	53.4	Con	26.3	All.	20.3
512	Sheffield Hillsborough	YH	5.5	Lab	44.0	All.	38.5	Con	17.5
513	Sherwood	EM	7.7	Con	45.9	Lab	38.2	All.	16.0
514	Shipley	YH	23.2	Con	49.5	All.	26.3	Lab	23.3
515	Shoreham	SE	30.9	Con	60.9	All.	30.0	Lab	9.1
516	Shrewsbury & Atcham	WM	16.7	Con	47.8	All.	31.2	Lab	19.8
517	Shropshire North	WM	24.8	Con	52.2	All.	27.4	Lab	20.4
518	Skipton & Ripon	YH	30.6	Con	59.0	All.	28.4	Lab	11.2
519	Slough	SE	7.3	Con	47.0	Lab	39.6	All.	13.4
520	Solihull	WM	37.1	Con	61.1	All.	24.0	Lab	15.0
521	Somerton & Frome	SW	17.5	Con	53.7	All.	36.3	Lab	10.0
522	Southampton Itchen	SE	12.2	Con	44.3	Lab	32.1	All.	23.6

PA No.	Seat name	Region	% Majority	Winner	% of Vote	Second	% of Vote	Third	% of Vote
523	Southampton Test	SE	12.3	Con	45.6	Lab	33.3	All.	21.2
524	Southend East	SE	33.8	Con	58.0	All.	24.2	Lab	17.8
525	Southend West	SE	16.3	Con	54.4	All.	38.1	Lab	7.6
526	South Hams	SW	21.3	Con	55.4	All.	34.1	Lab	8.2
527	Southport	NW	3.4	All.	47.9	Con	44.5	Lab	6.4
528	South Ribble	NW	14.2	Con	47.2	Lab	33.1	All.	19.7
529	South Shields	N	32.2	Lab	57.9	Con	25.7	All.	15.5
530	Southwark & Bermondsey	GL	7.7	All.	47.4	Lab	39.7	Con	12.6
531	Spelthorne	SE	37.1	Con	60.0	All.	22.9	Lab	17.1
532	Stafford	WM	23.8	Con	51.3	All.	27.5	Lab	21.2
533	Staffordshire Mid*	WM	25.9	Con	50.6	Lab	24.7	All.	23.2
534	Staffordshire Moorlands	WM	24.2	Con	52.9	Lab	28.8	All.	18.3
535	Staffordshire South	WM	40.8	Con	60.9	All.	20.1	Lab	19.1
536	Staffordshire South East	WM	20.5	Con	47.2	All.	26.7	Lab	26.1
537	Stalybridge & Hyde	NW	11.2	Lab	48.4	Con	37.1	All.	14.5
538	Stamford & Spalding	EM	25.5	Con	56.5	All.	31.0	Lab	12.5
539	Stevenage	SE	9.5	Con	42.1	All.	32.5	Lab	25.4
541	Stockport	NW	6.1	Con	41.4	Lab	35.3	All.	22.1
542	Stockton North	N	16.6	Lab	49.1	Con	32.5	All.	18.3
543	Stockton South	N	1.3	Con	35.0	All.	33.7	Lab	31.3
544	Stoke on Trent Central	WM	21.5	Lab	52.5	Con	31.0	All.	16.4
545	Stoke on Trent North	WM	15.7	Lab	47.1	Con	31.3	All.	21.6
546	Stoke on Trent South	WM	9.7	Lab	47.5	Con	37.8	All.	14.7
548	Stratford upon Avon	WM	34.1	Con	61.9	All.	27.9	Lab	10.2
550	Streatham	GL	5.7	Con	44.9	Lab	39.2	All.	15.8
551	Stretford	NW	22.7	Lab	55.2	Con	32.5	All.	12.4
552	Stroud	SW	18.9	Con	50.2	All.	31.3	Lab	18.5
553	Suffolk Central	EA	27.0	Con	53.7	All.	26.7	Lab	19.6
554	Suffolk Coastal	EA	25.9	Con	55.7	All.	29.8	Lab	12.8
555	Suffolk South	EA	25.6	Con	53.4	All.	27.9	Lab	18.7
556	Sunderland North	N	27.5	Lab	55.8	Con	28.3	All.	16.0
557	Sunderland South	N	23.7	Lab	54.1	Con	30.4	All.	14.6
558	Surbiton	GL	27.4	Con	55.9	All.	28.5	Lab	14.4
559	Surrey East	SE	39.5	Con	63.4	All.	23.9	Lab	10.4
560	Surrey North West	SE	39.1	Con	64.0	All.	24.8	Lab	11.2
561	Surrey South West	SE	25.1	Con	59.5	All.	34.4	Lab	5.6
562	Sussex Mid	SE	29.6	Con	61.1	All.	31.5	Lab	7.4
563	Sutton & Cheam	GL	32.1	Con	60.8	All.	28.6	Lab	10.6
564	Sutton Coldfield	WM	39.3	Con	64.0	All.	24.7	Lab	11.3
567	Swindon	SW	7.3	Con	43.8	Lab	36.6	All.	19.6
568	Tatton	NW	31.0	Con	54.6	All.	23.6	Lab	21.3
569	Taunton	SW	17.6	Con	51.4	All.	33.8	Lab	14.9
571	Teignbridge	SW	18.1	Con	53.2	All.	35.1	Lab	11.1
572	Thanet North	SE	34.7	Con	58.0	All.	23.3	Lab	16.7
573	Thanet South	SE	29.6	Con	54.3	All.	24.8	Lab	20.9
574	Thurrock	SE	1.4	Con	42.5	Lab	41.0	All.	16.5
575	Tiverton	SW	16.9	Con	55.0	All.	38.0	Lab	6.3
576	Tonbridge & Malling	SE	27.5	Con	56.9	All.	29.4	Lab	13.1
577	Tooting	GL	3.0	Lab	44.2	Con	41.3	All.	13.2
578	Torbay	SW	16.4	Con	54.0	All.	37.6	Lab	8.4

PA No.	Seat name	Region	% Majority	Winner	% of Vote	Second	% of Vote	Third	% of Vote
580	Tottenham	GL	8.2	Lab	43.6	Con	35.4	All.	17.9
581	Truro	SW	8.2	All.	49.0	Con	40.8	Lab	10.2
582	Tunbridge Wells	SE	28.5	Con	58.4	All.	30.0	Lab	11.6
584	Twickenham	GL	13.5	Con	51.9	All.	38.3	Lab	8.4
585	Tyne Bridge	N	42.4	Lab	63.0	Con	20.6	All.	16.4
586	Tynemouth	N	4.5	Con	43.2	Lab	38.8	All.	18.0
588	Upminster	GL	33.6	Con	55.8	Lab	22.1	All.	22.1
590	Uxbridge	GL	33.0	Con	56.5	Lab	23.4	All.	19.0
592	Vauxhall*	GL	21.2	Lab	50.2	Con	29.0	All.	18.2
593	Wakefield	YH	5.3	Lab	46.6	Con	41.3	All.	12.1
594	Wallasey	NW	0.5	Con	42.5	Lab	42.0	All.	15.6
595	Wallsend	N	33.7	Lab	56.8	Con	23.2	All.	20.0
596	Walsall North	WM	3.6	Lab	42.6	Con	39.0	All.	18.4
597	Walsall South	WM	2.2	Lab	44.9	Con	42.7	All.	12.4
598	Walthamstow	GL	4.3	Con	39.0	Lab	34.7	All.	25.1
599	Wansbeck	N	34.4	Lab	57.5	All.	23.1	Con	19.4
600	Wansdyke	SW	26.4	Con	51.6	All.	25.2	Lab	23.3
601	Wanstead & Woodford	GL	39.1	Con	61.3	All.	22.1	Lab	16.6
602	Wantage	SE	23.5	Con	54.0	All.	30.5	Lab	15.6
603	Warley East	WM	14.4	Lab	50.2	Con	35.8	All.	14.0
604	Warley West	WM	13.4	Lab	49.2	Con	35.8	All.	15.0
605	Warrington North	NW	14.1	Lab	48.2	Con	34.1	All.	17.7
606	Warrington South	NW	6.1	Con	42.0	Lab	35.9	All.	22.2
607	Warwick & Leamington	WM	25.3	Con	49.8	All.	24.5	Lab	23.5
608	Warwickshire North	WM	5.0	Con	45.1	Lab	40.1	All.	14.9
609	Watford	SE	20.5	Con	48.7	Lab	28.2	All.	23.0
610	Waveney	EA	18.4	Con	48.4	Lab	30.0	All.	21.6
611	Wealden	SE	36.7	Con	64.2	All.	27.5	Lab	8.3
612	Wellingborough	EM	25.6	Con	52.8	Lab	27.2	All.	20.1
613	Wells	SW	16.0	Con	53.5	All.	37.6	Lab	8.7
614	Welwyn Hatfield	SE	18.3	Con	45.6	All.	27.3	Lab	26.4
615	Wentworth	YH	43.4	Lab	65.2	Con	21.8	All.	13.0
616	West Bromwich East	WM	2.3	Lab	42.6	Con	40.3	All.	17.1
617	West Bromwich West	WM	13.3	Lab	50.5	Con	37.2	All.	12.4
618	Westbury	SW	15.2	Con	51.6	All.	36.4	Lab	12.0
620	Westminster North	GL	7.9	Con	47.3	Lab	39.5	All.	12.1
621	Westmorland & Lonsdale	N	28.4	Con	57.6	All.	29.2	Lab	13.3
622	Weston super Mare	SW	13.9	Con	49.4	All.	35.6	Lab	11.4
623	Wigan	NW	37.1	Lab	61.5	Con	24.5	All.	14.0
624	Wiltshire North	SW	17.1	Con	55.2	All.	38.1	Lab	6.8
625	Wimbledon	GL	23.4	Con	50.9	All.	27.5	Lab	21.6
626	Winchester	SE	12.2	Con	52.4	All.	40.2	Lab	6.6
627	Windsor & Maidenhead	SE	29.8	Con	56.8	All.	27.0	Lab	11.2
628	Wirral South	NW	22.2	Con	50.2	Lab	28.0	All.	21.8
629	Wirral West	NW	25.7	Con	51.9	Lab	26.3	All.	20.2
630	Witney	SE	31.7	Con	57.5	All.	25.8	Lab	16.7
631	Woking	SE	26.7	Con	58.1	All.	31.4	Lab	10.6
632	Wokingham	SE	31.4	Con	61.4	All.	30.0	Lab	8.7
633	Wolverhampton North East	WM	0.4	Con	42.1	Lab	41.7	All.	16.2

PA No.	Seat name	Region	% Majority	Winner	% of Vote	Second	% of Vote	Third	% of Vote
634	Wolverhampton South East	WM	15.8	Lab	48.9	Con	33.1	All.	18.0
635	Wolverhampton South West	WM	19.9	Con	50.7	Lab	30.8	All.	18.6
636	Woodspring	SW	29.6	Con	56.6	All.	27.0	Lab	14.5
637	Woolwich	GL	4.7	All.	41.7	Lab	37.0	Con	21.2
638	Worcester	WM	19.7	Con	48.2	Lab	28.4	All.	23.4
639	Worcestershire Mid	WM	24.2	Con	51.6	Lab	27.4	All.	21.0
640	Worcestershire South	WM	23.4	Con	55.3	All.	31.9	Lab	10.9
641	Workington	N	15.3	Lab	52.4	Con	37.1	All.	10.6
642	Worsley	NW	13.0	Lab	48.1	Con	35.1	All.	16.8
643	Worthing	SE	33.0	Con	61.7	All.	28.7	Lab	9.6
644	Wrekin, The	WM	2.3	Lab	42.8	Con	40.6	All.	16.6
646	Wycombe	SE	26.4	Con	53.9	All.	27.5	Lab	18.7
647	Wyre	NW	29.0	Con	53.0	All.	24.0	Lab	21.2
648	Wyre Forest	WM	13.2	Con	47.1	All.	34.0	Lab	18.9
649	Yeovil	SW	10.2	All.	51.4	Con	41.3	Lab	7.3
651	York	YH	0.2	Con	41.6	Lab	41.4	All.	15.9

Scotland

PA No.	Seat name	% Majority	Winner	% of Vote	Second	% of Vote	Third	% of Vote
2	Aberdeen North	36.9	Lab	54.7	All.	17.8	Con	14.3
3	Aberdeen South	2.8	Lab	37.7	Con	34.8	All.	20.9
9	Angus East	3.4	SNP	42.4	Con	39.0	Lab	10.8
13	Argyll & Bute	3.8	All.	37.3	Con	33.5	SNP	17.1
19	Ayr	0.3	Con	39.4	Lab	39.1	All.	14.8
21	Banff & Buchan	5.6	SNP	44.3	Con	38.7	All.	9.6
110	Caithness & Sutherland	36.9	All.	53.6	Con	16.7	Lab	14.9
124	Carrick, Cumnock & Doon Valley	39.3	Lab	60.1	Con	20.8	SNP	9.6
144	Clackmannan	32.8	Lab	53.7	SNP	20.9	Con	14.9
147	Clydebank & Milngavie	41.2	Lab	56.9	Con	15.7	All.	14.9
148	Clydesdale	21.8	Lab	45.3	Con	23.5	All.	16.4
169	Cumbernauld & Kilsyth	40.4	Lab	60.0	SNP	19.6	All.	11.4
170	Cunninghame North	10.3	Lab	44.4	Con	34.0	All.	12.1
171	Cunninghame South	44.5	Lab	60.8	Con	16.3	All.	11.9
201	Dumbarton	11.4	Lab	43.0	Con	31.7	All.	13.2
202	Dumfries	16.7	Con	41.9	Lab	25.2	All.	18.0
203	Dundee East	2.2	Lab	42.3	SNP	40.1	Con	12.9
204	Dundee West	35.4	Lab	53.4	Con	18.0	SNP	15.3
205	Dunfermline East	50.0	Lab	64.8	Scon	14.8	All.	10.5
206	Dunfermline West	23.9	Lab	47.1	Con	23.1	All.	21.1
215	East Kilbride	25.3	Lab	49.0	All.	23.7	Con	14.7
217	East Lothian –	19.8	Lab	48.0	Con	28.3	All.	15.5
218	Eastwood	12.3	Con	39.5	All.	27.2	Lab	25.1
221	Edinburgh - Central	5.5	Lab	40.2	Con	34.7	All.	17.9
222	Edinburgh - East	25.6	Lab	50.4	Con	24.7	All.	15.4
223	Edinburgh - Leith	26.5	Lab	49.3	Con	22.9	All.	18.3
224	Edinburgh - Pentlands	8.3	Con	38.3	Lab	30.0	All.	24.5
225	Edinburgh - South	3.8	Lab	37.7	Con	33.8	All.	22.5
226	Edinburgh - West	2.5	Con	37.4	All.	34.9	Lab	22.2

PA No.	Seat name	% Majority	Winner	% of Vote	Second	% of Vote	Third	% of Vote
239	Falkirk East	35.6	Lab	54.2	Con	18.7	SNP	15.4
240	Falkirk West	35.6	Lab	53.2	Con	17.6	SNP	16.5
246	Fife Central	36.8	Lab	53.4	Con	16.7	All.	15.2
247	Fife North-East	3.6	All.	44.8	Con	41.2	Lab	7.4
254	Galloway & Upper Northsdale	9.0	Con	40.4	SNP	31.5	All.	14.6
259	Glasgow - Cathcart	29.8	Lab	52.1	Con	22.4	All.	15.2
260	Glasgow - Central*	51.5	Lab	64.5	Con	13.0	All.	10.5
261	Glasgow - Garscadden	55.4	Lab	67.7	SNP	12.3	Con	10.7
262	Glasgow - Govan*	52.5	Lab	64.8	All.	12.3	Con	11.9
263	Glasgow - Hillhead	7.8	Lab	42.9	All.	35.1	Con	14.5
264	Glasgow - Maryhill	54.8	Lab	66.4	All.	11.7	SNP	11.0
265	Glasgow - Pollock	48.8	Lab	63.1	Con	14.3	All.	12.1
266	Glasgow - Provan	60.8	Lab	72.9	SNP	12.1	Con	7.7
267	Glasgow - Rutherglen	31.6	Lab	56.0	All.	24.4	Con	11.5
268	Glasgow - Shettleston	50.3	Lab	63.6	Con	13.3	SNP	12.7
269	Glasgow - Springburn	63.4	Lab	73.6	SNP	10.2	Con	8.3
272	Gordon	17.6	All.	49.5	Con	31.9	Lab	11.5
279	Greenock & Port Glasgow	46.0	Lab	63.9	All.	17.9	Con	9.6
287	Hamilton	45.3	Lab	59.7	Con	14.4	All.	13.2
332	Inverness Nairn & Lochaber	11.5	All.	36.8	Lab	25.3	Con	23.0
343	Kilmarnock & Loudoun	28.9	Lab	48.5	Con	19.6	SNP	18.2
344	Kincardine & Deeside*	4.3	Con	40.7	All.	36.3	Lab	15.9
347	Kirkcaldy	28.3	Lab	49.6	Con	21.3	All.	17.4
373	Linlithgow	22.5	Lab	47.4	SNP	24.9	Con	14.8
381	Livingston	26.5	Lab	45.6	All.	19.1	Con	18.7
402	Midlothian	26.2	Lab	48.3	All.	22.0	Con	18.2
407	Monklands East	44.1	Lab	61.0	Con	16.9	SNP	12.9
408	Monklands West	46.6	Lab	62.3	Con	15.7	All.	11.2
411	Moray	8.2	SNP	43.2	Con	35.0	Lab	11.3
413	Motherwell North	53.0	Lab	66.9	SNP	14.0	Con	11.1
414	Motherwell South	43.0	Lab	58.3	SNP	15.3	Con	14.5
449	Orkney & Shetland	18.4	All.	41.7	Con	23.3	Lab	18.7
453	Paisley North*	39.7	Lab	55.5	Con	15.8	All.	15.8
454	Paisley South*	41.0	Lab	56.2	All.	15.1	Con	14.7
459	Perth & Kinross	12.0	Con	39.6	SNP	27.6	All.	16.9
477	Renfrew West & Inverclyde	9.0	Lab	38.7	Con	29.8	All.	21.4
486	Ross, Cromarty & Skye	29.7	All.	49.4	Con	19.7	Lab	19.1
490	Roxburgh & Berwickshire	12.0	All.	49.2	Con	37.2	Lab	8.8
540	Stirling	1.2	Con	37.8	Lab	36.6	All.	14.9
549	Strathkelvin & Bearsden	4.8	Lab	38.1	Con	33.4	All.	21.4
570	Tayside North	12.4	Con	45.4	SNP	32.9	All.	12.9
583	Tweeddale Ettrick & Lauderdale	20.3	All.	49.9	Con	29.6	Lab	11.4
619	Western Isles	14.2	Lab	42.7	SNP	28.5	All.	20.7

Wales

1	Aberavon	50.7	Lab	66.8	All.	16.0	Con	14.4
7	Alyn & Deeside	13.5	Lab	48.6	Con	35.0	All.	15.4
66	Blaenau, Gwent	64.4	Lab	75.9	Con	11.5	All.	8.9
83	Brecon & Radnor	0.1	All.	34.8	Con	34.7	Lab	29.2

PA No.	Seat name	% Majority	Winner	% of Vote	Second	% of Vote	Third	% of Vote
89	Bridgend	9.5	Lab	47.5	Con	38.0	All.	12.1
108	Caernarfon	36.0	PC	57.1	Con	21.1	Lab	15.9
109	Caerphilly	39.0	Lab	58.4	Con	19.4	All.	14.1
118	Cardiff Central	4.8	Con	37.1	Lab	32.3	All.	29.4
119	Cardiff North	18.6	Con	45.3	Lab	26.7	All.	26.5
120	Cardiff South & Penarth	10.2	Lab	46.7	Con	36.5	All.	15.4
121	Cardiff West	9.1	Lab	45.5	Con	36.5	All.	16.4
123	Carmarthen	8.0	Lab	35.4	Con	27.4	PC	23.0
127	Ceredigion & Pembroke North	9.7	All.	36.6	Con	26.9	Lab	18.6
145	Clwyd North-West	23.7	Con	48.5	Lab	24.8	All.	22.7
146	Clwyd South West	2.2	Lab	35.4	Con	33.3	All.	22.9
153	Conwy	7.4	Con	38.7	All.	31.3	Lab	22.3
172	Cynon Valley	56.7	Lab	68.9	Con	12.2	All.	12.2
178	Delyn	2.3	Con	41.4	Lab	39.1	All.	17.0
274	Gower	12.1	Lab	46.6	Con	34.5	All.	16.1
337	Islwyn	56.6	Lab	71.3	Con	14.7	All.	9.2
382	Llanelli	42.0	Lab	59.2	Con	17.2	All.	13.5
398	Meirionnydd Nant Conwy	11.7	PC	40.0	Con	28.4	Lab	16.9
400	Merthyr Tydfil & Rhymney	63.5	Lab	75.4	Con	11.9	All.	8.1
409	Monmouth*	19.9	Con	47.5	Lab	27.7	All.	24.0
410	Montgomery	8.1	All.	46.6	Con	38.5	Lab	10.5
415	Neath*	47.2	Lab	63.4	Con	16.1	All.	14.1
426	Newport East	16.9	Lab	49.1	Con	32.2	All.	17.7
427	Newport West	6.0	Lab	46.1	Con	40.1	All.	13.0
445	Ogmore	54.3	Lab	69.4	Con	15.0	All.	9.6
456	Pembroke	10.0	Con	41.0	Lab	31.0	All.	26.1
465	Pontypridd*	36.8	Lab	56.3	Con	19.5	All.	18.9
478	Rhondda	64.4	Lab	73.3	PC	9.0	All.	8.3
565	Swansea East	44.8	Lab	63.7	Con	18.9	All.	14.8
566	Swansea West	15.5	Lab	48.5	Con	33.0	All.	15.4
579	Torfaen	38.8	Lab	58.7	All.	19.9	Con	19.1
591	Vale of Glamorgan*	12.1	Con	46.8	Lab	34.7	All.	16.7
645	Wrexham	8.2	Lab	43.9	Con	35.6	All.	19.4
650	Yns Mon	10.0	PC	43.2	Con	33.2	Lab	16.9

Northern Ireland

PA No.	Seat name	% Majority	Winner	% of Vote	Second	% of Vote	Third	% of Vote
10	Antrim East	45.9	UU	71.6	APNI	25.7	TWP	2.8
11	Antrim North	56.3	DUP	68.7	SDLP	12.5	APNI	12.4
12	Antrim South	53.8	UU	69.8	APNI	16.0	SDLP	9.9
38	Belfast East	29.8	DUP	61.9	APNI	32.1	TWP	4.0
39	Belfast North	23.3	UU	39.0	SDLP	15.7	I.UDUP	15.4
40	Belfast South	36.6	UU	57.8	APNI	21.3	SDLP	13.1
41	Belfast West	5.4	SF	41.2	SDLP	35.7	UU	18.7
196	Down North	9.7	DUP	45.1	Ind UU	35.4	APNI	19.4
197	Down South	1.3	SDLP	47.0	UU	45.7	SF	4.2
245	Fermanagh & South Tyrone	23.2	UU	49.6	SF	26.4	SDLP	19.1
250	Foyle	20.3	SDLP	48.8	DUP	28.6	SF	17.9
350	Lagan Valley	56.2	UU	70.0	APNI	13.8	SDLP	6.9
383	Londonderry East	41.4	UU	60.5	SDLP	19.2	SF	11.2
428	Newry & Armagh	10.2	SDLP	48.1	UU	37.9	SF	11.8
547	Strangford	55.6	UU	75.9	APNI	20.3	TWP	3.7

PA No.	Seat name	% Majority	Winner	% of Vote	Second	% of Vote	Third	% of Vote
587	Ulster Mid	18.0	DUP	44.2	SDLP	26.2	SF	23.9
589	Upper Bann*	41.0	UU	61.5	SDLP	20.5	SF	7.4

Balance of Payments
Seasonally adjusted

Quarter	Visible trade balance (£ million)	Current account balance (£ million)
1979 Q1	-1,472	-642
1979 Q2	-458	26
1979 Q3	-588	331
1979 Q4	-825	-168
1980 Q1	-444	-73
1980 Q2	-179	-120
1980 Q3	865	1,150
1980 Q4	1,115	1,886
1981 Q1	1,684	2,935
1981 Q2	1,281	1,974
1981 Q3	-148	521
1981 Q4	435	1,318
1982 Q1	262	1,419
1982 Q2	138	605
1982 Q3	549	896
1982 Q4	961	1,729
1983 Q1	-217	1,713
1983 Q2	-575	97
1983 Q3	-142	1,380
1983 Q4	-603	575
1984 Q1	-448	1,310
1984 Q2	-1,387	-148
1984 Q3	-1,534	-95
1984 Q4	-1,967	744
1985 Q1	-1962	-405
1985 Q2	-214	1,530
1985 Q3	-538	1,121
1985 Q4	-631	632
1986 Q1	-1,585	1,323
1986 Q2	-2,162	81
1986 Q3	-2,895	-591
1986 Q4	-2,917	-626

Quarter	Visible trade balance (£ million)	Current account balance (£ million)
1987 Q1	-1,848	323
1987 Q2	-2,791	-844
1987 Q3	-3,071	-1,215
1987 Q4	-3,872	-2,423
1988 Q1	-4,364	-3,258
1988 Q2	-4,836	-3,100
1988 Q3	-5,683	-3,331
1988 Q4	-6,741	-5,832
1989 Q1	-6,354	-4,778
1989 Q2	-6,672	-4,990
1989 Q3	-6,732	-6,065
1989 Q4	-4,840	-4,572
1990 Q1	-6,073	-5,287
1990 Q2	-5,391	-5,142
1990 Q3	-4,035	-2,552
1990 Q4	-3,176	-2,219
1991 Q1	-2,988	-2,688
1991 Q2	-2,104	-127
1991 Q3	-2,345	-1,335

Source: Central Statistical Office

Interest and Inflation Rates
Not seasonally adjusted

Quarter	Retail banks base rate	Retail Prices Index (all-items)
1979 Q1	12.9%	9.6%
1979 Q2	12.4%	10.6%
1979 Q3	14.0%	16.0%
1979 Q4	15.4%	17.3%
1980 Q1	17.0%	19.1%
1980 Q2	17.0%	21.5%
1980 Q3	16.1%	16.4%
1980 Q4	15.2%	15.3%
1981 Q1	13.6%	12.7%
1981 Q2	12.0%	11.7%
1981 Q3	12.3%	11.3%
1981 Q4	15.2%	11.9%
1982 Q1	13.8%	11.1%
1982 Q2	12.9%	9.4%
1982 Q3	11.4%	8.0%
1982 Q4	9.7%	6.2%

Quarter	Retail banks base rate	Retail Prices Index (all-items)
1983 Q1	10.8%	5.0%
1983 Q2	10.0%	3.8%
1983 Q3	9.5%	4.6%
1983 Q4	9.0%	5.1%
1984 Q1	8.9%	5.2%
1984 Q2	8.9%	5.1%
1984 Q3	10.9%	4.7%
1984 Q4	10.0%	4.8%
1985 Q1	13.1%	5.5%
1985 Q2	12.7%	7.0%
1985 Q3	11.7%	6.3%
1985 Q4	11.5%	5.5%
1986 Q1	12.3%	4.9%
1986 Q2	10.4%	2.8%
1986 Q3	10.0%	2.6%
1986 Q4	10.9%	3.4%
1987 Q1	10.8%	3.9%
1987 Q2	9.4%	4.2%
1987 Q3	9.6%	4.3%
1987 Q4	9.2%	4.1%
1988 Q1	8.8%	3.5%
1988 Q2	8.2%	4.3%
1988 Q3	11.1%	5.5%
1988 Q4	12.4%	6.5%
1989 Q1	13.0%	7.7%
1989 Q2	13.4%	8.2%
1989 Q3	14.0%	7.7%
1989 Q4	15.0%	7.6%
1990 Q1	15.0%	7.8%
1990 Q2	15.0%	9.7%
1990 Q3	15.0%	10.4%
1990 Q4	14.1%	10.0%
1991 Q1	13.6%	8.7%
1991 Q2	11.9%	6.0%
1991 Q3	10.9%	4.8%
1991 Q4	10.5%	n.a.

Source: Central Statistical Office

Employees by sex - Great Britain
not seasonally adjusted

Quarter	Males 000's	% of all	Females 000's	%	of which part time 000's	% of all
Mar 1979	13,100	58.5%	9,295	41.5%	3,771	16.8%
Jun 1979	13,183	58.2%	9,455	41.8%	3,870	17.1%
Sept1979	13,252	58.3%	9,476	41.7%	3,821	16.8%
Dec 1979	13,180	58.0%	9,544	42.0%	3,918	17.2%
Mar 1980	13,036	58.1%	9,402	41.9%	3,882	17.3%
Jun 1980	13,018	58.0%	9,440	42.0%	3,941	17.5%
Sept1980	12,895	58.0%	9,344	42.0%	3,834	17.2%
Dec 1980	12,641	57.7%	9,269	42.3%	3,871	17.7%
Mar 1981	12,384	57.7%	9,082	42.3%	3,790	17.7%
Jun 1981	12,278	57.4%	9,107	42.6%	3,817	17.8%
Sept1981	12,224	57.4%	9,084	42.6%	3,781	17.7%
Dec 1981	12,052	57.1%	9,057	42.9%	3,835	18.2%
Mar 1982	11,941	57.2%	8,941	42.8%	3,772	18.1%
Jun 1982	11,930	57.0%	8,985	43.0%	3,783	18.1%
Sept1982	11,921	57.2%	8,917	42.8%	3,743	18.0%
Dec 1982	11,766	57.0%	8,879	43.0%	3,748	18.2%
Mar 1983	11,648	57.1%	8,754	42.9%	3,685	18.1%
Jun 1983	11,670	56.7%	8,901	43.3%	3,776	18.4%
Sept1983	11,723	56.7%	8,960	43.3%	3,779	18.3%
Dec 1983	11,652	56.2%	9,070	43.8%	3,881	18.7%
Mar 1984	11,571	56.2%	9,008	43.8%	3,833	18.6%
Jun 1984	11,619	56.0%	9,123	44.0%	3,889	18.7%
Sept1984	11,699	56.1%	9,147	43.9%	3,858	18.5%
Dec 1984	11,678	55.8%	9,247	44.2%	3,967	19.0%
Mar 1985	11,595	55.8%	9,170	44.2%	3,908	18.8%
Jun 1985	11,632	55.6%	9,288	44.4%	3,976	19.0%
Sept1985	11,666	55.6%	9,310	44.4%	3,957	18.9%
Dec 1985	11,603	55.3%	9,384	44.7%	4,040	19.3%
Mar 1986	11,472	55.2%	9,294	44.8%	4,001	19.3%
Jun 1986	11,477	54.9%	9,409	45.1%	4,081	19.5%
Sept1986	11,498	54.9%	9,427	45.1%	4,047	19.3%
Dec 1986	11,409	54.4%	9,555	45.6%	4,158	19.8%
Mar 1987	11,324	54.5%	9,472	45.5%	4,119	19.8%
Jun 1987	11,431	54.2%	9,647	45.8%	4,169	19.8%
Sept1987	11,558	54.3%	9,713	45.7%	4,121	19.4%
Dec 1987	11,606	53.9%	9,910	46.1%	4,263	19.8%

Quarter	Males 000's	% of all	Females 000's	%	of which part time 000's	% of all
Mar 1988	11,623	54.1%	9,871	45.9%	4,214	19.6%
Jun 1988	11,698	53.8%	10,042	46.2%	4,288	19.7%
Sept1988	11,773	53.7%	10,153	46.3%	4,291	19.6%
Dec 1988	11,712	53.1%	10,328	46.9%	4,439	20.1%
Mar 1989	11,675	53.0%	10,348	47.0%	4,458	20.2%
Jun 1989	11,718	52.9%	10,416	47.1%	4,494	20.3%
Sept1989	11,798	53.1%	10,436	46.9%	4,474	20.1%
Dec 1989	11,804	52.8%	10,550	47.2%	4,604	20.6%
Mar 1990	11,741	52.9%	10,447	47.1%	4,560	20.6%
Jun 1990	11,775	52.7%	10,550	47.3%	4,645	20.8%
Sept1990	11,797	52.9%	10,501	47.1%	4,568	20.5%
Dec 1990	11,634	52.5%	10,529	47.5%	4,659	21.0%
Mar 1991	11,407	52.4%	10,357	47.6%	4,571	21.0%
Jun 1991	11,313	52.2%	10,355	47.8%	4,606	21.3%

Source: Department of Employment

Unemployed Claimants – United Kingdom

Seasonally adjusted – consistent with current coverage

Month	Male No.	%	Female No.	%	All No.	%
Mar 1979	820,600	5.1	296,600	2.9	1,117,200	4.2
Jun 1979	770,300	4.7	297,200	2.9	1,067,500	4.0
Sep 1979	749,500	4.6	295,700	2.8	1,045,200	3.9
Dec 1979	752,600	4.6	302,400	2.9	1,055,000	4.0
Mar 1980	806,300	4.9	330,100	3.1	1,136,400	4.2
Jun 1980	910,400	5.6	363,400	3.5	1,273,800	4.7
Sep 1980	1,090,500	6.7	417,500	4.0	1,508,000	5.6
Dec 1980	1,308,500	8.0	484,600	4.6	1,793,100	6.7
Mar 1981	1,469,200	9.0	532,400	5.1	2,001,600	7.5
Jun 1981	1,605,100	9.8	570,900	5.5	2,176,000	8.1
Sep 1981	1,695,400	10.4	609,600	5.9	2,305,000	8.6
Dec 1981	1,758,600	10.8	635,400	6.1	2,394,000	9.0
Mar 1982	1,795,600	11.0	652,400	6.3	2,448,000	9.2
Jun 1982	1,848,100	11.4	673,300	6.5	2,521,400	9.4
Sep 1982	1,907,600	11.7	698,600	6.7	2,606,200	9.8
Dec 1982	1,970,700	12.1	726,700	7.0	2,697,400	10.1
Mar 1983	1,994,700	12.4	754,300	7.2	2,749,000	10.3
Jun 1983	2,027,600	12.6	777,600	7.4	2,805,200	10.5
Sep 1983	2,019,400	12.5	793,800	7.6	2,813,200	10.6
Dec 1983	2,021,500	12.6	818,500	7.8	2,840,000	10.7

Month	Male No.	%	Female No.	%	All No.	%
Mar 1984	2,040,900	12.5	844,200	7.7	2,885,100	10.6
Jun 1984	2,040,400	12.5	856,900	7.8	2,897,300	10.6
Sep 1984	2,072,600	12.7	880,400	8.0	2,953,000	10.8
Dec 1984	2,087,900	12.8	896,800	8.2	2,984,700	10.9
Mar 1985	2,100,300	12.7	907,500	8.1	3,007,800	10.9
Jun 1985	2,100,000	12.7	919,400	8.2	3,019,400	10.9
Sep 1985	2,105,300	12.8	930,100	8.3	3,035,400	11.0
Dec 1985	2,122,900	12.9	940,400	8.4	3,063,300	11.1
Mar 1986	2,165,500	13.2	954,800	8.4	3,120,300	11.2
Jun 1986	2,153,700	13.1	967,300	8.5	3,121,000	11.2
Sep 1986	2,133,500	13.0	967,500	8.5	3,101,000	11.2
Dec 1986	2,105,000	12.8	943,000	8.3	3,048,000	11.0
Mar 1987	2,054,400	12.6	902,100	7.8	2,956,500	10.6
Jun 1987	1,980,100	12.1	858,700	7.4	2,838,800	10.1
Sep 1987	1,886,400	11.5	812,800	7.0	2,699,200	9.6
Dec 1987	1,785,300	10.9	771,700	6.6	2,557,000	9.1
Mar 1988	1,691,900	10.3	740,700	6.3	2,432,600	8.6
Jun 1988	1,602,500	9.8	696,300	5.9	2,298,800	8.1
Sep 1988	1,519,800	9.3	651,600	5.5	2,171,400	7.7
Dec 1988	1,421,400	8.7	600,300	5.1	2,021,700	7.2
Mar 1989	1,346,700	8.3	556,500	4.6	1,903,200	6.7
Jun 1989	1,279,600	7.8	511,600	4.2	1,791,200	6.3
Sep 1989	1,218,600	7.5	466,100	3.9	1,684,700	5.9
Dec 1989	1,194,700	7.3	441,400	3.6	1,636,100	5.8
Mar 1990	1,177,900	7.2	428,700	3.5	1,606,600	5.6
Jun 1990	1,193,500	7.3	424,900	3.5	1,618,400	5.7
Sep 1990	1,246,600	7.7	423,900	3.5	1,670,500	5.9
Dec 1990	1,385,800	8.5	456,500	3.7	1,842,300	6.5
Mar 1991	1,581,200	9.7	509,800	4.2	2,091,000	7.4
Jun 1991	1,744,600	10.7	555,700	4.6	2,300,300	8.1
Sept 1991	1,862,600	11.5	594,600	4.9	2,457,200	8.6

Note: Percentages are proportions of workforce
Source: Department of Employment

Gross Domestic Product per capita

Seasonally adjusted

Quarter	1985 facto cost	Change on year before	Quarter	1985 facto cost	Change on year before
1979 Q1	1,232	1.7%	1988 Q1	1,497	4.8%
1979 Q2	1,280	4.4%	1988 Q2	1,509	4.1%
1979 Q3	1,265	2.5%	1988 Q3	1,524	3.3%
1979 Q4	1,272	2.2%	1988 Q4	1,532	3.3%
1980 Q1	1,258	2.1%	1989 Q1	1,539	2.8%
1980 Q2	1,243	-2.9%	1989 Q2	1,537	1.9%
1980 Q3	1,228	-2.9%	1989 Q3	1,546	1.4%
1980 Q4	1,210	-4.9%	1989 Q4	1,550	1.2%
1981 Q1	1,208	-4.0%	1990 Q1	1,557	1.2%
1981 Q2	1,216	-2.2%	1990 Q2	1,566	1.9%
1981 Q3	1,226	-0.2%	1990 Q3	1,546	0.0%
1981 Q4	1,230	1.7%	1990 Q4	1,531	-1.2%
1982 Q1	1,230	1.8%	1991 Q1	1,516	-2.6%
1982 Q2	1,244	2.3%	1991 Q2	1,504	-4.0%
1982 Q3	1,244	1.5%	1991 Q3	1,505	-2.7%
1982 Q4	1,250	1.6%			

Source: Central Statistical Office

Quarter	1985 facto cost	Change on year before
1983 Q1	1,273	3.5%
1983 Q2	1,282	3.1%
1983 Q3	1,291	3.8%
1983 Q4	1,303	4.2%
1984 Q1	1,313	3.1%
1984 Q2	1,300	1.4%
1984 Q3	1,302	0.9%
1984 Q4	1,317	1.1%
1985 Q1	1,339	2.0%
1985 Q2	1,359	4.5%
1985 Q3	1,357	4.2%
1985 Q4	1,362	3.4%
1986 Q1	1,375	2.7%
1986 Q2	1,395	2.6%
1986 Q3	1,406	3.6%
1986 Q4	1,421	4.3%
1987 Q1	1,428	3.9%
1987 Q2	1,449	3.9%
1987 Q3	1,475	4.9%
1987 Q4	1,483	4.4%

Productivity
Seasonally adjusted

	Output per person employed				Output per hour	
	Whole economy		Manufacturing		Manufacturing	
	Index	*Change*	*Index*	*Change*	*Index*	*Change*
	1985=	*on year*	*1985=*	*on year*	*1985=*	*on year*
Quarter	*100*	*before*	*100*	*before*	*100*	*before*
1979 Q1	86.9	0.2%	78.1	-0.4%	77.7	-0.3%
1979 Q2	90.2	3.1%	81.9	1.9%	81.4	1.5%
1979 Q3	88.9	1.1%	79.1	-1.6%	79.2	-1.2%
1979 Q4	89.1	1.0%	80.7	1.8%	80.4	1.8%
1980 Q1	88.3	1.6%	79.5	1.8%	79.6	2.4%
1980 Q2	87.7	-2.8%	77.4	-5.5%	78.5	-3.6%
1980 Q3	87.3	-1.8%	75.8	-4.3%	77.9	-1.6%
1980 Q4	87.0	-2.4%	74.7	-7.4%	78.1	-2.9%
1981 Q1	87.7	-1.7%	76.3	-4.0%	80.0	0.5%
1981 Q2	89.2	1.7%	78.3	1.2%	81.3	3.6%
1981 Q3	90.5	3.7%	81.1	7.0%	83.4	7.1%
1981 Q4	91.3	4.9%	82.5	10.4%	84.5	8.2%
1982 Q1	91.5	4.3%	83.3	9.2%	85.1	6.4%
1982 Q2	93.0	4.3%	84.6	8.0%	86.5	6.4%
1982 Q3	93.4	3.2%	85.4	5.3%	87.3	4.7%
1982 Q4	94.5	3.5%	86.0	4.2%	87.8	3.9%
1983 Q1	96.5	5.5%	89.6	7.6%	91.5	7.5%
1983 Q2	97.2	4.5%	90.8	7.3%	92.6	7.1%
1983 Q3	97.6	4.5%	92.6	8.4%	93.9	7.6%
1983 Q4	98.0	3.7%	94.7	10.1%	95.6	8.9%
1984 Q1	98.3	1.9%	96.6	7.8%	97.2	6.2%
1984 Q2	97.0	1.2%	96.5	6.3%	97.0	4.8%
1984 Q3	96.9	0.7%	97.6	5.4%	98.1	4.5%
1984 Q4	97.6	0.4%	97.3	2.7%	97.8	2.3%
1985 Q1	98.9	0.9%	100.2	3.7%	100.2	3.1%
1985 Q2	100.3	3.4%	101.0	4.7%	101.0	4.1%
1985 Q3	100.1	3.3%	99.9	2.4%	99.8	1.7%
1985 Q4	100.6	3.1%	99.0	1.7%	98.9	1.1%
1986 Q1	101.7	2.8%	99.7	-0.5%	100.0	-0.3%
1986 Q2	103.2	2.9%	102.6	1.6%	103.0	2.0%
1986 Q3	104.0	3.9%	104.1	4.2%	104.3	4.5%
1986 Q4	104.9	4.3%	107.7	8.8%	108.1	9.3%
1987 Q1	105.2	3.4%	106.7	7.0%	106.8	6.9%
1987 Q2	105.9	2.6%	109.1	6.3%	108.6	5.4%
1987 Q3	107.1	3.0%	111.2	6.8%	110.9	6.3%
1987 Q4	106.8	1.8%	112.4	4.4%	111.8	3.4%

	Output per person employed		Output per hour Manufacturing		Manufacturing	
	Whole economy					
	Index 1985=	Change on year	Index 1985=	Change on year	Index 1985=	Change on year
Quarter	100	before	100	before	100	before
1988 Q1	106.9	1.6%	113.3	6.2%	112.5	5.3%
1988 Q2	107.1	1.1%	114.6	5.0%	113.5	4.5%
1988 Q3	107.3	0.2%	117.5	5.7%	116.6	5.1%
1988 Q4	107.4	0.6%	119.3	6.4%	118.1	5.6%
1989 Q1	107.2	0.3%	120.5	6.4%	119.9	6.6%
1989 Q2	106.7	-0.4%	120.8	5.4%	120.3	6.0%
1989 Q3	107.0	-0.3%	121.1	3.1%	120.7	3.5%
1989 Q4	107.0	-0.4%	120.9	1.3%	120.7	2.2%
1990 Q1	107.7	0.5%	121.6	0.9%	121.2	1.1%
1990 Q2	108.2	1.4%	123.3	2.1%	122.6	1.9%
1990 Q3	106.9	-0.1%	121.9	0.7%	121.2	-0.4%
1990 Q4	106.6	-0.4%	119.2	-1.4%	118.8	-1.6%
1991 Q1	106.6	-1.0%	119.4	-1.8%	120.3	-0.7%
1991 Q2	106.7	-1.4%	120.9	-1.9%	121.8	-0.7%
1991 Q3	n.a.	n.a.	123.1	1.0%	123.9	2.2%

Source: Central Statistical Office

Output of the Production Industries

Seasonally adjusted

	Index 1985=	Change on year	Index 1985=	Change on year	Index 1985=	Change on year
Quarter	100	before	100	before	100	before
1979 Q1	96.7	4.1%	59.3	56.9%	103.9	-0.6%
1979 Q2	101.3	5.9%	65.7	50.0%	108.7	1.7%
1979 Q3	99.2	2.8%	70.2	48.1%	105.0	-2.1%
1979 Q4	99.2	3.0%	66.1	23.6%	106.4	0.5%
1980 Q1	97.6	0.9%	66.3	11.8%	103.5	-0.4%
1980 Q2	93.9	-7.3%	64.6	-1.7%	99.0	-8.9%
1980 Q3	90.5	-8.8%	65.2	-7.1%	94.4	-10.1%
1980 Q4	88.4	-10.9%	68.8	4.1%	90.3	-15.1%
1981 Q1	88.4	-9.4%	71.1	7.2%	89.8	-13.2%
1981 Q2	88.9	-5.3%	71.6	10.8%	90.2	-8.9%
1981 Q3	90.2	-0.3%	73.7	13.0%	91.9	-2.6%
1981 Q4	91.2	3.2%	75.7	10.0%	92.2	2.1%
1982 Q1	90.4	2.3%	75.0	5.5%	91.8	2.2%
1982 Q2	92.0	3.5%	83.9	17.2%	91.9	1.9%
1982 Q3	92.0	2.0%	87.2	18.3%	91.1	-0.9%
1982 Q4	91.1	-0.1%	86.6	14.4%	90.2	-2.2%

Quarter	Index 1985= 100	Change on year before	Index 1985= 100	Change on year before	Index 1985= 100	Change on year before
1983 Q1	93.1	3.0%	86.8	15.7%	92.7	1.0%
1983 Q2	94.0	2.2%	88.2	5.1%	92.9	1.2%
1983 Q3	95.2	3.5%	93.7	7.5%	94.0	3.3%
1983 Q4	96.5	5.9%	95.8	10.6%	95.6	6.1%
1984 Q1	97.2	4.4%	97.5	12.3%	97.1	4.7%
1984 Q2	94.1	0.1%	96.7	9.6%	97.0	4.4%
1984 Q3	93.3	-2.0%	95.1	1.5%	97.9	4.1%
1984 Q4	94.4	-2.2%	100.3	4.7%	97.7	2.2%
1985 Q1	97.8	0.6%	101.4	4.0%	100.4	3.4%
1985 Q2	101.7	8.1%	101.3	4.8%	101.1	4.2%
1985 Q3	100.6	7.8%	97.3	2.3%	99.9	2.0%
1985 Q4	99.9	5.8%	99.9	-0.4%	98.6	0.9%
1986 Q1	101.2	3.6%	102.4	1.0%	98.8	-1.6%
1986 Q2	102.2	0.5%	101.0	-0.3%	100.8	-0.3%
1986 Q3	103.0	2.4%	105.0	7.9%	101.3	1.4%
1986 Q4	103.5	3.4%	96.4	-3.5%	104.4	5.9%
1987 Q1	103.7	2.6%	100.6	-1.8%	103.0	4.3%
1987 Q2	104.8	2.5%	97.6	-3.4%	105.6	4.8%
1987 Q3	106.7	3.6%	99.0	-5.7%	108.1	6.7%
1987 Q4	107.8	4.2%	97.2	0.8%	109.6	5.0%
1988 Q1	107.9	4.1%	96.5	-4.1%	110.9	7.7%
1988 Q2	109.5	4.5%	96.6	-1.0%	112.4	6.4%
1988 Q3	110.3	3.4%	85.7	-13.4%	115.5	6.8%
1988 Q4	110.4	2.4%	81.4	-16.3%	117.4	7.1%
1989 Q1	109.6	1.6%	72.2	-25.2%	118.7	7.0%
1989 Q2	109.1	-0.4%	66.6	-31.1%	118.9	5.8%
1989 Q3	110.5	-0.2%	76.5	-10.7%	119.2	3.2%
1989 Q4	110.4	0.0%	78.2	-3.9%	118.9	1.3%
1990 Q1	109.8	0.2%	75.6	4.7%	119.3	0.5%
1990 Q2	111.8	2.5%	80.4	20.7%	120.4	1.3%
1990 Q3	108.7	-1.6%	67.8	-11.4%	118.8	-0.3%
1990 Q4	106.8	-3.3%	69.8	-10.7%	115.0	-3.3%
1991 Q1	106.5	-3.0%	74.6	-1.3%	113.4	-4.9%
1991 Q2	105.3	-5.8%	68.4	-14.9%	112.6	-6.5%
1991 Q3	106.2	-2.3%	77.5	14.3%	112.5	-5.3%

Source: Central Statistical Office